Investing with Exchange-Traded Funds Made Easy, Second Edition

"Possessing a rare skill set amongst professional investors and authors, Dr. Appel has successfully managed to provide readers with the perfect mix of up-to-date details on the various types and asset classes of ETFs, crucial, tried, and true concepts of risk management, and just the right mix of backing historical data to pull it all together—all in a "user-friendly" package. Upon conclusion of this book, readers will have experienced a paradigm shift in the thought process of their own current investment strategies. Taking it to the next level and actually implementing the concepts will automatically cause readers to experience a higher level of profitability and consistency; one they might never have thought possible from the utilization of concepts in just one small book."

—**Deron Wagner**, Founder and Portfolio Manager,
MorpheusTrading.com, author, *Trading ETFs: Gaining An Edge
With Technical Analysis*

INVESTING
with

EXCHANGE-
TRADED FUNDS
MADE EASY

SECOND EDITION

INVESTING
with
EXCHANGE-TRADED FUNDS
MADE EASY

SECOND EDITION

A Start-to-Finish Plan to Reduce Costs
and Achieve Higher Returns

MARVIN APPEL

Vice President, Publisher:	**Cover Designer**
Tim Moore	Chuti Prasertsith
Associate Publisher and	**Managing Editor:**
Director of Marketing:	Kristy Hart
Amy Neidlinger	**Project Editor:**
Executive Editor:	Todd Taber
Jim Boyd	**Copy Editor:**
Editorial Assistants:	Karen A. Gill
Pamela Boland and Myesha Graham	**Proofreader:**
Operations Manager:	Water Crest Publishing
Gina Kanouse	**Senior Indexer:**
Digital Marketing Manager:	Cheryl Lenser
Julie Phifer	**Senior Compositor:**
Publicity Manager:	Gloria Schurick
Laura Czaja	**Manufacturing Buyer:**
Assistant Marketing Manager:	Dan Uhrig
Megan Colvin	

© 2009 by Pearson Education, Inc.
Publishing as FT Press
Upper Saddle River, New Jersey 07458

This book is sold with the understanding that neither the author nor the publisher is engaged in rendering legal, accounting or other professional services or advice by publishing this book. Each individual situation is unique. Thus, if legal or financial advice or other expert assistance is required in a specific situation, the services of a competent professional should be sought to ensure that the situation has been evaluated carefully and appropriately. The author and the publisher disclaim any liability, loss, or risk resulting directly or indirectly, from the use or application of any of the contents of this book.

FT Press offers excellent discounts on this book when ordered in quantity for bulk purchases or special sales. For more information, please contact U.S. Corporate and Government Sales, 1-800-382-3419, corpsales@pearsontechgroup.com. For sales outside the U.S., please contact International Sales at international@pearson.com.

Printed in the United States of America

First Printing October 2008

ISBN-10: 0-13-236009-8
ISBN-13: 978-0-13-236009-8

Pearson Education LTD.
Pearson Education Australia PTY, Limited.
Pearson Education Singapore, Pte. Ltd.
Pearson Education North Asia, Ltd.
Pearson Education Canada, Ltd.
Pearson Educación de Mexico, S.A. de C.V.
Pearson Education—Japan
Pearson Education Malaysia, Pte. Ltd.

Library of Congress Cataloging-in-Publication Data
Appel, Marvin.
  Investing with exchange-traded funds made easy : a start to finish plan to reduce costs and achieve higher returns / Marvin Appel. — 2nd ed.
     p. cm.
  Includes index.
  ISBN 0-13-236009-8 (pbk. : alk. paper) 1. Exchange traded funds. 2. Stock index futures. I. Title.
  HG6043.A67 2009
  332.63'27—dc22
                              2008026743

To my children—Emily, Caroline, and Alexandra.
You brighten my world just by being yourselves.

Contents

Acknowledgments xv

About the author xvii

Chapter 1   Exchange-Traded Funds (ETFs): Now
Individuals Can Invest Like the
Big Players 1

ETFs Are a Special Type of Mutual Fund 2

ETFs Avoid the Expense of Fund Managers 2

ETFs Are Traded on Exchanges 4

ETF Investors Have Hidden Costs Through
the Bid-Ask Spread 7

The Creation/Redemption Process Keeps ETF
Share Prices Close to the Market Value of the
Underlying Shares 16

ETF Performance Is Not Weighed Down
by Transaction Costs 21

ETF Shares Are Often More Tax-Efficient
Than Mutual Funds 21

Special Risks of ETFs 22

Conclusion 23

Endnotes 24

Chapter 2   The Multifaceted Stock Market: A Guide
to Different Investment Styles 25

The First Decision: Stocks, Bonds, or Cash 26

Size Matters 29

Each Investment Style Has Multiple ETFs 34

Conclusion 40

Endnotes 40

Chapter 3   A One-Step Strategy for Selecting Superior
               Investments: Indexing 43

               Investments That Track Market Indexes Have
               Outperformed Most Mutual Funds 46

               The Evidence in Favor of Indexing 47

               Indexing Has Delivered Greater Profits Than
               the Average Mutual Fund, Except in the
               Small-Cap Area 49

               How a Few Mutual Fund Managers Have
               Beaten the Indexes 50

               Conclusion 52

               Appendix to Chapter 3—Index Construction
               Methodologies 53

               Endnotes 56

Chapter 4   Investment Risk: A Visit to the
               Dark Side 57

               Drawdown—An Intuitive Measure of
               Investment Risk 58

               A 43-Year History of Bear Markets 64

               What if Your Investment Was Not Around
               During a Bear Market? 70

               Example of Risk Assessment: An Emerging
               Market ETF 73

               Market Risks and Planning for Your Future 77

               Appendix 4A: Where to Find Quantitative
               Investment Risk Information 79

               Appendix 4B: Calculation of Drawdown
               with a Spreadsheet 79

               Appendix 4C: Volatility of Past Returns
               as a Risk Measure 83

               Endnotes 86

Chapter 5   How Well Are Your Investments Really
               Doing? Risk-Adjusted Performance 87

               The First Risk-Adjusted Performance Measure—
               Annual Gain-to-Drawdown Ratio 88

               Another Risk-Adjusted Performance Measure—
               The Sharpe Ratio 91

Risk Adjusted Performance Review 94
Conclusion 96
Appendix 5A—Calculation of the Compounded
Annual Rate of Return 96
Appendix 5B—Calculation of the
Sharpe Ratio 98
Endnote 101

Chapter 6   **Diversification: The Only Free Lunch
on Wall Street** 103
Reduce Risk, Not Profits, with
Diversification 104
Diversification Versus Picking Only
the Best 106
How to Determine What Should Be in
the Optimal Portfolio 107
Example—Determining a Good Mix
of Stocks and Bonds 108
Interpretation of the Sharpe Ratio 110
The Uncertainty of Future Investment
Returns 110
Conclusion 113
Endnote 113

Chapter 7   **The One-Decision Portfolio** 115
A Risk-Reducing Investment Mix 116
Indexes Used to Test the One-Decision
Portfolio 119
Performance History for the One-Decision
Portfolio 119
The One-Decision Portfolio for Less
Conservative Investors 123
ETFs You Can Use to Create Your Own
One-Decision Portfolio 124
Rebalancing 126
Why Are Only U.S. Investments Included
in the One-Decision Portfolio? 127
Conclusion 128

Appendix to Chapter 7—A Brief Discussion
of the Bond Market 129
Endnotes 133

Chapter 8   **When to Live Large: An Asset
Allocation Model for Small- versus
Large-Cap ETFs 135**
Why Market Capitalization Matters 136
Trading Rules 138
Results 139
Real-World Implementation with ETFs 142
Conclusion 145
Appendix to Chapter 8—ETF Distributions
and Taxes 146

Chapter 9   **Boring Bargains or Hot Prospects?
Choosing between Growth and
Value ETFs 151**
The Concept of Relative Strength 154
History of Relative Strength Changes between
Growth and Value 156
Recognizing the Emergence of a New Trend
Using the Relative Strength Ratio 161
Results with Small-Cap Value versus
Growth 165
Results with Large Cap Value versus
Large Cap Growth 168
Real-World Implementation with ETFs 169
Conclusion 171

Chapter 10 **When Is It Safe to Drink the Water?
International Investing 173**
How to Identify Whether the Long-Term
Trend Favors U.S. or Developed-Country
Foreign Stocks 179
Results of Using the EAFE/S&P 500 Asset
Allocation Model 182

Emerging Market ETFs—Investing for
the Future 185
Outlook for International Investing 188
Conclusion 189

**Chapter 11 What Bonds Can Tell You about Stocks:
How to Use Interest Rates 191**
A Basic Introduction to the Bond Market 192
Why Rising Interest Rates Have Usually
(But Not Always) Been Bad for Stocks 193
An Indicator of Rising Interest Rates 196
Yield Curve Indicator 197
Composite Interest Rate Indicator 203
Conclusion 205

**Chapter 12 It's a Jungle Out There: Selecting from
Among Different ETFs with Similar
Investment Objectives 207**
The Drawdown Chart—A New Tool 208
Example 1—Small-Cap ETFs 211
Example 2—Growth Versus Value ETFs 214
Example 3—Utility Sector ETFs 218
Conclusion 221
Endnotes 222

**Chapter 13 The Ultimate ETF Investment Program
for 30 Minutes per Month 223**
The Ultimate ETF Investment Program 224
Results of the Ultimate ETF Strategy 230
Conclusion 231

**Chapter 14 ETF Strategies for Investment
Income 237**
The Ideal Income Investment—A Payout
That Grows over Time 238
If You Want High Dividends, You Have to
Like Financial Stocks 239
Where to Find High-Dividend ETFs 240

A Unique High-Dividend Portfolio 243

Preferred Stock ETFs 244

Conclusion 248

Chapter 15 **The Hottest Investments Around:**
Commodity ETFs **251**

Primer on Commodity Investing 254

Absentee Ownership of Precious Metals 255

Become a Futures Trader 257

A Virtual Commodity Investment 260

How to Invest in Commodity ETFs 261

The Outlook for Commodities 263

Conclusion 264

Appendix **Internet Resources for ETF Investors** . . **267**

ETF Sponsor Web Sites 268

General ETF Web Sites 269

Index Provider Web Sites 270

Current and Historical Market Data
Web Sites 271

Fundamental Economic Data Web Sites 272

Index **273**

Acknowledgments

It is with love and gratitude that I acknowledge my father, Gerald Appel, for teaching me everything I know about investing and for establishing an ethical and intellectually challenging business environment in our offices in Great Neck. I have also been blessed with unwavering love and support from my mother, Judith Appel.

Joanne Quan Stein read every draft each step of the way, assisted with the research, and held me to the production schedule. Without her keen eye for logical gaps in my exposition, many explanations in these pages would have remained in my mind, accessible to the reader only through ESP.

Bonnie Gortler and Audrey Deifik also reviewed my drafts on short notice despite their many other work commitments. Their insights improved the book. I am grateful (and relieved) that the editorial commentary from my three colleagues, Joanne, Bonnie, and Audrey, was tougher than the comments I received from the professional editors at FT Press.

Russ Hall, Rudy Morando, and Karen Gill suggested numerous improvements to make the material more readily accessible to the reader. Their feedback was thorough and prompt. Last and certainly not least, I am grateful for the encouragement I received from Jim Boyd.

About the Author

Dr. Marvin Appel, CEO of Appel Asset Management Corporation, is a leading expert on ETF selection and active asset allocation. Together with his father, Gerald Appel (a world-famous authority on investing and technical analysis), he manages $250 million in assets. Dr. Appel also edits *Systems and Forecasts*, a top investment newsletter. He has been featured on CNBC, CNNfn, CBS Marketwatch.com and Forbes.com, and has presented at conferences ranging from the New York State Legislature's Consensus Economic Forecasting Conference to the American Association of Individual Investors. Dr. Appel is also coauthor of the book *Beating the Market, 3 Months at a Time* (FT Press, 2008).

1

EXCHANGE-TRADED FUNDS (ETFs): NOW INDIVIDUALS CAN INVEST LIKE THE BIG PLAYERS

Exchange-traded funds (ETFs) are one of the fastest-growing investments in the United States. Their rapid growth is all the more remarkable because, unlike mutual funds, ETFs do not pay sales loads to financial intermediaries. Advisors who recommend ETFs rarely have financial incentive to do so.

ETFs are a powerful investment tool. However, before you use them, you should understand how they work and what makes them different from other mutual funds. This chapter introduces you to ETFs but only begins to discuss why you should use them. Chapter 2, "The Multifaceted Stock Market: A Guide to Different Investment Styles," completes the presentation of the background necessary for you to fully appreciate the evidence in Chapter 3, "A One-Step Strategy for Selecting Superior Investments: Indexing," showing that ETFs have outperformed and are likely to continue to outperform a majority of comparable mutual funds.[1]

ETFs Are a Special Type of Mutual Fund

ETFs hold a basket of individual stocks, just as mutual funds do. Each ETF share represents a proportional piece of the portfolio of stocks, as with mutual funds. Therefore, many of the advantages of mutual funds also characterize ETFs:

- Ability to diversify with a single investment
- Ability to gain exposure to a particular investment style (small versus large company stocks, for example) or to a specific industry (utilities, technology, etc.) with a single investment, without having to select individual companies

Saving the effort needed to select individual stocks can be helpful because the selection of individual stocks has been a less important determinant of investment performance than the selection of particular industries. For example, the steep rise in oil prices that started in 2003 has lifted shares in a wide variety of energy companies. During the same period, U.S. automotive stocks have faced great difficulties. As a result, even relatively uninformed energy investors are far more likely to have nice gains to show for the 2003–2006 period because any stock they picked is likely to have done well. On the other hand, even the most astute automotive analyst would have had a rough time making money by holding stocks in that sector. This is not to say that competition between two companies has never resulted in gains for one stock and losses for the other. Rather, industry-wide developments that move stocks across an entire sector have had a larger impact on the stock market than have company-specific events. (Even a takeover bid for a particular company often leads other companies in that sector to move.)

ETFs Avoid the Expense of Fund Managers

Most open-end mutual funds (which will be referred to simply as *mutual funds* throughout the rest of the book) are actively managed. This means that most funds have managers who pick which stocks to buy and sell, and when, according to their own judgments. Active managers generally keep their stock selections secret until they have finished making transactions for their own funds. In this way, they avoid having to compete in the market when placing transactions against free riders, who might want to copy the managers' ideas.

In contrast, ETFs are passively managed. Passive management means that a predetermined set of rules is used to select the individual stocks that are held in each ETF. An ETF sponsor can update the selection of stocks in a passively managed portfolio, but only on dates that it specified in advance. Anybody who knows what the rules are can anticipate the changes that an ETF will be making to its portfolio on the dates specified for portfolio update. Because the rules for selecting a passively managed portfolio are available to everyone, it is unnecessary to hire a manager.

The fund sponsor for each passively managed ETF selects a set of rules that govern which stocks the ETF will hold. After these rules are in place, the ETF does not deviate. So, unlike the case with an actively managed fund, investors in a passively managed fund or ETF know at any time exactly which stocks are in the fund and when that portfolio is scheduled to change. (Although some actively managed ETFs are in development, passively managed ETFs are likely to dominate the landscape for the foreseeable future.) The accurate knowledge by individual fund investors of their funds' holdings is called *investment transparency*. For many investors, this transparency is considered an advantage, because when you buy an ETF, you know exactly what you are getting.[2]

Another term used to describe passive investment management is indexing. The connotation of a market index, in addition to being passively managed and enjoying the attendant advantages of low cost and transparency, is that it usually aims to represent the performance of a particular market sector. Broadly based indexes can represent the entire universe of publicly traded shares in the United States, or even in the world (such as the MSCI World Index). At the other end of the spectrum, a number of market indexes have been designed to represent the behavior of fairly narrow industry sectors, such as the S&P Select Homebuilders Industry Index. (The latter is tracked by an ETF, the SPDR Homebuilders ETF, whose ticker symbol is XHB.)

ETFs Are Traded on Exchanges

The big difference between ETFs and regular mutual funds is that as an individual investor, you buy ETFs on a stock exchange. You do not deal directly with the sponsoring mutual fund company, and you bear the full costs of every transaction you make. Whether this is an advantage to you depends on how you are using ETFs.

For example, when you purchase shares of a regular mutual fund, such as Vanguard's S&P 500 Index Fund (VFINX), you send your money to Vanguard, and it creates new shares of its fund for you. The price per share is based on the value at the market close of the fund's holdings on the date of your purchase. Conversely, if you want to redeem from a Vanguard fund, Vanguard eliminates your shares and sends you the cash value, again based on the value of the assets in the fund at the market close on that day.

With regular (open-end) mutual funds, buyers and sellers receive the same price for their shares on any given day, regardless of how the market behaved, and regardless of how many other shareholders in the fund might be buying or selling on that day. If you buy new shares, the mutual fund manager might be unable to put your money to work until the next day, when the fund will have the chance to purchase additional shares. If you redeem mutual fund shares, the fund manager might have to raise the cash you have requested by selling some of the fund's holdings the next day. The necessity of engaging in such transactions to accommodate shareholder additions or redemptions might hurt the performance of the mutual fund, but it does not affect the price per share you pay or receive.

In contrast, when you purchase an ETF, you call or e-mail your stockbroker just as you would to buy stock in an individual company. When you purchase an ETF, you must pay a broker's commission, similar to the charge you would incur to buy an individual stock. Note the difference between the likely size of a commission on the purchase of ETF shares and the sales charge on the purchase of a mutual fund with a sales load. Competition among brokers has driven the cost of buying ETF shares to low levels at many brokerage firms (including online brokerages and discount brokerages). However, the sales loads on mutual funds remain far larger than the cost of buying shares through a discount broker. Sales loads are generally as high as 5 percent of the assets you are investing.

You pay this sales charge either as a lump sum up front or over a period of years. When the sales charge is collected over a period of years (for example, 0.75 percent of assets per year for seven years in a typical class B load mutual fund share), you pay a "deferred sales charge" if you try to exit the fund before the full sales charge has been paid to the broker.[3]

When you purchase shares of an open-end mutual fund, the number of outstanding fund shares increases because the fund company takes your cash and creates new shares that are delivered to your account. The mutual fund generally puts the cash it received from you to work by using it to buy stock. Similarly, when you redeem shares of an open-end mutual fund, the fund company takes your shares and eliminates them, thereby decreasing the number of outstanding shares. In return for your shares, the fund company places cash in your account. The mutual fund generally sells shares of stock it owns to raise the cash it has to give to you.

Unlike mutual funds, which need to create new shares to meet your purchases and to eliminate existing shares to meet your redemptions, when you buy or sell ETF shares, you conduct the transaction with another investor. You and the other investor exchange ETF shares for cash, but the number of outstanding ETF shares does not change as a result of your transaction. Only the list of shareholders changes.

As an example, let us compare what happens when an investor purchases 100 SPY at $127/share to what happens if the same investor instead purchases shares in an open-end S&P 500 Index Fund (ticker ABCDX) that sells for $50/share. The outline that follows compares the purchase of ETF shares to the purchase of shares in an open-end mutual fund.

Case 1	Case 2
Investor A has $12,700 that he wants to invest in the ETF that tracks the S&P 500 Index (ticker SPY). Investor B has 100 shares of SPY that she wants to sell at $127.00/share.	Investor A has $12,700 to invest in an open-end mutual fund (ticker ABCDX) that tracks the S&P 500 Index. The share price of ABCDX is $50/share.
Before purchase by Investor A:	**Before purchase by Investor A:**
• Investor A has $12,700 cash. • Investor B has 100 SPY. • Total SPY outstanding = 100 shares.	• Investor A has $12,700 cash. • Fund ABCDX has 2,000 shares outstanding at $50/each, for total assets of $100,000. This $100,000 in fund assets is entirely invested in the basket of stocks that tracks the S&P 500 Index.
After purchase by Investor A:	**After purchase by Investor A:**
• Investor A has 100 SPY. • Investor B has $12,700 cash. • Total SPY outstanding = 100 shares. (No change from before the purchase by Investor A.)	• Investor A has 254 shares of fund ABCDX. • Fund ABCDX holds shares of stock worth $100,000 plus $12,700 cash, for total assets of $112,700 (an increase from before the purchase by Investor A). The new cash in the fund will be used to purchase more shares during the next trading day. • Total number of ABCDX shares outstanding has increased from 2,000 to 2,254, but each share is still worth $50.

Every transaction in an open-end fund for the entire day receives the same price. An order placed with a fund at 9:00 a.m. gets the same closing price for the day as one placed at 3:59 p.m. That closing price is set based on data from the market close at 4:00 p.m. Any order received at a mutual fund after 4:00 p.m.—even 4:01 p.m.— receives the next day's closing price.

With ETFs, as with stocks, the price you get for your order can change throughout the day. Suppose that you buy an ETF early in the trading day (say, at 10:00 a.m.), and then at 11:00 a.m., some news comes out that drives the market higher. In this case, you will profit from the timing of your order. However, mutual fund purchasers will not. Of course, the reverse can also be true—namely, that the timing of your order can result in your getting a less favorable price than would have been the case if you had waited until the end of the trading day.

If you are a day trader, the ability to trade ETFs throughout the day makes them useful to you in a way that other mutual funds are not. Indeed, many hedge funds use ETFs specifically to be able to day-trade. If you trade more slowly, holding positions for days or weeks or longer, or if you are a long-term investor, the ability to trade during the day will probably not affect your investment performance one way or the other, on average.

For investors who utilize end-of-day trading strategies, ETFs have a big advantage that does not apply to individual stocks or mutual funds: Many ETFs trade until 4:15 p.m.—15 minutes after the regular market closes at 4:00 p.m. This allows you to wait until the market close to collect data and then use that data to decide which trades to execute on the same day.

In my experience, any trading model that utilizes daily data from the market close is likely to perform more poorly if trades are not executed on that same day. Investors who use mutual funds that allow unlimited trading (such as those offered by Rydex, Profunds, and Direxion that are designed to accommodate active trading) must submit their buy or sell orders to the mutual fund before the market closes. There is a chance that some trading decisions made before the close will turn out to be different from the decisions that would have been made if the final closing data had been known earlier.

ETF Investors Have Hidden Costs Through the Bid-Ask Spread

From the earlier discussion, you can infer that the price you pay for your ETF depends on the balance of supply and demand for that ETF at the time your order hits the trading floor. An ETF's share price is usually slightly different from the market value of the fund's underlying holdings. Moreover, the price a buyer pays is generally higher than the price a seller receives.

Selling a used car is a useful analogy. If you know how much you want for your car, you can sell it yourself. If a willing buyer sees your advertisement, he may take the car off your hands at a price you both feel is fair. However, you might not be able to locate a buyer.

If that is the case, you might decide to sell your car to a dealer. The dealer then pays a price low enough for him to expect to turn a profit when he resells your car. The dealer's knowledge of the car's value comes from observing the used-car market. Ideally (for the dealer), he would like to offer you as little as possible, but if the offer is too low for your liking, you will simply look for another dealer. On the other hand, if your demands are too high to leave room to profit, the dealer will let you walk.

If you accept the dealer's offer on your car, he will try to resell it at a higher price. Suppose the dealer is extremely lucky—the second after you leave the lot, a buyer enters, looking for exactly the car you just sold. Naturally, the dealer will sell it at a profit. The same car on the same day was worth less to you, the seller, than it was to the buyer.

Trading ETFs on exchanges works much the same way. If you as an ETF buyer are offering the same price that a different seller is demanding, the stock exchange is supposed to match up the two of you so that each of your orders can be filled. (However, exchanges have not always functioned this way, giving rise to periodic scandals and investigations. As a result, you should pay attention to the quality of your trade execution.)

However, suppose you want to buy an ETF at a time when a willing seller is not around. In that case, a dealer or specialist in a stock exchange offers to fill your order. Just as with a car dealer, a stock dealer transacts with you only at a price that allows him to make a profit. With the advent of electronic trading, you (through your broker) can look for the best price available for the ETF you want on more than one exchange. This is analogous to shopping around for the best price at multiple car dealerships.

If the dealer sells you the shares you want, he immediately tries to repurchase them from someone else at a lower price. If you turn around and try to resell your shares to a dealer (or specialist, or market maker), you receive less than you paid, even if the market has not moved one iota in the interim.

The price you pay to buy shares at the lowest available price is called the asking price, or *ask*. The price you receive when you sell shares at the highest available price is the *bid*. As with cars, stock dealers stand ready at any time to sell you shares at the ask price or to buy shares from you at the bid price.

The difference between the price you have to pay to buy shares and what a seller would receive to sell shares is called the *bid-ask spread*. The bid-ask spread is no less a cost to you than a broker's commission, despite being less visible (see Table 1.1). But to the unwary investor, the bid-ask spread is a hidden cost. Before you decide to buy an ETF, you should ask your broker for both the bid and ask so that you can get a feel for the cost per trade.

TABLE 1.1 Bid-Ask Spreads as a Percentage of the Share Price for Selected U.S. Equity ETFs During Normal Midday Market Conditions in the Fall of 2005*

ETF Name	ETF Ticker Symbol	Investment Objective	Bid Price ($)	Ask Price ($)	Bid-Ask Spread as % of Midpoint	Size of Market (Shares in 100s, Bid×Ask)
S&P 500 Depository Receipts	SPY	Large cap	123.81	123.83	.02%	750×400
iShares Russell 100 Index Fund	IWB	Large cap	67.08	67.16	.12%	100×132
Vanguard Large Cap ETF	VV	Large cap	54.77	54.84	.13%	500×600
Diamonds Trust	DIA	Large cap	107.06	107.08	.02%	600×300
iShares Russell 1000 Growth Index Fund	IWF	Large growth	50.62	50.69	.14%	100×600

TABLE 1.1 (*continued*)

ETF Name	ETF Ticker Symbol	Investment Objective	Bid Price ($)	Ask Price ($)	Bid-Ask Spread as % of Midpoint	Size of Market (Shares in 100s, Bid×Ask)
iShares S&P 500 Growth Index Fund	IVW	Large growth	58.71	58.81	.17%	600×900
Vanguard Growth ETF	VUG	Large growth	53.06	53.11	.09%	300×379
iShares Russell 1000 Value Index Fund	IWD	Large value	68.40	68.49	.13%	600×620
iShares S&P 500 Value Index Fund	IVE	Large value	64.40	64.51	.17%	300×600
Vanguard Value ETF	VTV	Large value	56.39	56.44	.09%	491×94
iShares S&P 400 Midcap Index Fund	IJH	Midcap	72.12	72.16	.06%	30×30
S&P Midcap SPDR	MDY	Midcap	131.46	131.49	.02%	300×125
Vanguard Extended Market Index ETF	VXF	Midcap	89.13	89.25	.13%	600×600
iShares Russell Midcap Index Fund	IWR	Midcap	85.83	85.91	.09%	490×1000
iShares Russell Midcap Growth Index Fund	IWP	Midcap growth	90.99	91.10	.12%	300×900

TABLE 1.1 (*continued*)

ETF Name	ETF Ticker Symbol	Investment Objective	Bid Price ($)	Ask Price ($)	Bid-Ask Spread as % of Midpoint	Size of Market (Shares in 100s, Bid×Ask)
iShares S&P 400 Midcap Growth Index Fund	IJK	Midcap growth	73.33	73.43	.14%	300×300
iShares Russell Midcap Value Index Fund	IWS	Midcap value	122.22	122.28	.05%	10×74
iShares S&P 400 Midcap Value Index Fund	IJJ	Midcap value	69.34	69.45	.16%	300×300
iShares S&P 600 Index Fund	IJR	Small cap	57.42	57.47	.09%	50×50
iShares Russell 2000 Index Fund	IWM	Small cap	66.21	66.22	.02%	500×32
iShares Russell Microcap Index Fund	IWC	Small cap	50.51	50.59	.16%	200×300
Vanguard Small Cap ETF	VB	Small cap	58.93	59.02	.15%	300×300
Vanguard Small Cap Growth ETF	VBK	Small cap growth	56.99	57.15	.28%	500×500
StreetTracks Small Cap Growth	DSG	Small cap growth	79.71	79.87	.20%	50×50

TABLE 1.1 (*continued*)

ETF Name	ETF Ticker Symbol	Investment Objective	Bid Price ($)	Ask Price ($)	Bid-Ask Spread as % of Midpoint	Size of Market (Shares in 100s, Bid×Ask)
iShares S&P 600 Small Cap Growth	IJT	Small cap growth	114.60	114.70	.09%	3×25
iShares Russell 2000 Growth	IWO	Small cap growth	68.55	68.59	.06%	130×60
Vanguard Small Cap Value ETF	VBR	Small cap value	61	61.11	.18%	900×600
StreetTracks Small Cap Value	DSV	Small cap value	62.01	62.17	.26%	50×100
iShares S&P 600 Small Cap Value	IJS	Small cap value	63.89	63.98	.14%	300×300
iShares Russell 2000 Value	IWN	Small cap value	65.88	65.92	.06%	95×40
Select Energy Sector SPDR	XLE	Sector energy	47.6	47.65	.10%	200×315
iShares Dow Jones U.S. Financial Index Fund	IYF	Sector financial	100.77	100.91	.14%	300×900
iShares Dow Jones U.S. Financial Services Index Fund	IYG	Sector financial	113.54	113.68	.12%	300×900

TABLE 1.1 (*continued*)

ETF Name	ETF Ticker Symbol	Investment Objective	Bid Price ($)	Ask Price ($)	Bid-Ask Spread as % of Midpoint	Size of Market (Shares in 100s, Bid×Ask)
Select Financial Sector SPDR	XLF	Sector financial	31.58	31.59	.03%	600×1000
Vanguard Financial ETF	VFH	Sector financial	55.78	55.87	.16%	300×300
Vanguard Health Care ETF	VHT	Sector health care	53.07	53.16	.17%	300×600
Select Health Care Sector SPDR	XLV	Sector health care	30.96	30.98	.06%	900×100
iShares Dow Jones U.S. Healthcare Index Fund	IYH	Sector heath care	61.76	61.85	.15%	300×600
iShares Cohen & Steers Realty Majors Fund	ICF	Sector REITs	73.28	73.37	.12%	110×120
iShares Dow Jones U.S. Real Estate Index Fund	IYR	Sector REITs	64	64.02	.03%	56×130
Vanguard REIT ETF	VNQ	Sector REITs	59.79	60.04	.42%	100×100
iShares Dow Jones U.S. Technology Index Fund	IYW	Sector technology	49.55	49.62	.14%	900×100
Select Technology Sector SPDR	XLK	Sector technology	21.10	21.12	.09%	330×1400
iShares Goldman Sachs Technology Index Fund	IGM	Sector technology	46.97	47.04	.15%	101×230

TABLE 1.1 (*continued*)

ETF Name	ETF Ticker Symbol	Investment Objective	Bid Price ($)	Ask Price ($)	Bid-Ask Spread as % of Midpoint	Size of Market (Shares in 100s, Bid×Ask)
Vanguard Information Technology ETF	VGT	Sector technology	48.03	48.12	.19%	600×600
Utilities HOLDRs	UTH	Sector utilities	109.22	109.30	.07%	100×65
Select Utilities Sector SPDR	XLU	Sector utilities	30.45	30.48	.10%	1200×800
Vanguard Utilities ETF	VPU	Sector utilities	63.34	63.46	.19%	900×600
iShares Russell 3000 Index Fund	IWV	Total market	74.32	74.42	.13%	100×100
iShares Dow Jones Total Market Index Fund	IYY	Total market	62.51	62.59	.13%	100×100
Vanguard Total Market ETF	VTI	Total market	121.95	122.07	.10%	100×900
iShares Lehman Aggregate Bond Index Fund	AGG	Bond	99.39	99.79	.40%	300×350
iShares Lehman 7-10 Year Treasury Note Fund	IEF	Bond	82.47	82.55	.10%	350×1000
iShares Lehman TIPS Fund	TIP	Bond	102.26	102.46	.20%	400×400

TABLE 1.1 (continued)

ETF Name	ETF Ticker Symbol	Investment Objective	Bid Price ($)	Ask Price ($)	Bid-Ask Spread as % of Midpoint	Size of Market (Shares in 100s, Bid×Ask)
iShares Goldman Sachs Investop Corp Bond Fund	LQD	Bond	106.09	106.76	.63%	300×250
iShares Lehman 20-Year Treasury Bond Fund	TLT	Bond	88.72	88.82	.11%	2500×2500
iShares 1–3 Year Treasury Note Fund	SHY	Bond	80.08	80.13	.06%	1000×1000

°The size of the market is the number of shares available to sell at the bid price by the number of shares available to buy at the ask price, in hundreds of shares. (So, for example, 100×50 means that 10,000 shares are available to sell at the bid and that 5,000 are available to buy at the ask.) Note that the bid-ask spreads and the size of the market on any ETF can vary from minute to minute. The data in Table 1.1 is only a snapshot of the market at a particular time in the past. Future conditions might differ.

Bid-ask spreads and brokers' commissions are disadvantages of ETFs compared to regular mutual funds, which you can purchase without incurring either expense. However, mutual fund investors also bear these costs, albeit in a less visible way.

If the mutual fund must make transactions as a result of share purchases or redemptions from any shareholder or on the basis of investment decisions that the portfolio manager makes, the fund bears the costs of a bid-ask spread in addition to the brokerage commissions for whatever stocks it trades. These expenses of the fund are not reported as part of its expense ratio. The typical equity mutual fund turns over 100 percent of its portfolio each year.

Because ETFs are passively managed, the underlying stock portfolios turn over slowly compared to most mutual funds. Therefore, ETF performance is far less impaired by transactions in the underlying stocks than is the case with most mutual funds. (This advantage some-what offsets the burden that an ETF investor has of paying for his own transaction costs.) The extent to which mutual funds suffer from trans-action costs in their stock portfolios varies widely, depending on the manager's investment style, the type of stocks in which the fund invests, and the level of shareholder additions and redemptions. Information about how much a regular mutual fund spends on brokerage commis-sions and adverse market impact is difficult to uncover and is not included in the mutual fund's expense ratio.

As you might expect, dealers respond to changes in the balance between supply and demand. If everyone wants to sell at the same time but no one wants to buy, the price falls. That is to say, the bid price drops. Again, all this is independent of the actual market value of the underlying stocks that the ETF holds.

The question then arises, what is to stop ETFs from trading well above or below the market value of the underlying stocks? The next section discusses the unique feature of ETFs that keeps them in line with fair market values.

The Creation/Redemption Process Keeps ETF Share Prices Close to the Market Value of the Underlying Shares

The unique feature of ETFs compared to mutual funds is that shares can be created or redeemed in exchange for the basket of underlying stocks. You and I cannot do this, but a number of large financial firms called *authorized participants* can by transacting with the ETF custo-dian, as explained next.

All shares of stocks in individual companies need to be housed somewhere. As individual investors, we rarely hold stock certificates for ourselves these days. Rather, a custodial bank or brokerage firm holds shares for us and keeps track of how much it is holding on our behalf. Because ETFs represent partial ownership of a metaphorical basket of stocks, the actual shares in the basket need to be held some-where, just as our own individual stocks do.

For this purpose, each ETF has a custodian who holds the shares. However, rather than keeping track of which shares belong to which individual investor, all the custodian has to do is make sure that the number of ETF shares in circulation is exactly the right amount for the custodian's holdings of underlying shares. In this regard, an ETF share (in the hands of an authorized participant) is like a claim check. Whoever submits the claim check can retrieve the stored item, which in this case is a basket of stocks. Because all investors know what goods the claim check represents, they can trade claim checks among themselves without needing to inspect the underlying merchandise for each transaction, while the custodian simply guards the merchandise until someone claims it.

Even though ETF shares are traded between investors far more frequently than they are exchanged for the underlying basket of stocks, authorized participants do have the option of switching between ETFs and the actual underlying shares in individual companies. If an authorized participant wants to create shares of an ETF, it can deliver the basket of stocks to the ETF custodian. Conversely, if the authorized participant wants to redeem shares of an ETF, it can deliver the ETF shares to the custodian, who transfers the underlying stocks' shares in exchange. Creation or redemption of ETFs usually occurs in lots of 50,000 ETF shares.

The ability of authorized participants to create or redeem ETF shares in exchange for the underlying stocks gives them a financial incentive to keep the price of ETFs close to the market value of the underlying shares. To see how this occurs, consider the example of an ETF facing a lot of selling pressure. As discussed earlier, an overabundance of sellers drives the ETF price down, regardless of what is happening to the underlying shares.

Let us consider the hypothetical (and unrealistically simple) case of an ETF that holds only one stock—say, shares in GE. The ETF is priced so that one share of GE-ETF equals one share of GE stock. Suppose that panic selling has driven the ETF price a full 1 percent below the market value of its underlying GE shares.

An authorized participant firm happens to own 50,000 shares of GE in its own capital account. This firm, when it perceives the disparity between the GE-ETF and the true price of GE stock, can buy 50,000 shares of GE-ETF at a 1 percent discount and simultaneously sell its 50,000 shares of GE.

At the end of the day, the authorized participant firm asks to redeem its 50,000 shares of GE-ETF. It receives 50,000 shares of GE. The firm started and ended the day with 50,000 shares of GE. But in the course of the day's trading, it locked in a profit of 1 percent.

Obviously, no ETF is created as a basket of one stock. However, authorized participants can achieve the same result with a basket of stocks. If strong selling drives the price of the ETF far enough below the market value of its underlying stocks, an authorized participant can step in and buy the discounted ETF while simultaneously selling (or selling short) the equivalent basket of stocks.

Conversely, if strong buying pushes the price of an ETF far enough above the fair value of its underlying stocks, the authorized participant can sell or short-sell shares of the ETF while simultaneously buying the basket of stocks in the open market.

The process of simultaneously buying and selling essentially identical baskets of stocks in different places at the same time to profit from price discrepancies is called *arbitrage*. Firms that practice arbitrage help maintain a narrow gap between the ETF's market price and the value of its underlying shares.

The size of the discrepancy between an ETF's price and its fair value depends on the character of the stocks in the ETF. An S&P 500 ETF holds stocks for which there are almost always willing buyers and sellers for a large number of shares. Such stocks are said to be very liquid. All else being equal, it is easier to be an investor in a liquid stock than the opposite—an illiquid stock. Suppose you want to buy $1 million worth of shares in ExxonMobil, a company whose outstanding shares are worth a total of $349 billion. Compared to the entire company, $1 million is an insignificantly small amount, and it is usually easy to find someone with whom to transact. Most of the dollar value of the stocks in the S&P 500 consists of easy-to-trade stocks like XOM. As a result, the cost of arbitrage by an authorized participant is low, allowing S&P 500 ETFs to trade close to their fair values.

On the other hand, an ETF that holds only small company stocks imposes higher costs on arbitrageurs. If you want to buy $1 million worth of stock in a company whose outstanding shares are worth

$100 million in total, you have to locate a seller for fully 1 percent of the company's shares. Although in the case of ExxonMobil, it is not hard to find sellers for less than 1/3,000th of 1 percent of a company, it is a far more difficult undertaking to find someone who owns 1 percent of a small company and is willing to sell that much all at once to you. To attract that large a fraction of the outstanding shares, you might have to raise the price you are willing to pay. Conversely, if you want to sell 1 percent of a company's stock, you have to accept a fairly low price to attract that many buyers all at once. Although this is an extreme example, these considerations usually do cause the share price of a small-cap ETF to deviate further from its fair value before it becomes profitable to arbitrage, compared to the situation with large company stocks, which are almost always more liquid.

The market provides two types of information throughout the trading day for you to consult when you are considering making a trade. First are the current bid and ask prices. (If you want to sell immediately "at the market," you should get the bid price. If you want to buy immediately "at the market," you should pay the ask price. In reality, delays in transmitting your order to the exchange might result in your getting a price different from the bid-ask quote you saw when you placed the order.)

The second bit of information is the Indicative Optimized Portfolio Value (IOPV), which in later chapters of this book is referred to by the more descriptive term *fair value*. IOPV is the fair market value of the underlying basket of stocks in the ETF. This is updated every 15 seconds. Normally, the bid price should be lower than the IOPV, and the ask price should be above it.

To understand why this is, we can turn back to the used car example. There is usually a true wholesale price at which a dealer knows she can buy or sell a car at auction. This price is analogous to the IOPV, which is what the basket of stocks in an ETF is worth in the absence of transaction costs. Generally speaking, a car dealer will not pay more than the auction price to buy a used car and will not sell one off the lot for less, because transacting with other dealers at a car auction remains an option. If a dealer did put up a car for sale for less than the auction price, another dealer could simply buy the car and resell it at auction, pocketing a profit at no risk (again, neglecting transaction costs, which for cars are significant).

Similarly, the ask price on an ETF is what you would have to pay to purchase it. Insiders (authorized participants, specialists, etc.) ordinarily will not sell you an ETF for less than it would cost them to reassemble the underlying basket of stocks through purchases on the open market. If one authorized participant were to ask less for an ETF than the underlying basket of stocks was worth on the open market, which is the IOPV, another trader would snap up the shares at the too-low ask price and simultaneously sell short the underlying basket of stocks at the IOPV, locking in a profit. This actually does occur on rare occasions when one trader's attention might lapse. At such times, other traders swoop in like vultures to take advantage of the riskless profit opportunity. The trader who lets himself get taken advantage of is said to have been *picked off*, in the language of floor traders.

It is wise to check the IOPV before placing an order. If the bid-ask quote is very different from the IOPV, you might want to try to understand why before making the trade. In some cases, especially when the market is moving quickly, the 15-second delay in updating the IOPV can account entirely for discrepancies between it and the bid-ask quote.

IOPV is reported under a different ticker symbol than the ETF. Other ticker symbols exist for ETFs that report more arcane data, such as the number of shares outstanding, the prior day's closing fair market value, and the cash component of the ETF holdings. (Because the stocks in an ETF pay dividends at various dates, each ETF might have small cash holdings in addition to the basket of shares.)

Good sources of information on the ticker symbols for this additional ETF data are available online from Indexfunds.com[4] and from www.amex.com[5] (the American Stock Exchange Web site). Barclay's iShares Web site (www.ishares.com) also provides ticker symbols for price quotes and intra-day fair market values for all of its ETFs.

ETF Performance Is Not Weighed Down by Transaction Costs

As mentioned earlier, all mutual fund shareholders bear the costs incurred as a result of purchases or redemptions by every other shareholder. Such costs are typically modest for any transaction that an individual investor might request. However, if large numbers of shareholders request redemptions or make purchases at the same time, the fund might incur significant costs.

Many funds restrict the number of transactions that each investor can make in a given year to avoid these types of costs. However, the larger problem for mutual fund investors is what would happen if a large number of long-term shareholders decided to run for the exits at the same time. That could happen on a day of a significant market decline, such as occurred on October 19, 1987, when the S&P 500 Index lost more than 20 percent of its value during just that one day.

ETFs do not suffer from this risk because the only way for ETF shares to be redeemed is with a transfer of shares of individual stocks. No cost is involved in simply transferring stocks from one account to another, so the performance for remaining ETF shareholders is not adversely affected when ETF shares are redeemed. Those costs fall entirely on the authorized participant firms if they elect to liquidate shares they have received from a creation or redemption.

ETF Shares Are Often More Tax-Efficient Than Mutual Funds

The exchange of ETF shares for shares of stock also avoids realizing capital gains when many shareholders want to unload the fund. In a regular mutual fund, when shareholder redemptions force the fund to sell stock holdings to raise the cash needed to meet those redemptions, any profits on the stock sale generate capital gains that are passed on to the remaining shareholders of the fund at the time of its annual capital gains distribution. This means that long-term shareholders might have to pay capital gains taxes because some other shareholders sold out.

In some instances, fund managers might decide to realize the gains from one of their holdings. That, too, creates a taxable capital gain for the fund shareholders, whether or not they actually sell their shares. The extent to which this is an issue depends on how frequently a fund manager turns over his portfolio and whether the market has been in an uptrend. (At the tail end of a bear market, there might be no profits to tax, in which case portfolio turnover does not create tax liabilities for the shareholders.)

The exchange of ETF shares for shares of the underlying stocks does not create a taxable event. The only way for a long-term shareholder of an ETF to realize capital gains without selling his own shares is when a change in the basket of stocks forces the sale of some shares. Because all ETFs that are currently trading in the United States are passively managed and therefore have low portfolio turnover, the risk of a large capital gains distribution is minimal. In contrast, a regular mutual fund can generate a large taxable distribution in either of two situations: first, if the portfolio manager makes a big change in his holdings, or second, if a large number of shareholder redemptions force the fund to sell stock.

Special Risks of ETFs

As already discussed, ETF share prices are sensitive to the balance between supply and demand—a risk absent from regular mutual funds. ETF investors face the additional risk of relying on authorized participants to keep ETF prices in line with the underlying share values. During *fast markets*—periods marked by an overwhelming imbalance between supply and demand—authorized participant firms and specialists have been known to be slow to step up and fill the wave of orders. The result is that at the time you are most anxious to sell, you might not be able to get as fair a price (relative to the value of the underlying shares) as you thought you would. The bid-ask spreads illustrated in Table 1.1 were obtained during a normal market. If you buy or sell during a fast market, your bid-ask spread costs will be higher than normal.

Actually, if you like to trade against the crowd, ETF pricing can work in your favor. You might be able to buy the ETF you want at a discount to its fair value if panic selling is occurring. If you are looking to sell ETF shares, you might be able to get more than fair value if buyers are clamoring for what you are selling.

Conclusion

This chapter has described the ways in which ETFs possess characteristics of both traditional open-end mutual funds and shares in individual companies. Like mutual funds, ETF shares represent a proportional ownership in a portfolio of individual stocks or bonds. All the ETFs currently listed have investment transparency—you know exactly what you are buying. Although it is usually not important for an individual mutual fund investor to know precisely what stocks are in his fund's portfolio, in the past, some mutual funds deviated from their original objectives, leading investors to assume risks of which they were unaware when they selected the fund.

Like individual stocks and in contrast to open-end mutual funds, ETFs trade on exchanges. This means that your transaction costs are likely to be greater with an ETF than with a no-load mutual fund purchased directly from the fund company. For long-term shareholders, their transaction costs might ultimately be offset by an improvement in ETF performance compared to a comparable mutual fund because ETF shareholders do not bear transaction costs arising from buy and sell orders from other shareholders.

Another difference between ETFs and mutual funds is that ETF share prices are subject to shifts in the balance between supply and demand at the time you place your order. This represents an additional risk that is nonexistent with open-end funds.

The flexibility of ETFs has led a wide range of investors to utilize them. We have, however, just barely begun to discuss the advantages of ETFs. Specifically, we have referred to potentially greater tax efficiency compared to regular mutual funds and to the benefits to long-term shareholders of not having their long-term performance eroded if other shareholders effect large or frequent transactions.

The next two chapters teach you how to evaluate mutual fund and ETF performance and show you in which areas ETFs have outperformed a majority of their actively managed competition.

Endnotes

1 The past results presented in this book, either real or hypothetical, do not guarantee future investment performance.

2 During the 1990s, a number of ostensibly low-volatility equity mutual funds stretched their mandates to be able to participate in the boom in technology stocks. These funds did boost their gains by doing so for as long as the tech boom lasted, but then they delivered unexpectedly large losses during the ensuing bear market. Shareholders who thought they were diluting their risk from exposure to technology stocks by investing in nontechnology funds found out that they were not as protected as they had expected.

3 Many mutual funds that normally charge sales loads are also available through discount brokers with mutual fund supermarkets such as Schwab or T.D. Ameritrade. These discount brokerages frequently do not impose the normal brokerage sales load on mutual fund purchases, which is a big advantage compared to using a full-service broker. However, the discount brokers do impose a range of charges of their own. Many funds purchased through supermarkets are free of transaction costs, but others might carry prohibitive costs. Be careful about purchasing mutual funds through brokers.

4 The exact URL for Indexfunds.com is www.indexfunds.com/data/tickerzone.php.

5 On the home page for the American Stock Exchange, you can use its ETF screener to find the ticker symbol for the shares you want. For further information about each ETF, enter its ticker symbol into the dialog box as if requesting a quote. Finally, on the quote screen, select the "tear sheet," which has all the secondary ticker symbols as well as other information.

2

THE MULTIFACETED STOCK MARKET: A GUIDE TO DIFFERENT INVESTMENT STYLES

More than 475 ETFs are trading in the United States. Considering that most ETFs are low-margin businesses for their sponsors, why should there be so many? The answer, not surprisingly, is that a large number of investment objectives can be filled with ETFs. In medicine, when a condition has a multiplicity of treatments available, the implication is usually that no single treatment has demonstrated clearly superior results. The same is true in investing. If a strategy had a clearly superior record, nobody would invest using any other method. The fact that so many choices are available to the individual investor reflects that each investment strategy has its advantages and its drawbacks, its past successes and failures. You, the reader, are left with a bewildering array of choices. The good news is that the range of options might present the opportunity to outperform the market. Here we begin to lay out the choices you have that are the building blocks of a successful investment strategy. Later chapters of the book show you how to take advantage of the options available to you.

The First Decision: Stocks, Bonds, or Cash

ETFs represent different areas of the stock and investment grade bond markets. For cash holdings, you will likely be best off in a low-cost money market fund.[1] The closest alternative to a money market fund available through ETFs is the iShares Lehman 1–3-Year Treasury Index Fund, ticker symbol SHY. Although the 2.5 percent yield paid by SHY is higher than that paid by most money market funds, the yield advantage is small compared to the best money market funds. Moreover, SHY has some price risk, and you do have to pay commissions to buy and sell SHY, whereas the best money market funds incur neither of these disadvantages. In particular, during periods when the Federal Reserve has boosted short-term interest rates, the total return available from a good money market fund has actually been higher than that from short-term bond funds such as SHY. (Of course, the converse is also likely to be true. If the Federal Reserve is on a well-telegraphed campaign of lowering interest rates, SHY could potentially generate capital gains in addition to its yield.)

The first decision that the individual investor must make is how much to invest in each of these areas. The optimal asset allocation in general will be different at different points in the life of an investor and will depend on the economic outlook. Table 2.1 provides a brief summary of how stocks, bonds, and cash have performed historically in the United States.

TABLE 2.1   Long-Term Performance Histories for Three Different Broad Classes of Investments in the United States (Stocks, Bonds, or Cash), and the Relative Performance of These Different Investments According to the Level of Inflation

	Stocks (Large Company)	Bonds	Treasury Bills
Long-term annual compounded growth rate 1926–2004°	10.4%	Long-term corporate: 5.9% Long-term government: 5.4% Intermediate-term government: 5.4%	3.7%

TABLE 2.1 (continued)

	Stocks (Large Company)	Bonds	Treasury Bills
Worst losses based on calendar year results	64% (1929–1932); 35% (1937); 37% (1973–1974); 38% (2000–2002)	11% (1967–1969) 7% (1978–1980) 7% (1999) (Risk figures for long-term corporate bonds only)	0
Moderate inflation	Best		
Severe inflation		Worst	Best
Deflation	Worst	Best	

*Source: Ibbotson, Stocks, Bonds, Bills, and Inflation, 2005 Yearbook.

Although a discussion of personal financial planning is beyond the scope of this book, Chapter 7, "The One-Decision Portfolio," presents a one-decision portfolio suitable for relatively conservative investors. The one-decision portfolio allocates 50 percent to equity investments and 50 percent to income investments. Historically, all but the most conservative investors would have benefited from having exposure to U.S. equities.

Table 2.2 shows more recent annual return data. Based on calendar year total returns 1979 to 2007, stocks have been the most profitable investment. Nonetheless, bonds beat stocks in 9 out of 29 years. Cash also beat stocks in 8 out of 29 years. Cash beat bonds in 10 out of the past 29 years. The compounded gains per year during this period have averaged 13.1 percent for stocks, 8.8 percent for bonds, and 6.5 percent for cash. Note that the returns from these investments have been higher since 1979 than they were in the decades before 1979.

Even though stocks have been significantly more profitable over the years, the fact that bonds have had less than half the risk of stocks and have outperformed stocks almost one-third of the time suggests that all but the most aggressive investors should maintain some exposure to bonds in addition to stocks to improve their balance of risk versus reward.

TABLE 2.2   Annual Total Returns for U.S. Stock, Bond, and Cash Benchmarks, 1979 to 2007

	Lehman Aggregate Bond Index	90-Day T-Bills	Russell 3000 Index
1979	1.9%	10.5%	24.1%
1980	2.7%	12.1%	32.5%
1981	6.3%	15.0%	−4.4%
1982	32.6%	11.4%	20.7%
1983	8.4%	9.0%	22.7%
1984	15.2%	10.0%	3.4%
1985	22.1%	7.8%	32.2%
1986	15.3%	6.2%	16.7%
1987	2.8%	5.9%	1.9%
1988	7.9%	6.9%	17.8%
1989	14.5%	8.2%	29.3%
1990	9.0%	7.8%	−5.1%
1991	16.0%	5.6%	33.7%
1992	7.4%	3.5%	9.6%
1993	9.8%	3.0%	10.9%
1994	−2.9%	4.4%	.2%
1995	18.5%	5.7%	36.8%
1996	3.6%	5.2%	21.8%
1997	9.7%	5.2%	31.8%
1998	8.7%	4.9%	24.1%
1999	−.8%	4.8%	20.9%
2000	11.6%	6.0%	−7.5%
2001	8.4%	3.5%	−11.5%
2002	10.3%	1.6%	−21.5%
2003	4.1%	1.0%	31.1%
2004	4.3%	1.4%	12.%
2005	2.4%	3.3%	6.1%
2006	4.3%	4.8%	15.7%
2007	7.0%	5.0%	5.5%

Unfortunately, it has been difficult to predict when bonds are likely to outperform stocks. However, Chapter 11, "What Bonds Can Tell You About Stocks: How to Use Interest Rates," presents an interest rate indicator that tells you when to increase cash positions. The main function of cash in an investment portfolio is to provide a source of consistently positive performance and to reduce volatility. Conservative investors can use the one-decision portfolio of Chapter 7, which includes a cash position to reduce the risk of having a losing year. Growth-oriented investors can use cash only when other investments appear likely to underperform or to maintain a rainy-day fund for emergencies.

Size Matters

The first distinction between different stocks is the size of the company. From an investment perspective, company size is measured as the dollar value of all outstanding shares. For example, if a company has 10 million shares outstanding, and the recent closing price was $20/share, the total market capitalization is 10 million × $20 = $200 million.

ETFs and mutual funds are available for large, midsized, and small companies. (Small companies are often referred to as small-cap, midsized companies as midcap, and large companies as large-cap.) No universally accepted range of market capitalizations defines large-, mid-, and small-cap stocks. Generally, large-cap stocks are those with market capitalizations over $10 billion. Midcap stocks have market caps ranging from $2–$10 billion, and small-cap stocks are those with less than $2 billion in total market capitalization. These dollar amounts are not strict rules but rather are soft guidelines that suggest which type of stock will appear in which type of index. Approximately 10 percent of all stocks are considered large-cap. However, this 10 percent represents some 80 percent of the dollar value of outstanding shares. Another 10 percent of stocks qualify as midcaps, and the remaining 80 percent are small-caps and microcaps. Midcap stocks represent approximately 10 percent of the total market cap of the U.S. market, and small-caps represent the remaining 10 percent.

Many large-cap stocks are extremely well known. WalMart, ExxonMobil, and General Electric are a few. As an example of how to calculate a market capitalization, consider Microsoft. There are 10.38 billion shares of Microsoft outstanding. At a current share price of $27.25, the market capitalization of Microsoft is

10.38 billion shares×$27.25/share = $282.86 billion

which is approximately 2.1 percent of the value of all publicly traded stocks in the United States.

Many midcap stocks are also well known. Examples include Clorox Co., Nordstrom, E-Trade Financial, and Royal Caribbean Cruises. All these shares have market capitalizations in the $8–11 billion range, which places them at the larger end of the midcap universe.

Small-cap stocks, although numerous, are generally far less recognizable. Examples include Shurguard Storage Centers, the Men's Wearhouse, Toro Co., Jack in the Box Inc., Ethan Allen Interiors, and Phillips-Van Heusen. These companies have market capitalizations in the $1–3 billion range.

A new category of ETF was launched in August 2005 to represent the behavior of microcap stocks, which are the smallest of the small-caps. The two microcap offerings that are currently available are the iShares Russell Microcap Index Fund (ticker symbol IWC) and the PowerShares Zacks Microcap Portfolio (ticker symbol PZI). The Russell Microcap Index consists of the smallest 1,000 stocks in the Russell 2000 Index plus the next 2,000 stocks smaller than those in the Russell 2000 Index. The largest company in the Russell Microcap Index has a market cap of $540 million, and the smallest has shares totaling $55 million.[2]

The underlying microcap index represents the broad universe of microcap stocks listed on national exchanges. The ETF, however, does not attempt to hold all 3,000 microcap stocks. Rather, with the goal of improving liquidity, IWC holds a subset of the Russell Microcap Index (approximately 1,200 shares).[3]

In contrast to the Russell Microcap Index, the Zacks Microcap Index uses a proprietary (nonpublic) stock selection algorithm in an attempt to outperform the broad microcap market. Zacks selects

000–500 stocks with market capitalizations ranging from $58 million to $575 million. Roughly equal dollar amounts of each stock are invested in the hypothetical index portfolio. PZI in general holds most or all of the stocks in the Zacks Index.[4]

Microcap stock ETFs must overcome two inherent difficulties. First, the underlying individual stocks are difficult to trade, which in finance is called *poor liquidity*. At any one time, relatively few shares are available to buy, and, conversely, relatively few buyers are willing to purchase shares put up for sale. As a result, the act of placing a buy or sell order for a microcap stock can easily move the market against you. (That is, the arrival of a buy order at a stock exchange can easily drive the price significantly higher before all the desired shares are purchased, or the arrival of a sell order can easily drive the share price significantly lower before all the desired shares are sold.)

Note that a large buy or sell order can move the market against you in even a widely traded stock. The difference between an easily traded (liquid) stock and a difficult-to-trade (illiquid) stock is the size of the order that can be filled without affecting the prevailing price. For blue-chip stocks such as XOM, an order of $1 million (approximately 17,000 shares) can be filled without adverse price impact.

At the other end of the spectrum lie stocks such as Steinway Musical Instruments Company (ticker symbol LVB), which is a component of the Russell Microcap Index ETF. Although this brand name is well known to pianists, the company is small, with a total market capitalization of $250 million. On a typical, quiet morning two hours into the trading day, the total volume in this stock has been only 800 shares. One hundred shares are available for purchase at $31.18, but if you want more stock than that, you have to pay the next lowest ask price of $31.22 (at which 900 shares are currently available). What this means is that an order of more than 100 shares drives up the stock's price by 4 cents, or almost 1/8 percent. If, on the other hand, you want to sell some shares, you have to accept a price of only $31.01. A simple calculation shows that the bid-ask spread is huge:

(bid price – ask price)/(midpoint of bid-ask prices)

($31.18 – $31.01)/($31.095) = 0.55 percent

Liquidity concerns apply not only to individual stocks, but also to ETFs. As a general rule, ETFs whose portfolios consist of highly liquid stocks are highly liquid. ETFs whose portfolios consist of illiquid stocks are difficult to trade. Most individual investors are unlikely to move the market against them when buying ETFs. However, for an investment professional who trades ETFs for many clients simultaneously, liquidity is an important concern.

The second challenge to microcap ETFs is the sheer number of microcap stocks that are available. Both of the available microcap ETFs hold fewer than half of the microcap stocks that are listed on exchanges. In the case of the Russell Microcap Index Fund (IWC), the ETF is attempting to match the performance of its index by holding only 40 percent of the index's constituents. As a result, there is a risk that the ETF will not succeed in its objective. The PowerShares Zacks Microcap Index Fund (PZI) has set for itself the goal of outperforming the broad microcap market. Even though it is passively managed (in that Zacks lists the shares it has selected every quarter and makes its selections public), it's always possible that Zacks' methods will lag rather than beat the broader microcap market. PZI does start off with a cost advantage: PowerShares Zacks Microcap Index Fund has an expense ratio of 0.7 percent. Royce Microcap Investor Class has an expense ratio of 1.5 percent, and Perritt Microcap has an expense ratio of 1.25 percent.

Because microcap stocks are so numerous, and because it is generally difficult to find buyers or sellers of significant numbers of shares at an attractive price (which ETFs are liable to have to do more frequently than mutual funds, which have the option of limiting the frequency of their shareholders' redemptions), it remains to be seen whether the microcap ETFs will be able to compete with microcap mutual funds such as Royce Microcap (RYOTX) or Perritt Microcap Opportunity (PRCGX). Several other microcap funds exist, but these two have among the longest track records of those available to individual investors.[5]

The distinction between different market capitalizations is relevant to the individual investor for a number of reasons. First, academic research has suggested and experience has demonstrated that market capitalization is an independent predictor of investment performance.[6] Since 1926, small-cap stocks have returned 2.3 percent per year more than large-caps.[7] During the entire historical period, small-caps were riskier than large-caps. (Note, however, that during the 2000–2003 bear market, small-caps were safer than large-caps— an exception to the historical pattern.)

More importantly, small-cap stocks have not been more profitable than large-caps every year. Rather, there have been long stretches of time when large company stocks as a group were more profitable, and other stretches of time when small company stocks were more profitable. For example, small-cap stock mutual funds outperformed large-cap funds from 1977–1983, 1991–1993, and 1999–2005. Large-cap mutual funds outperformed from 1970–1976, 1984–1990, and 1995–1998.

There have even been times when stocks of one size were profitable overall while the other lost money. For example, in 1998, the Russell 2000 Index of small-cap stocks *lost* 2.6 percent (including dividends), whereas the S&P 500 Index (representing large-cap stocks) returned 28.6 percent during the same year. However, in 2001, the Russell 2000 Index showed a profit (2.5 percent), whereas the large-cap S&P 500 Index lost 11.9 percent.

The point to draw from these examples is that the success of a small- or large-cap investment can depend critically on when you make it. Clearly, it has been important to be in the right place at the right time. As you will see in Chapter 8, "When to Live Large: An Asset Allocation Model for Small- versus Large-Cap ETFs," a successful strategy that allocates investments to large versus small stocks might by itself significantly increase investment performance.

A number of fundamental explanations have been advanced as to why thousands of stocks across so many different industries should share performance characteristics based only on size.[8,9] One issue is interest rates. Small companies have a harder time borrowing than large companies. Therefore, during periods of easy credit, small companies derive a relatively greater benefit than large companies.

Currency exchange rates might also have different impacts on large versus small companies. Large companies are more likely to do business internationally and to derive profits from operations abroad. A weaker U.S. dollar inflates the value of earnings from foreign operations—a benefit not enjoyed by small-caps in general.

Another important consideration in allocating between small- and large-cap stocks is trading costs. A truly long-term investor (multiple-year holding period) need not worry about this, but anyone who is more active will quickly discover that the cost of trading ETFs that hold small-cap stocks is significantly greater than the cost of trading large-cap ETFs. Multiple ETFs are available for each investment style, and as discussed next, the basis for selecting one over another should include a consideration of trading costs.

Each Investment Style Has Multiple ETFs

So far, we have treated the behavior of small- or large-cap stocks as if there were only one universally accepted performance result. Although there are relatively few sources of remote historical data, since the development of the Russell Indexes in 1979 and the more recent development of competing Standard & Poor's Indexes (beyond the S&P 500) and Wilshire Indexes, among others, there are now at least two and often more measures of the performance of large-cap and small-cap stocks. Moreover, at least two ETFs can track each market capitalization.

This is a potential benefit to the individual investor (after you sort through the confusion of having multiple indexes purporting to represent the same investment style). Given a decision to invest in small-cap stocks, for example, you can pick the best-performing ETF, or the ETF that is cheapest to trade (in terms of bid-ask spread and liquidity, if your order is large enough for liquidity to be an issue).

The selection of one ETF over another in the same investment style is not entirely objective. Chapter 12, "It's a Jungle Out There: Selecting from Among Different ETFs with Similar Investment Objectives," delves into how I analyze which ETF to select when more than one is available.

Midcap ETFs

As an investment style, midcaps have had the best performance in the past 25 years compared to large- or small-caps. (See Figure 2.1.) Four ETFs track three midcap stock market indexes. Both the Midcap SPDR (MDY) and the iShares S&P 400 Midcap Index Fund (IJH) track the S&P 400 Midcap Stock Index. The iShares Russell Midcap Index Fund (IWR) tracks the Russell Midcap Index. The Midcap Viper (VO) tracks the Morgan Stanley Capital International (MSCI) U.S. Midcap 450 Index.

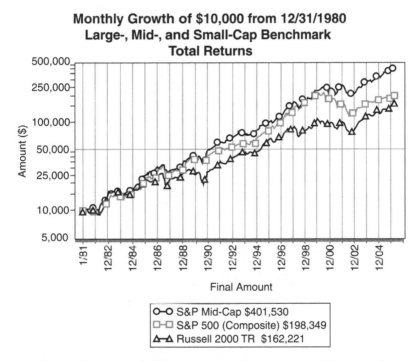

FIGURE 2.1   Growth of $10,000 invested in small-cap, midcap, and large-cap benchmarks 1981–2005.

In addition, there is another ETF that on the face of it would not appear to be a midcap ETF—the S&P 500 equal-weighted ETF, ticker RSP, sponsored by Rydex Funds. However, when you examine its performance histories, you see that it most closely matches that investment style.

RSP holds the same stocks as the S&P 500. However, unlike the S&P 500 Index, in which larger company stocks are given more weight in the index, each of the 500 stocks has an equal 0.2 percent weight in the RSP. (By way of comparison, the top 100 stocks in the S&P 500 account for 57 percent of the entire index.)

The amazing observation is that RSP is more closely correlated with the S&P 400 Midcap Index than with the S&P 500 Index even though the RSP and the S&P 400 Index have no stocks in common, whereas the RSP and the S&P 500 Index have every stock in common. (See Figure 2.2.) This is a stunning example of how market capitalization is an independent and important determinant of investment performance.

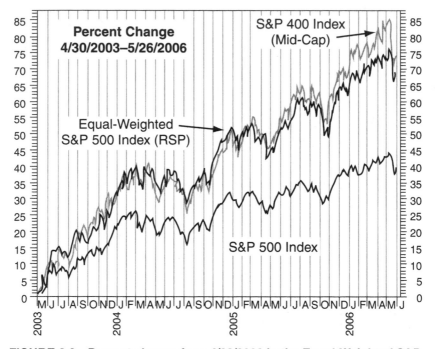

FIGURE 2.2 Percent change from 4/30/2003 in the Equal-Weighted S&P 500 Index ETF (RSP), compared to the S&P 500 Index and the S&P 400 Midcap Index.

All-Cap or Total-Market ETFs

Four ETFs capture the behavior of almost the entire market capitalization of the United States: the iShares Russell 3000 Index Fund (IWV), the Total Market Vipers (VTI), the StreetTracks Total Market ETF (TMW), and the iShares Dow Jones Total Market Index Fund (IYY). These can be useful proxies for the overall stock market, but you should not lose sight of the implicit allocation decision you make when you purchase any of these ETFs.

All of these ETFs reflect an average of publicly traded stocks that place heavier weight on companies with higher market capitalizations. (Actually, they weight stocks by the dollar value of outstanding shares available for trading, which excludes closely held shares. See Chapter 3, "A One-Step Strategy for Selecting Superior Investments.") For example, the Russell 1000 Index (large-cap) accounts for 91 percent of the Russell 3000 Total Market Index. The S&P 500 accounts for 77 percent of the Wilshire Total Market Index.

Because so much more market capitalization resides in large-cap stocks than in small-cap stocks, the behavior of these total-market ETFs correlates much more closely with the behavior of large-caps than with small-caps. This is clearly demonstrated in Figure 2.3, which shows the behavior of different all-cap ETFs compared to a small- and large-cap benchmark from 2001–2005. During this period, small-cap stocks were much stronger than large-caps. The four all-cap ETFs that appear in Figure 2.3 had results far closer to that of the S&P 500 (large-caps) than to the Russell 2000 Index (small-caps).

As a practical matter, it might be easier just to use a large-cap ETF than a total-market ETF whenever the trading costs for the total-market ETF are higher. Conversely, if you want to allocate to both small- and large-caps for diversification, you might be better advised to purchase small- and large-cap ETFs separately so that you can achieve the portfolio mix you desire rather than the roughly 80 percent large-cap/20 percent small-cap mix implicit in buying a total-market ETF.

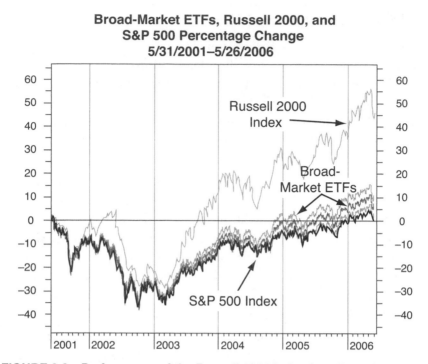

FIGURE 2.3   Performance of the Russell 2000 Index (small-cap bench-mark), the S&P 500 Index (large-cap benchmark), and the four broad-market ETFs (ticker symbols IWV, VTI, TMV, IYY) from 2001–2005. Note that the broad-market ETFs moved much more closely to the S&P 500 than to the Russell 2000 Index, reflecting the significantly greater impact of large-cap stocks compared to small-caps on the behavior of total-market ETFs.

If you wanted to allocate more to small-caps at a time when you considered them to be undervalued as a group, a total-market ETF would be a poor choice. The total-market would have a relatively low (by historical standards) exposure to small-caps precisely when you wanted to overweight them.

Although total-market ETFs have not been around long enough to demonstrate a performance advantage compared to either large- or small-cap ETFs, one situation where they are attractive are for small investors for whom each brokerage commission has a significantly negative impact. Such investors can achieve some diversification with a single transaction.

Growth and Value ETFs

Other criteria are available with which to segregate groups of stocks besides market capitalization. An important category is the group of market indexes called *value indexes*, which represent the collective behavior of stocks that appear cheap compared to the overall market in terms of their *current* earnings, dividends, or value of the company's underlying assets (called *book value*). Although in principle, any company's stock could be a value stock if the share price dropped low enough, in practice, certain industries, such as banks, energy, and cyclical stocks, have been disproportionately represented in value indexes.

Complementing value indexes are *growth indexes*. Growth stocks generally appear expensive relative to the overall market in terms of their current earnings, dividends, or book values. Investors buy these stocks because the companies appear to have better *future* prospects than the typical company. Industries represented most heavily in growth stock indexes have included technology, health care, and consumer staples.

Indexes that do not attempt to separate growth and value stocks are called *blend indexes*. The S&P 500, composed of large-cap stocks, is an example of a large-cap blend index. The Russell 2000 Index is a small-cap blend index that consists of 2,000 small company stocks, again without regard to growth or value characteristics.

Over the long term, large-cap value has outperformed large-cap growth. However, as is the case with small- versus large-caps, growth and value stocks have done better at different times. As a general rule, when the stock market has been weak, large-cap value stocks have fared better than large-cap growth stocks. During strong market climates, large-cap growth has generally beaten large-cap value.

Small-cap growth and value have also fared differently from one another during different periods. However, it is hard to make a generic statement that small-cap value has generally done better than small-cap growth during bear markets. Certainly, from 2000–2003, small-cap value performed well compared to the other investment styles. However, during the bear market years of 1969–1970, small-cap growth actually held up better.

It turns out that the same strategy has been successful in guiding long-term asset allocation decisions between growth and value, whether using small- or large-cap ETFs. The growth-versus-value asset allocation model is discussed in Chapter 9, "Boring Bargains or Hot Prospects? Choosing between Growth and Value ETFs."

Conclusion

Growth and value, large cap and small cap are all examples of different *investment styles*. ETFs offer you exposure to all the major investment styles, allowing you to choose the one with the best investment prospects at the time, and to change the amount you have invested in different areas whenever you want. The ability to move assets from one style to another is an important tool you can use to increase your investment performance. You will learn how to use this tool starting in Chapter 8.

Endnotes

1 Vanguard and Fidelity offer the best money market funds that are available to the general investment public. A number of other companies offer good money markets, but they are available only to restricted classes of investors such as participants in certain retirement plans or to very large clients of the fund. Note that although the risk of money markets is listed as zero based on historical experience, the value of money market funds is nonetheless not guaranteed.

2 www.russell.com/US/Indexes/US/Definitions.asp (Russell U.S. Equity Index Definitions, 11/8/2005).

3 http://moneycentral.msn.com/content/invest/mstar/P129015.asp.

4 www.powershares.com/images/pdf/PZIZacks_PreProspectus.pdf (PowerShares prospectus for PZI dated 8/18/2005).

5 DFSCX goes back to 1982 but is available only to institutional investors with a minimum investment of $2 million and prior approval of the investor by DFA.

6 Perhaps the most famous example is the work of Fama and French. Their historical data on the performance difference between large- and small-cap stocks is available online at http://mba.tuck.dartmouth.edu/pages/faculty/ken.french/data_library.html.

7 Ibbotson, Stocks, Bonds, Bills, and Inflation, 2005 Yearbook.

8 It might be useful to discuss some terminology here. *Fundamental analysis* reflects the discipline of making investment decisions based on underlying data (subjective or quantitative), such as industry prospects, economic environment and projections, regulatory climate, source of competition, and so on. Many fundamental analysts visit individual companies, attend industry conferences, and generally form subjective opinions of the important players in the investments they are analyzing. The goal is for the fundamental analyst to estimate a fair value for his investments. When those fair values differ from the market values, the analyst makes recommendations to capture the economic benefit of the market's mispricing.

Technical analysis is the discipline of using quantitative data or visual chart patterns to guide investment decisions. Classically, technical analysts used chart patters to make investment decisions. Then, the advent of calculators and computers led to the widespread use of quantitative data among technical analysts. Quantitative asset allocation models lend themselves to hypothetical testing on historical data in a way that is more difficult to achieve by looking at past visual patterns. The underlying assumption is that past patterns of market behavior will repeat themselves to enough of an extent to allow the technical analyst to beat the market.

Both fundamental and technical analysis assume that markets are "inefficient"— that stock prices do not accurately reflect the true worth of every traded stock. Fundamental and technical analyses are not mutually exclusive. For example, an asset allocation model that uses changes in interest rates to guide investment decisions could qualify as an example of either fundamental or technical analysis. The approach used in this book reflects technical analysis.

9 See, for example, Richard Anderson, *Market Timing Models*, Irwin Professional Publishing, 1997, Chapter 6.

3

A ONE-STEP STRATEGY FOR SELECTING SUPERIOR INVESTMENTS: INDEXING

If you have been reading the financial press, you have no doubt learned that the typical equity mutual fund lags the S&P 500 a majority of the time. This observation has been borne out repeatedly. Indeed, if you decided to limit your stock market investments to a low-cost S&P 500 Index fund[1] and do nothing else, you would be ahead of the pack.

Nonetheless, it is not always fair (or informative) to compare the diverse universe of equity funds against one particular standard. The S&P 500 represents mainly the behavior of large U.S. company stocks. Although the companies in the S&P 500 represent the bulk of the dollar value of all publicly traded stocks, in fact, more than 6,000 different issues are listed on the New York and NASDAQ Stock Exchanges. Small company stocks (total market value less than $2 billion, also called *small-cap stocks*) are far more numerous than large company stocks (large-caps).

The fact that many different investment styles exist means that if your ETF or mutual fund happens to have a different investment style than that of the S&P 500, the fund's performance relative to the

S&P 500 might have little to do with the skill of the fund manager and a lot to do with which style happens to be in favor.

It is important for you to understand how to make investments that perform like market indexes, because for most investment styles, such investments have outperformed the majority of actively managed mutual funds. One of the reasons why ETFs can be valuable is that most of them are designed to mimic the behavior of a market index. This chapter goes into more detail about exactly what a market index is, how different market indexes in widespread use are calculated, and which types of indexes have been most likely to beat mutual funds with similar objectives. In those areas where market indexes have a consistent history of outperforming the majority of mutual funds, ETF investing might be your best bet.

Market indexes define a stock market index as just the average price of a group of stocks. The selection of stocks in an index and the contribution each stock makes to the overall index are specified by objective rules that the public knows in advance.

Typically, indexes represent the behavior of specific groups of stocks: the entire U.S. market (Wilshire 5000), a cross section of the U.S. economy (Dow Jones Averages), small publicly traded U.S. stocks (Russell 2000, S&P 600), large U.S. stocks (S&P 500, Russell 1000), and so on. Some indexes represent specific industry sectors (SOX—the Semiconductor Index, XAU—an index of gold mining companies, XOI—oil companies, and so on).

By design, many mutual funds represent only a specific investment style or market sector. If such a mutual fund does well, is it because the manager is skilled or because every manager in the area outperformed? Conversely, if a fund with a well-defined type of portfolio fares poorly, is it the manager's fault?

You can answer these questions by using benchmarks. A *benchmark* is an index—passively managed—whose performance serves as the standard by which other investments can be judged. In general, the investment style of the index benchmark should be the same as the style of the investment whose performance you are trying to evaluate. Mutual funds that invest in large company stocks should be compared to large-cap indexes.

Whereas the stocks in the portfolio of an actively managed mutual fund are kept secret, the constituents of a market index are available to the public. Because anyone can replicate a stock market index, the only reason to hire an active manager is the expectation that he can outperform an index investment in the same area of the market. Therefore, an easy way to determine if an active manager is earning his salary is to see if his fund is delivering better returns relative to risk compared to a benchmark market index with the same investment style.

To see why the use of benchmarks can help you determine if an investment is successful and why it is important to choose the right benchmark, consider the example of the Legg Mason Value Trust (LMVTX)—a large-cap value fund. Its manager since 1982, Bill Miller, is legendary for his 15-year streak (1991–2005) of beating the S&P 500 Index. Despite Miller's acclaim, since the beginning of his winning streak, the *average* financial services sector fund has beaten the Legg Mason Value Trust. (See Figure 3.1.) Does this mean that the average fund manager among financial services sector funds is better than Bill Miller?

Probably not. Far more likely, financial services turned out to be one of the best areas in which to invest. Many reasons explain why, including the 18-year bull market that began in 1982 and drew ever-increasing numbers of Americans into stocks; the demutualization of savings and loans, which provided fertile ground for investors in regional banks; and the waves of mergers and acquisitions that occurred starting in the 1980s.

The financial services sector has been so strong that almost everyone in it has outperformed large company stocks generally, and the mutual fund industry recognized this fairly late in the game. Indeed, of the 115 financial services funds listed in the Mutual Fund Expert Database of 9/30/2005, only 13 (12 percent) were incorporated before 1996. By way of comparison, 5,583 of 18,864, or 30 percent, of all existing U.S. mutual funds were incorporated before 1996.

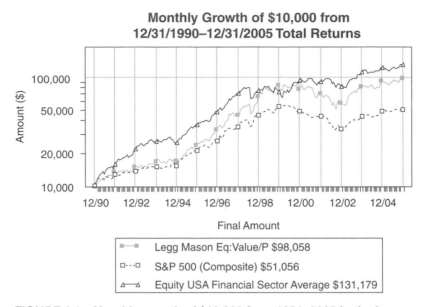

FIGURE 3.1   Monthly growth of $10,000 from 1991–2005 in the Legg Mason Value Trust (LMVTX), the average financial sector fund, and the S&P 500. All data is total return. Source: Mutual Fund Expert database.

The best way to judge the Legg Mason Value Trust fairly is to compare it to a broad index of large-cap value stocks, or at least to the average performance of mutual funds with similar objectives. Either of these would be a reasonable benchmark. By those standards, the fund has been a strong performer.[2]

Investments That Track Market Indexes Have Outperformed Most Mutual Funds

Investing in mutual funds or ETFs that track market indexes has outperformed the majority of regular mutual funds, mainly because index mutual funds and ETFs have much lower expenses than other mutual funds.

The list of stocks that comprise an index and their weights in the index are determined at infrequent intervals (sometimes as infrequently as once per year) by the index sponsor and then are distributed to the public. As a result, an index fund does not need a manager to pick stocks. All that is necessary is the intervention of a trader to make sure that the fund or ETF portfolio contains the right stocks in the right proportions. Although this is not a trivial undertaking, it is nowhere near as expensive as maintaining a research staff to pick stocks.

In theory, the average investor can do only as well as the market. It turns out that most mutual funds managers do not fare very differently from the universe of stocks from which they select. As a result, the index fund has an immediate advantage. Its performance before fees is by definition average, but it saves the considerable cost of a manager, giving its performance net of expenses a head start compared to the average mutual fund.

The only way that the average fund can overcome the handicap of higher expenses (compared to ETFs and other low-cost index funds) is for other market participants to have consistently below-average performance. This might once have been the case when many individual retail investors picked their own stocks. Now, however, institutional investors dominate the stock market, so a source of consistently underperforming investors to help mutual funds deliver above-average performance is unlikely to emerge. As a rule, therefore, a mutual fund that has a well-defined index benchmark should be more likely to lag than to beat the benchmark, particularly over the long term. The evidence in the next section shows that in most stock market categories, indexing has beaten the majority of actively managed funds.

The Evidence in Favor of Indexing

The data used here covers a ten-year period (12/31/1995–12/31/2005), as reported in the Mutual Fund Expert Database. The results show that index benchmarks have outperformed a majority of actively managed funds with similar objectives. (Exceptions include large-cap growth, and small-cap blend and growth if you consider the Russell 2000 Index and the Russell 2000 Growth Index as benchmarks.) Moreover, the indexes that have outperformed the funds are available to individual investors through ETFs. The data is summarized in Table 3.1.

TABLE 3.1   Comparison of Mutual Fund Performance to Benchmark Index Performance, Based on Ten Years of Risk-Adjusted Returns (Sharpe Ratio)*

Investment Objective	Benchmark	Percentage of Actively Managed Funds That Benchmark Beat	ETFs Available to Track Benchmark
Balanced fund	60% S&P 500 + 40% Lehman Aggregate	67%	60% SPY (or IVV) + 40% AGG
Information technology	NASDAQ 100 Index	84%	QQQQ
Large-cap blend	S&P 500 Index	75%	SPY, IVV
Large-cap growth	Russell 1000 Growth Index	43%	IWF
Large-cap value	Russell 1000 Value Index	87%	IWD
Midcap blend	S&P 400 Index	84%	MDY, IJH
Midcap growth	S&P 400 Growth Index	95%	IJK
Midcap value	S&P 400 Value Index	91%	IJJ
Small-cap blend	Russell 2000 Index or S&P 600 Index	25% 66%	IWM IJR
Small-cap growth	Russell 2000 Growth Index or S&P 600 Growth Index	20% 80%	IWO IJT
Small-cap value	Russell 2000 Value Index or S&P 600 Value Index	46% 58%	IWN IJS

*The performance of mutual funds that charge sales loads is included in the performance statistics, but the impact of the sales load was not taken into account. Source: Mutual Fund Expert database, 12/31/2005. The greater the percentage of funds beaten by the benchmark, the greater the past hypothetical benefit of indexing would have been.

Indexing Has Delivered Greater Profits Than the Average Mutual Fund, Except in the Small-Cap Area

The large proportion of mutual funds that have been beaten by an index should encourage the ETF investor. However, the size of the advantage is also important to consider. ETFs have their own generally low expenses, so they, too, will of necessity underperform their benchmark indexes. Fortunately, index investing has afforded a large-enough advantage to make ETFs attractive alternatives. The data is summarized in Figure 3.2, which shows that the advantage of indexing compared to the average mutual fund has exceeded 1 percent per year for most categories. This amount of profit advantage is more than sufficient to cover the expenses that an ETF investor incurs.

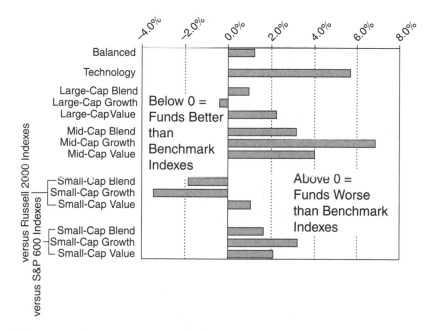

FIGURE 3.2 Profit advantage or disadvantage of investing in the benchmarks listed in Table 3.1 versus the average mutual fund with similar objectives, adjusted for risk.

How a Few Mutual Fund Managers Have Beaten the Indexes

A handful of mutual fund managers have consistently beaten their benchmarks in a number of ways. First, a creative (and successful) manager can deviate from rigid guidelines and exercise greater flexibility in selecting stocks than could be captured in a single market index. For example, a large-cap manager might choose mainly from S&P 500 stocks but might hold a different mix of industry sectors than is present in the benchmark. Fidelity Contrafund (FCNTX) is an example of a mutual fund that has succeeded in this way.

Some mutual funds have distinguished themselves with unconventional strategies. Hussman Strategic Growth (HSGFX) takes both long and short positions. Gateway Fund (GATEX) has achieved an outstanding balance between risk and reward by selling index options against its stock selection. Mairs and Powers Growth invest in companies of all sizes but emphasize small companies based in the Midwest.

I suspect that numerous talented fund managers have original ideas but do not want to take the risk of implementing them. There is safety in numbers. If a fund comes close to its benchmark, the manager's performance is hard to criticize, and he might feel his job is more secure. On the other hand, if a manager sticks his neck out by deviating from a benchmark and the gamble does not pay off, his job might be on the line.

This happened to Jeffrey Vinik, the former manager of Fidelity Magellan (then the largest mutual fund), who in 1995–1996 believed the stock market to be overvalued. As a result, he placed a significant portion of the fund's assets in bonds. When the market correction that Vinik feared did not materialize, Fidelity Magellan underperformed the S&P 500 by a margin of more than 10 percent in 1996—the only time in the past 30 years that the fund lagged by such a large amount. As a result, Vinik lost his job at Fidelity in 1996. Since then, Fidelity Magellan has performed much like the S&P 500, for better or worse.

Another type of manager who has consistently beaten the market is a small-cap stock picker, particularly a small company growth fund manager. That's because the vast majority of publicly traded stocks are small-caps (companies for which the total value of outstanding shares is below $2 billion). Recall that the large-cap S&P 500 Index has only 500 out of the more than 5,000 NYSE and NASDAQ stocks, and the behavior of the largest 50 of the 500 dominate the index. Approximately 10 percent of traded stocks constitute midcaps, and 80 percent—more than 3,500 issues—make up the universe of small-caps.

With so many different stocks, of which each represents a relatively small investment opportunity, a fund manager has a good chance of unearthing an undiscovered gem and accumulating a significant position in the small company before the competition catches on. In contrast, large company stocks are followed by a number of analysts. Particularly in the age of fair and full disclosure, any insight that an analyst might have about a large company quickly becomes disseminated throughout the market.

As revealed in Table 3.1 and Figure 3.2, the historical success of small-cap managers has been relative to the Russell 2000 Index and the Russell 2000 Growth Index. The Russell 2000 Indexes, the first small-cap benchmarks, provide a fairly complete representation of the small-cap market.

In terms of investment returns from small-cap indexes, the S&P 600 Index has performed more strongly than the Russell 2000 Index. Indeed, the S&P 600 Index, the S&P 600 Growth Index, and the S&P 600 Value Index have all outperformed a majority of mutual funds with similar objectives during the past ten years. With only 600 stocks, the S&P 600 Index is far from a complete representation of the small-cap universe. Its composition reflects the insights of the Standard and Poor's investment committee in deciding which small fraction of stocks to select from among the many available. Apparently those insights, even though made public, have added significant value. Even though past results do not predict future performance, it appears that investors could avail themselves of a potentially superior small-cap investment by holding the ETFs that correspond to the S&P 600 Indexes listed in Table 3.1.

Insofar as large-cap growth managers have been relatively successful in beating the benchmark Russell 1000 Index during the past ten years, you might be better off holding a top-performing fund than holding a large-cap growth ETF. Table 3.2 lists no-load large-cap growth mutual funds selected from large-cap growth funds in operation for at least ten years. All the funds listed have been in the top 25 percent of large-cap growth funds in risk-adjusted performance for the one-, three-, five-, and ten-year periods that ended 12/31/2005. Even though it's not guaranteed that these funds will continue their winning streaks, their track record is impressive.

TABLE 3.2   Large-Cap Growth Mutual Funds That Have Been Consistently in the Top Quarter of Their Peers*

Fund Name	Ticker Symbol
Fidelity Contrafund	FCNTX
Fidelity Fund	FFIDX
Fidelity Disciplined Equity	FDEQX
Fidelity Growth Company	FDGRX
Janus Growth and Income	JAGIX
Northeast Investors Growth	NTHFX
Rainier Core Equity	RIMEX

*These funds were selected from among U.S. large-cap growth funds with at least ten years' history from the 12/31/2005 Mutual Fund Expert database.

Conclusion

Indexes that ETFs track have a long-term history of outperforming the majority of actively managed mutual funds with similar objectives. With the exception of large-cap growth, market benchmarks have outperformed the average mutual fund by at least 1 percent per year (risk-adjusted). Although ETFs would be expected to lag the indexes that they are trying to match because of their own modest expense ratios and because of trading costs incurred when the stocks comprising an index change, the margin of past outperformance in the underlying indexes should be more than sufficient to overcome ETF expenses. As a result, if past patterns repeat themselves in the future, ETFs could beat the majority of actively managed diversified equity mutual funds (except possibly in the large-cap growth area).

Appendix to Chapter 3—Index Construction Methodologies

Example of Index Construction—Equal Weighting

This is the most straightforward methodology conceptually. The performance of each stock in an index is averaged to arrive at the change in the overall index. For example, consider a hypothetical two-stock index consisting of General Electric (NYSE: GE, $36/share) and Altria (NYSE: MO, $66/share). If GE gains 2 percent and MO loses 1 percent on a given day, the change in the index is simply the average of these changes: +1/2 percent.

Few indexes in wide use are actually constructed this way, because as a practical matter, not all stocks are equally easy to trade or equally important to the economy or the stock market. However, two equal-weighted indexes that you might encounter include the Value Line Arithmetic Index (which represents the average behavior of 1,700 stocks) and the equal-weighted S&P 500 Index, which is tradeable through an ETF sponsored by Rydex Mutual Funds with the ticker symbol RSP. Compared to the regular S&P 500 Index, which represents the behavior of large company stocks, RSP behaves more like midcap stock benchmarks even though its components are the same as those in the large-cap S&P 500.

Example of Index Construction—Price Weighting

Suppose that I want to make a two-stock index: GE ($36/share) and MO ($66/share). The first issue is how to combine these two share prices into a single index.

The option that the Dow Jones Industrial Average used (because it was originally calculated and updated by hand throughout the day when the index began in 1896) was to add the prices. In this case, my index would have a value of 36+66=102. If GE gained 5 percent (rising from $36 to $37.80) while MO stayed flat, the index would rise from 102 to 103.80—a gain for the index of less than 1.8 percent. But if MO rose 5 percent while GE stayed flat, the index would gain more, rising from 102 to 105.9—a gain of almost 4 percent.

This example demonstrates that MO carries a larger weight in the index than GE does, simply because its shares are more expensive.

What if MO should split 2:1 so that its share price drops to $33? By the original formula, the index dropped from 36+66=102 down to 36+33=69—an apparent 33 percent drop due to a stock split (which historically has been bullish, if anything).

To correct for this type of artifact, Dow Jones rescales the index so that the occurrence of a stock split (or a substitution of one company for another) does not by itself change the index's level.

To restore an index value of 102 (which is what would result except for the stock split in this example), the value of 69 is multiplied by 1.48. After the split, the new formula for calculating the index is 1.48×(33+36). Now MO and GE have roughly equal weights in the index even though nothing about the underlying companies changed.

Example of Index Construction—Capitalization Weighting

The next development in index construction was weighting each stock by the total value of all its outstanding shares. In the Dow Industrials, calculated by price weighting, Caterpillar ($92/share) has more than 3.5 times the importance of Microsoft ($26/share). However, the value of all outstanding MSFT shares is more than $280 billion, whereas the value of Caterpillar's shares is only $31 billion.

So, in the case of the stocks MSFT and CAT, the index is calculated as follows:

(92)×(31 billion)+(26)×(280 billion)/(31 billion+280 billion) = 32.58

The advantage of this method is that indexes actually reflect the performance of the total pool of investment capital. Also, if your goal is to match an index portfolio, it is easier to take a proportionally larger position in a stock with a larger value of outstanding shares, because such stocks are generally more liquid than stocks that have smaller amounts of shares outstanding.

Most common stock market indexes have been capitalization-weighted: S&P 500, Russell 2000, NASDAQ Composite, NASDAQ 100, MSCI EAFE (an international stock benchmark), and so on.

The Newest Indexing Scheme—Free-Float Weighting

This method is the same as weighting by market capitalization, except that nontrading shares are excluded from determining how much each company should contribute to the index. The S&P 500 Index moved to free-float weighting in March 2005. Most of the newer indexes that have been used as benchmarks for ETFs are also free-float-weighted.

Float weighting was developed because the surge in assets allocated to index investments has become so large that distortions in the market can develop when investors who are tracking an index attempt to take proportional positions in companies with a significant portion of their shares not up for sale at nearly any price.

An example is Wal-Mart. The founding family holds 40 percent of the outstanding shares in this company. Although Wal-Mart represents approximately 2 percent of the market capitalization of all the companies in the S&P 500 Index, only 60 percent of its shares will be counted in determining its weighting in the index. That free-float weighting is 1.2 percent (which is 60 percent of 2 percent).

Moreover, most small company stock indexes are capitalization- or free-float-weighted. This can distort the behavior of indexes, especially near rebalancing. For example, in 1999, a number of small technology stocks rose so quickly that they were no longer rightly considered small companies. However, it was not until the small-cap benchmarks were rebalanced (for example, June 30, 1999 for the Russell 2000 Index) that these nouveau large-caps or nouveau mid-caps could be removed from the small-cap index. Until that time, the behavior of the cap-weighted Russell 2000 Index was dominated by hot stocks rather than by well-established small-caps. In fact, in 1999, the shares of profitable companies in the Russell 2000 were losing investments as a group, while shares in companies without earnings rose in value overall.

Endnotes

1 Examples include S&P 500 Index funds offered by Vanguard (VFINX), Fidelity (FSMKX), and ETFs (SPY or IVV). A complete online list of no-load index mutual funds is available from the Motley Fool Web site at www.fool.com/mutualfunds/indexfunds/table01.htm.

2 You might have noticed that the S&P 500, which includes both growth and value stocks, is not the most suitable benchmark for the Legg Mason Value Trust. According to its prospectus, it selects mainly large company stocks selling at discounts to their fair value. The Legg Mason Value Trust has been more profitable than the Russell 1000 Value Index during the past 15 years overall, but it has lagged this benchmark for 7 of the past 15 years.

4

INVESTMENT RISK: A VISIT TO THE DARK SIDE

As an individual investor, you are likely bombarded with advertisements that imply (but by law cannot explicitly state) that if you sign on with the advertiser, you will reap generous investment returns. After all, without high returns, how else would you be able to fulfill all the fantasies in the commercials—paying for your children's college, retiring to a house on the beach at age 55, and so on?

Unfortunately, picking an investment involves more than the quest for high returns. You need to consider the risks, too. However, the concept of investment risk is never mentioned in advertising, except perhaps by a speed-talker in the final seconds of a commercial, or in fine print at the bottom of the ad copy.

Don't let Madison Avenue cause you to take your eye off the ball. If you commit one point from this book to memory, it is that you cannot evaluate the merits of an investment until you have a thorough understanding of both its potential risk and return. Committing your money before obtaining such an understanding is like buying a house without first conducting an inspection.

This chapter acquaints you with an intuitive way of comparing the risks of different investments. It also looks back through decades of investment history to see what the worst losses have been in the past.

Drawdown—An Intuitive Measure of Investment Risk

A handy concept in describing risk is drawdown. *Drawdown* is the largest investment loss sustained in the past, from a high point to a low point in investment capital. This is most easily understood through some visual examples.

Figure 4.1 shows the Dow Jones Industrial Average from 1999–2004, a period that includes the 2000-2003 bear market. During this period, the worst loss in value occurred from the high of 11722 on January 14, 2000 through the low of 7286 on October 9, 2002—a drawdown of 37.8 percent (excluding dividends).

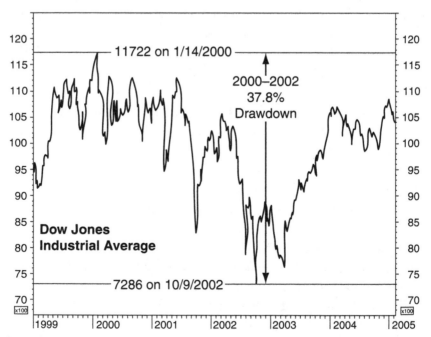

FIGURE 4.1   Daily prices of the Dow Jones Industrial Average showing the maximum extent of its loss during the most recent major bear market, from 2000–2004.

As bad as this was, the 2000–2003 bear market was hardly the worst in modern stock market history. The 1973–1974 bear market saw a 45.1 percent drawdown in the Dow Jones Industrial Average, from the January 11, 1973 high of 1051 to the December 6, 1974 low of 577. (See Figure 4.2.)

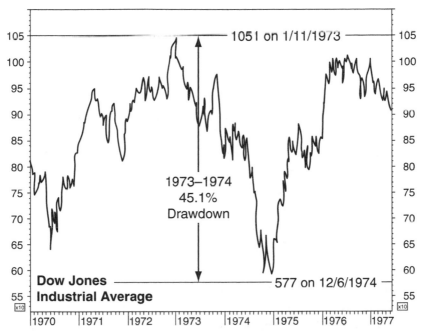

FIGURE 4.2   Daily prices of the Dow Jones Industrial Average showing the maximum extent of its loss during the 1973–1974 bear market. A comparison between Figures 4.1 and 4.2 shows that the 1973–1974 bear market was more severe for this market benchmark than was the 2000–2003 bear market.

How to Use Drawdown

The preceding examples raise the question of what a drawdown number really means if two different chart examples result in two different results.

The answer is that drawdown depends on the period over which you measure it. Many investors in the late 1990s made the mistake of looking at performance histories of technology funds that covered only the bull market. As a result, risk seemed insignificant. Even the sharp sell-offs in 1997 and 1998 reversed themselves in a matter of weeks.

A salesperson once visited our office to tout the five-year performance record of an emerging market bond fund, which was indeed impressive. However, knowing that emerging market bonds suffered during 1997 and 1998, I did not consider the five-year history (1999–2004) to be indicative of the potential pitfalls of this investment. It turned out that in 1998, this "hot" fund lost 30 percent. I would not have learned this except that I happened to know specifically what period to ask about.

Another important factor to consider in evaluating investment risk is the amount of time required to recover from a loss. One of the reasons why investors became complacent in the late 1990s is because every serious market correction from 1982–1999 resolved itself in a short time. The lesson learned from that period was that stocks always recover if you stick with them. However, during other periods, the recovery can be very protracted. For example, many market benchmarks have not yet recovered the full extent of their losses incurred during the 2000–2003 bear market. Figure 4.3 shows the S&P 500, its major bear markets, and the amount of time required to revisit the previous high points.

The length of a drawdown is the time required for the value of an investment to exceed its previous peak. An illustration of drawdown length appears in Figure 4.4. All else being equal, a shorter drawdown is preferable to a longer one. This is especially important for investors who need to withdraw from their investments to meet living expenses.

The importance of limiting drawdown for investors who rely on their holdings to generate income for living expenses is highlighted by the example of two different equity investments from the start of 1997 through the end of 2005 (nine years): utilities and large-cap value stocks. During this interval, the Dow Jones Utility Average was both more profitable and riskier than the Russell 1000 Value Index (a benchmark for large-cap value stocks). Table 4.1 shows the performances of these two investments.

FIGURE 4.3   The S&P 500 and the duration of its major bear markets 1957–2006.*

*The number of months indicated is the time taken for this index to fall from its peak, hit the bear market bottom, and recover. Note that this data does *not* include the effects of dividends, whereas the data in Table 4.2 *does* include dividends. As a result, recovery times listed in the table are longer here than they are in Table 4.2 for the 1969–1970, 1973–1974, and 1987 market declines.

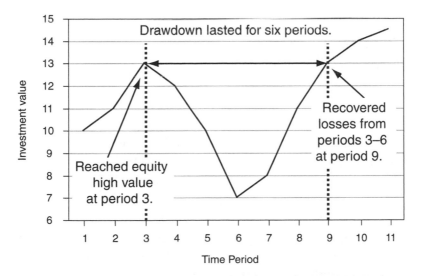

FIGURE 4.4   Measurement of the length of a drawdown for hypothetical data.

TABLE 4.1   Compounded Annualized Gains and Drawdowns for the Dow Jones Utility Average and the Russell 1000 Value Index (12/31/1996–12/31/2005)*

Hypothetical Investment	Compounded Annual Gain (Percent Per Year)	Drawdown 1997–2005 (Percent)
Dow Jones Utility Average	10.6%	49%
Russell 1000 Value Index	9.8%	28%

*Figures are based on monthly total return data from the 12/31/2005 edition of the Mutual Fund Expert database. These investments are hypothetical, and take no account of taxes or transaction costs.

The top part of Figure 4.5 shows how $100,000 invested in each of these investments would have fared from 1997–2005. Utilities were clearly more volatile, as evidenced by their greater drawdown of 49 percent from 2001–2002, but they were more profitable by the end of the period shown (1997–2005), assuming that all dividends were reinvested and no money was withdrawn during the period shown.

On the other hand, if the investor needed to withdraw $1,000/month for living expenses, the greater volatility in utilities would have left him with less money by the end of 2005 than would have been the case if he had invested in large-cap value stocks and had withdrawn the same $1,000/month from that. (See the bottom part of Figure 4.5.) The high rate of withdrawal made it impossible for the portfolio to recover from its losses in 2001–2002. This was more of a problem in volatile utility stocks than in quieter large-cap value stocks, even though utilities were more profitable on a buy-and-hold basis.

The greater drawdown reduced the amount of remaining investment capital even after the market recovered because a certain number of withdrawals had to be made when the account was near its low point (in 2002). The impact of these withdrawals was great enough to hinder the account's ability to recover from 2003–2005. As an extreme example, if an initial investment of $100,000 dwindled to $1,000 (losing 99 percent of its value), the next monthly withdrawal of $1,000 would wipe out the account. After that point, no matter how well the underlying investment recovered, the investor who needed to make his withdrawal would not recover financially.

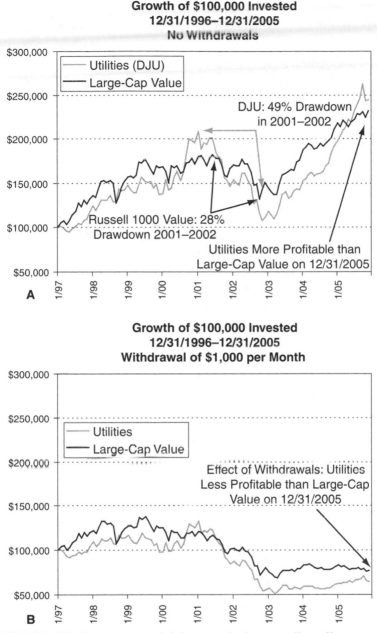

FIGURE 4.5   The importance of risk control when you live off your investments.*

*The top chart shows the buy and hold performance of utilities (Dow Jones Utility Average total return) versus large-cap value stocks (Russell 1000 Value Index total return). The bottom chart shows the results of hypothetical $100,000 investments in each of these indexes from which $1,000 is withdrawn at the start of each month.

Bottom line: You need to measure drawdown during the worst market climate for the investment you are evaluating: 1973–1974, 1987, and 2000–2002 for large-company stocks; 1998 for small-company stocks; and 1998–1999 for value stocks. Table 4.2 lists the most significant market declines for a variety of investments that can be made using ETFs.

A 43-Year History of Bear Markets

Table 4.2 lists important categories of investments that you can make using ETFs, and their important historical bear market drawdowns. (For stock market investments, only declines of at least 20 percent are listed.) The market risk history in Table 4.2 is based on both market benchmark indexes and on the historical average performance of mutual funds (as reported in the Mutual Fund Expert database). In many cases, the average performance of mutual funds goes back further than the performance of market benchmarks, so I have found it informative to use both sources of information.

TABLE 4.2   Major Bear Market for Selected Types of Investments

Investment Category	Benchmark and Period Examined°	Date of Bear Market Trough	Bear Market Drawdown	Duration of Drawdown Plus Recovery (Months)
U.S. large-cap stocks	S&P 500, 1965–2008	1970	20%	12
		1974	43%	45
		1987	30%	21
		2002	45%	74
Investment-grade U.S. bonds	Lehman Aggregate Bond Index, 1976–2008	1979–1980	13%	10
		1980–1981	9%	17
		1987	5%	10
		1994	5%	13
Emerging market stocks	Average Emerging Market Stock Fund, 1989–2008	1990	23%	33
		1995	25%	28
		1998	49%	31
		2001	47%	47

TABLE 4.2 (*continued*)

Investment Category	Benchmark and Period Examined°	Date of Bear Market Trough	Bear Market Drawdown	Duration of Drawdown Plus Recovery (Months)
International equities	Average Int'l Equity Mutual Fund, 1965–2008	1970	23%	22
		1974	44%	67
		1987	23%	19
		1990	20%	22
		2003	49%	69
Small-cap stocks	Average Small-Cap Blend Mutual Fund, 1969–2008	1974	52%	110
		1981	23%	17
		1983	22%	29
		1987	33%	21
		1990	24%	9
		1998	29%	20
		2003	25%	18
Small-cap stocks	Russell 2000 Index, 1979–2008	1982	22%	17
		1984	21%	25
		1987	36%	21
		1990	32%	20
		1998	30%	20
		2002	35%	46
Total U.S. stock market	Wilshire 5000 Index, 1971–2008	1974	46%	48
		1987	30%	20
		2002	42%	82
Technology stocks	Technology Fund Average, 1965–2008	1966	23%	12
		1970	42%	43
		1974	53%	73
		1987	33%	24
		2002	83%	>96
Small-cap value stocks	Small-Cap Value Fund Average, 1967–2008	1974	62%	134
		1984	21%	24
		1987	29%	20
		1990	25%	18
		1998	28%	28
		2003	25%	18
		2008	20%	>7
Small-cap value stocks	Russell 2000 Value Index, 1979–2008	1987	32%	20
		1990	33%	26
		1998	25%	32
		2003	27%	18
		2008	22%	>12

TABLE 4.2 *(continued)*

Investment Category	Benchmark and Period Examined°	Date of Bear Market Trough	Bear Market Drawdown	Duration of Drawdown Plus Recovery (Months)
Small-cap growth stocks	Small-Cap Growth Fund Average, 1965–2008	1970	38%	36
		1974	57%	71
		1978	20%	10
		1984	23%	25
		1987	34%	20
		1990	27%	9
		1998	29%	13
		2002	54%	72
		2008	20%	>7
Large-cap growth stocks	Russell 1000 Growth Index, 1979–2008	1982	26%	24
		1987	32%	23
		2002	62%	>77
Large-cap growth stocks	Large-Cap Growth Fund Average, 1965–2008	1970	38%	38
		1974	48%	64
		1987	29%	21
		2002	55%	>96
Large-cap value stocks	Russell 1000 Value Index, 1979–2008	1987	27%	17
		2002	28%	31
Large-cap value stocks	Large-Cap Value Fund Average, 1965–2008	1970	31%	38
		1974	40%	38
		1987	25%	19
		2002	29%	32
Utilities	Dow Jones Utility Average, 1965–2008	1974	62%^	242
		1988	24%^	33
		1994	27%	27
		2002	48%	51
Real estate (REITs)	Nareit Equity REIT Index, 1972–2008	1974	37%	49
		1990	24%	20
		1999	24%	37
		2008	26%	>16
Treasury bonds (all maturities)	Merrill Lynch Government Treasury Master, 1978–2008	1980	8% and 6%	10 and 16
		1987	5%	10
		1994	5%	15

°Mutual fund averages are from the 12/31/2005 and 1/31/2008 editions of the Mutual Fund Expert database. All the information presented here is based on monthly total return data except the dates marked with (^) under Dow Jones Utility Average, which represents price-only data.

Table 4.3 presents the history of the U.S. stock market in more detail, listing all 10 percent, 15 percent, and 20 percent market declines in the S&P 500 Index since 1941 (based on weekly closing price data, not counting dividends).

TABLE 4.3 Detailed History of Moves Up and Down in the S&P 500 from 1941 to 2008

Moves of at Least 10 Percent in S&P 500 from 1941 to 2008

Date of Trough	S&P 500 at Low	Date of Peak	S&P 500 at Peak	Gain during Advance	Decline to Next Trough
5/31/41	9.35	7/26/41	10.39	11.1%	−27.1%
4/25/42	7.57	7/17/43	12.56	65.9%	−11.5%
11/27/43	11.12	5/31/46	19.18	72.5%	−25.3%
11/23/46	14.33	2/8/47	16.20	13.0%	−15.4%
5/17/47	13.71	7/25/47	16.08	17.3%	−13.9%
2/14/48	13.84	6/18/48	16.96	22.5%	−18.6%
6/10/49	13.81	6/9/50	19.26	39.5%	−12.4%
7/14/50	16.87	1/2/53	26.54	57.3%	−13.5%
9/18/53	22.95	8/3/56	49.64	116.3%	−12.7%
2/8/57	43.32	7/12/57	49.08	13.3%	−19.6%
12/20/57	39.48	7/31/59	60.51	53.3%	−11.9%
10/21/60	53.32	12/8/61	72.04	35.1%	−26.9%
6/22/62	52.68	2/11/66	93.81	78.1%	−22.0%
10/7/66	73.20	11/29/68	108.37	48.0%	−33.3%
5/22/70	72.25	4/23/71	104.05	44.0%	−12.0%
11/19/71	91.61	1/5/73	119.87	30.8%	−15.5%
7/6/73	101.28	10/12/73	111.44	10.0%	−44.1%
10/4/74	62.34	11/8/74	74.91	20.2%	−13.2%
12/6/74	65.01	6/27/75	94.81	45.8%	−12.1%
9/12/75	83.30	12/31/76	107.46	29.0%	−18.6%
3/3/78	87.45	9/8/78	106.79	22.1%	−11.6%
11/17/78	94.42	2/8/80	117.95	24.9%	−14.8%
4/18/80	100.55	11/28/80	140.52	39.8%	−19.7%
9/25/81	112.77	12/4/81	126.26	12.0%	−17.9%
8/6/82	103.71	10/7/83	170.80	64.7%	−12.7%
6/15/84	149.03	8/21/87	335.90	125.4%	−33.3%
12/4/87	223.92	7/13/90	367.31	64.0%	−18.3%

TABLE 4.3 *(continued)*

Moves of at Least 10 Percent in S&P 500 from 1941 to 2008

Date of Trough	S&P 500 at Low	Date of Peak	S&P 500 at Peak	Gain during Advance	Decline to Next Trough
10/12/90	300.03	7/17/98	1186.75	295.5%	−17.9%
9/4/98	973.89	7/16/99	1418.78	45.7%	−12.1%
10/15/99	1247.41	3/24/00	1527.46	22.5%	−11.2%
4/14/00	1356.56	9/1/00	1520.77	12.1%	−25.8%
4/6/01	1128.43	5/18/01	1291.96	14.5%	−25.2%
9/21/01	965.80	1/4/02	1172.50	21.4%	−27.7%
7/19/02	847.75	8/23/02	940.85	11.0%	−14.9%
10/4/02	800.60	11/29/02	936.30	16.9%	−11.5%
3/7/03	828.90	10/09/07	1565.15	88.8%	−22.4%
7/15/08	1214.91				

36 declines of at least 10% in 67 years

Average move of at least 10%   **47.3%**   **−18.8%**

Moves of at Least 15 Percent in S&P 500 from 1941 to 2008

Date of Trough	S&P 500 at Low	Date of Peak	S&P 500 at Peak	Gain during Advance	Decline to Next Trough
4/25/42	7.57	5/31/46	19.18	153.4%	−28.5%
5/17/47	13.71	6/18/48	16.96	23.7%	−18.6%
6/10/49	13.81	8/3/56	49.64	259.4%	−20.5%
12/20/57	39.48	12/8/61	72.04	82.5%	−26.9%
6/22/62	52.68	2/11/66	93.81	78.1%	−22.0%
10/7/66	73.2	11/29/68	108.37	48.0%	−33.3%
5/22/70	72.25	1/5/73	119.87	65.9%	−48.0%
10/4/74	62.34	12/31/76	107.46	72.4%	−18.6%
3/3/78	87.45	11/28/80	140.52	60.7%	−26.2%
8/6/82	103.71	8/21/87	335.9	223.9%	−33.3%
12/4/87	223.92	7/13/90	367.31	64.0%	−18.3%
10/12/90	300.03	7/17/98	1186.75	295.5%	−17.9%
9/4/98	973.89	3/24/00	1527.46	56.8%	−36.8%
9/21/01	965.8	1/4/02	1172.5	21.4%	−31.7%

TABLE 4.3   (continued)

Moves of at Least 15 Percent in S&P 500 from 1941 to 2008

Date of Trough	S&P 500 at Low	Date of Peak	S&P 500 at Peak	Gain during Advance	Decline to Next Trough
10/4/02	800.6	10/9/07	1565.15	95.4%	−22.4%
7/15/08	1214.91				
15 declines of at least 15% in 67 years					
Average move of at least 15%				106.7%	−26.6%

Moves of at Least 20 Percent in S&P 500 from 1941 to 2008

Date of Trough	S&P 500 at Low	Date of Peak	S&P 500 at Peak	Gain during Advance	Decline to Next Trough
4/25/42	7.57	5/31/46	19.18	153.4%	−28.5%
5/17/47	13.71	8/3/56	49.64	262.1%	−20.5%
12/20/57	39.48	12/8/61	72.04	82.5%	−26.9%
6/22/62	52.68	2/11/66	93.81	78.1%	−22.0%
10/7/66	73.2	11/29/68	108.37	48.0%	−33.3%
5/22/70	72.25	1/5/73	119.87	65.9%	−48.0%
10/4/74	62.34	11/28/80	140.52	125.4%	−26.2%
8/6/82	103.71	8/21/87	335.9	223.9%	−33.3%
12/4/87	223.92	3/24/00	1527.46	582.1%	−36.8%
9/21/01	965.8	1/4/02	1172.5	21.4%	−31.7%
10/4/02	800.6	10/9/07	1565.15	95.4%	−22.4%
7/15/08	1214.91				
10 declines of at least 20% in 67 years					
Average move of at least 20%				**154.4%**	**−30.7%**

Since the start of 1941—a period of 67 years—there have been 36 market corrections of 10 percent or more in the S&P 500, representing one correction every 1.9 years on average. During the same 67 years, there have been 15 corrections of at least 15 percent, and 11 bear markets (declines of at least 20 percent in a broad market average). In other words, investors have on average faced a 15 percent market decline roughly once every four years, and a full-fledged bear market once every six years. The minimum loss (by definition) during a bear market is 20 percent, and the average historical loss has been 29.9 percent as of August 2008.

There are three steps to using drawdown to compare the risks of different investments:

1. **Identify the worst period for each of the investments you are comparing.**

2. **Measure the historical drawdown of your investment during this period, which might not be the same for each investment.** For example, small-company stock mutual funds fared worse in 1998 than during the 2000–2003 bear market, on average. So, to compare the risk of a large-company stock fund to a small-company stock fund, your data for both needs to include 1998–2003.

3. **The larger the historical drawdown during its worst period, the riskier you assess the investment to be.**

What if Your Investment Was Not Around During a Bear Market?

Most ETFs were launched in the late 1990s, or even more recently. As a result, in many cases there is not as much real-time bear market experience as there is for well-established mutual funds. Many mutual funds, too, are of recent vintage.

If a fund or ETF did not exist during the period that would be most informative to you, you need to find a comparable investment that has a sufficiently long history, and use that as a surrogate with which to measure risk.

Most mutual funds and ETFs describe themselves as adhering to a particular style of investing, such as those described in Chapter 2, "The Multifaceted Stock Market: A Guide to Different Investment Styles": large-company stocks, small-company value stocks, and so on. Another group of mutual funds focuses on particular industries, such as real estate investment trusts (REITs). Each major investment objective has one or more benchmarks. A *benchmark* is a price average of a basket of individual stocks selected to represent the market segment in which a fund invests. You encountered benchmarks in Table 3.1 of Chapter 3, "A One-Step Strategy for Selecting Superior Investments," where it was shown that the majority of mutual funds have not performed as well as benchmarks that are tracked by available ETFs.

You have no doubt heard about many benchmarks. For example, the Dow Jones Industrial Average consists of 30 large U.S. company stocks; therefore, it is a benchmark for large-caps. The NASDAQ Composite is most heavily weighted in technology stocks, so it is a technology stock benchmark.

The good news for investors is that numerous benchmarks have been around for a long time. You can use them to get an idea of how your current selection of ETFs or mutual funds *might* perform if similar market conditions arise. (Of course, it is not guaranteed that market history will repeat itself, or that your fund will behave in the same way as its benchmark.)

With many ETFs, the selection of a benchmark is especially simple because the ETFs are index funds. Many of the indexes that they attempt to replicate have been around from before the first ETF was launched in 1993.

When you think you have identified a benchmark for your fund, use charting software or Internet resources to plot the benchmark and the fund for the period when they were both actively trading. If they have experienced major dips and rallies of similar extents at the same times, it is reasonable to attempt to use the longer history of the benchmark to help you understand your fund. This process does require you to assume that the fund's risk will be at least as great as that of the best-fitting benchmark. In my experience, this assumption has almost always been justified.[1]

Let us look to the utilities sector as an example. The Utilities HOLDR (UTH) was launched in 2000. An investor who wants to investigate a longer utilities investment history could proceed as follows.

First, select a utilities benchmark. The Dow Jones Utility Average is a logical choice. Next, plot UTH and the Dow Utilities on the same chart, making sure that the same percentage range of data is displayed. For example, in Figure 4.6, the Dow Utilities are plotted in a vertical range of 50–450, whereas UTH is plotted in a range of 15–135. The upper limit of UTH (135) is 0.3 times the upper limit of the Dow Utilities (450). Similarly, the lower limit of UTH (15) is 0.3

times the lower limit of the plot of the Dow Jones Utility Average (50). In addition, both plots have a 9:1 ratio between their upper and lower limits (that is, 450/50 = 9, and 135/15 = 9). When all these conditions are met on a single chart with two vertical axes, the difference between the appearances of the two investments in the plots represents a true apples-to-apples comparison.

Plotted this way, Figure 4.6 makes it clear that during the five years (2000–2005) that both UTH and the Dow Utility Average were reported, they overlapped almost exactly. Therefore, it is reasonable to use the history of the Dow Jones Utility Average to evaluate the risk and reward potential of any investment strategy involving UTH. Note that it is not guaranteed that the Dow Jones Utility Average and UTH will continue to track each other so closely in the future just because they did from 2000–2005, but in my opinion this is a reasonable assumption to make.

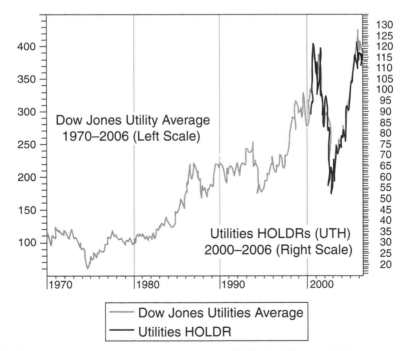

FIGURE 4.6   Dow Jones Utility Average (1970–2006) and Utilities HOLDRs (UTH, 2000–2006) plotted on the same time axis but on separate price axes.

Example of Risk Assessment: An Emerging Market ETF

The first ETF to track an index of *emerging market stocks* (which are stocks in companies from countries with developing economies) was the iShares M.S.C.I. Emerging Market Index Fund, ticker symbol EEM. From its inception in April 2003 through May 9, 2006, the share price more than tripled, rising from less than $34 per share to a high of more than $110 per share before pulling back to $93 per share by the end of May 2006. This represents an annualized rate of gain since inception of 38 percent per year. The four most severe market corrections in EEM have ranged from 10–18 percent. Investors required from two to six months to recover from these corrections. (During the same period, the S&P 500 gained 13 percent per year and had two corrections of only 8 percent and one correction of 6 percent.) Figure 4.7 shows the price growth in EEM since its inception and the four most significant price declines during the period.

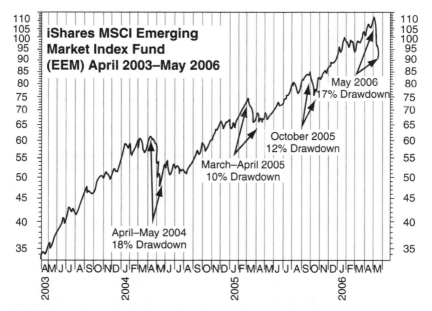

FIGURE 4.7   Price history of the iShares Morgan Stanley Capital International Emerging Market Index Fund (EEM) from its inception in April 2003 through May 2006.

When comparing the profits and drawdowns of emerging market stocks to the S&P 500 displayed in Figure 4.8, you might get the impression that emerging-market investing, although riskier than investing in industrialized-country stocks, has been far more profitable. On a risk-adjusted basis, EEM has far outperformed our own S&P 500 Index in its lifetime. (Note that in Figure 4.8, the right and left logarithmic scales are proportional to each other so that the same vertical displacement in either investment represents the same percentage change.)

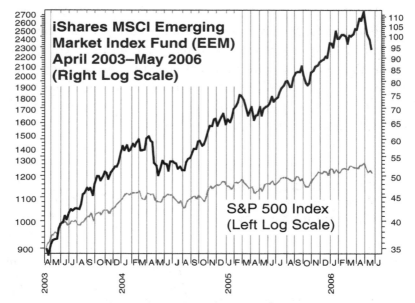

FIGURE 4.8   A chart of the performance of the S&P 500 Index overlaid with the iShares M.S.C.I. Emerging Market Index Fund (EEM) from April 2003–May 2006.

However, mutual fund performance averages afford us a longer-term look at stock markets in developing countries, and the picture is less attractive. Table 4.2 indicates that the emerging-market fund average has suffered four major declines between 1989 and 2005: 23 percent, 25 percent, 49 percent, and 47 percent. The duration of these drawdowns ranged from 28 to 47 months. The most recent bear market for emerging market stocks began in October 2007. As of August 2008, the iShares M.S.C.I. Emerging Market Index ETF had a 26% drawdown from its high point in October 2007.

Moreover, emerging-market mutual funds have not as a group
been nearly as profitable since 1989 as they have been since March
2003. From September 1989 to March 2003, the average emerging-
market fund gained only 2.9 percent per year, compared to a gain of
9 percent per year for the S&P 500 over the same period. The growth
of investments in the average emerging-market fund and the S&P
500 is shown in Figure 4.9. The longer-term data shows that by the
standard of market history from 1989–2005, the three years from
March 2003 through April 2006 have been a historically anomalous
period for emerging-market stocks.

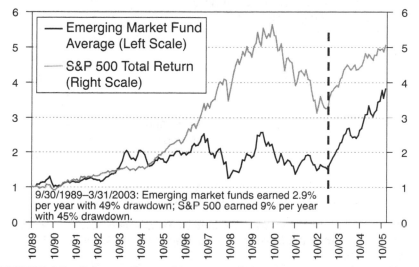

**FIGURE 4.9   Comparative performance of the average emerging-market
stock fund and the S&P 500 Index, 9/30/1989–12/30/2005, with the vertical
line placed at March 2003.**

Before we finish our discussion of emerging markets, you need to
consider two more things. First, is it reasonable to use the mutual
fund average as a proxy for the hypothetical past performance of
EEM? Second, is it possible that our look back to 1989 using the
mutual fund average might not be representative of future prospects
for emerging-market stocks as a whole?

The first question is easily settled by Figure 4.10, which shows
the total return of a hypothetical investment in the average emerging-
market fund (1989–2005) with the performance of EEM overlaid

(May 2003 through December 2005).[2] This chart is constructed so that on 4/30/2003, each had the same value of 1.0. The observation that EEM and the average emerging-market mutual fund behaved almost identically during the time that both were operating strongly suggests that it is reasonable to use the longer-history mutual fund average to gain insights about the possible behavior of EEM.

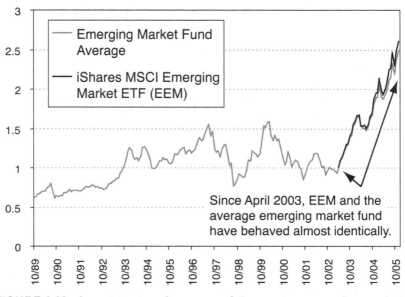

FIGURE 4.10   Investment performance of the average emerging market mutual fund and of the iShares M.S.C.I. Emerging Market Index ETF (ticker EEM).

The question of how well the past performance of emerging-market stocks reflects their future potential has no clear answer; it is a matter of subjective judgment. One major difference between the economic climate during the 1989–2002 period and the time since then is the price of commodities. From 1989–2002, commodity prices were generally falling; in fact, there was a fear of widespread deflation in many quarters. However, since 2002, commodity prices (especially energy and precious metals) have skyrocketed.

Figure 4.11 shows how major swings in commodity prices have been reflected in major moves in emerging-market stocks. This is logical, because the economies of many developing countries depend heavily on the production of raw materials. The emergence of commodity price inflation, reversing a trend of some 20 years, also makes it likely that emerging-market stocks will be more profitable for the next 15 years than they were in the past 15, although obviously the 38 percent annualized gains seen from May 2003–May 2006 cannot persist.

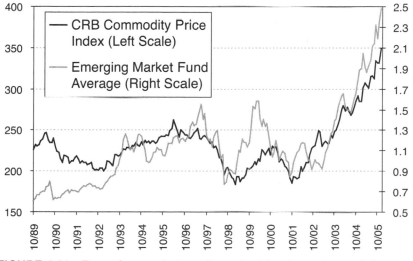

FIGURE 4.11   Emerging-market equity mutual fund average and the CRB Commodity Price Index.

Even though profit potential for emerging markets appears brighter than in the past, you cannot assume that risk will be lower in the future than during the 1989–2002 period. As a general rule, never assume that investments will be less risky in the future than they were in the past.

Market Risks and Planning for Your Future

The implication is that investors must factor in the occurrence of a major bear market when making retirement plans. What would happen if you retired at the top of the market and then proceeded to see your stock investments lose 30 percent? Would you be able to sleep at night? Would you be able to meet your anticipated rate of withdrawals? These are questions to address while you are still working.

Now that you understand drawdown, you will be able to understand why you will need to save more than you think to fulfill your financial goals for retirement. If you can accumulate enough money, the first strategy in securing a stable retirement for yourself is to wait until you have 40 percent more in equities than you think you will need to retire. That way, if a 30 percent correction hits at exactly the wrong time, you will still be on track. I realize that this is easier said than done for all of us.

Even if you cannot or will not continue working past the retirement age you envisioned, you can at least formulate a backup retirement plan for reduced spending in case your investments do not work out as well as you projected. For example, suppose you plan to withdraw 5 percent of your stock market assets each year for living expenses. If you need to take $25,000 per year from your equity investments, that means you need to have $500,000 in the stock market when you retire. (That is to say, 5 percent per year of $500,000 is $25,000 per year.)

If you happen to retire at a time such as early 2003 or 1982 (which were major market low points), your worries are over. However, suppose the reverse happens—that immediately upon retirement, your stock market investments proceed to lose 30 percent of their value. In that unfortunate case, you have only $350,000 working for you (30 percent less than the $500,000 you had to start retirement), so you can withdraw only $17,500 per year instead of $25,000. The financially safe thing to do is to cut your spending by $7,500 per year so that your initial rate of withdrawal remains just 5 percent. You are better off knowing how you would reduce your income (from the stock market) by 30 percent before you retire than after catastrophe strikes.

Many people might choose to withdraw the $25,000 per year they originally planned in the hope that the stock market will recover strongly enough to restore their original savings. The choice that most appeals to you depends on your temperament and many other factors, so there is no single correct response. The goal of the strategies in this book is to reduce the chances that you might ultimately find yourself financially between a rock and a hard place, by both potentially increasing your investment returns and reducing the risks.

Take-Home Messages

Drawdown is the percentage lost from a high point to the next low point. The significance of drawdown depends on the period over which you measure it.

Severe bear markets have been a recurring pitfall for investors, as shown in the two examples with the Dow Industrials. Your investment plan must include contingencies for bear markets of this severity.

Appendix A to Chapter 4: Where to Find Quantitative Investment Risk Information

The best way to measure drawdown is off a price chart, as in the examples shown. You can obtain such charts for free on the Web, such as from http://moneycentral.msn.com/investor/charts/charting.asp or http://finance.yahoo.com.

Otherwise, you have to download total return data into a spreadsheet program such as Excel and either create your own graph for a visual estimation of drawdown or use the formulas described in Appendix 4B to calculate the exact drawdown.

Appendix 4C describes the risk measure widely used in academic studies—standard deviation. Yahoo Finance provides standard deviation for ETFs and mutual funds under its "risk" menu, after you enter the ticker symbol for the ETF you want to look up. For open-end mutual funds but not ETFs, standard-deviation data is available in MSN investor (on the Portfolio Holdings page).

Appendix B to Chapter 4: Calculation of Drawdown with a Spreadsheet

Table 4.4 gives an example of the drawdown calculation. To calculate the drawdown in a spreadsheet, you start with one column of data that includes the values of the investment. For example, if you want to calculate the drawdown of the S&P 500 based on daily data, the first column should have the dates arranged from earliest to most recent, and the second column (Column B in Table 4.4) should contain the daily closing prices of the S&P 500.

The third column (Column C in Table 4.4) contains the highest prior value that the investment has obtained. Note that the number in Column C can be either a value in the same row or a value from an earlier row, but it can never be a value from a subsequent row. The fourth column (Column D in Table 4.4) contains the calculation of the current investment value divided by the highest prior peak value minus 1. In this way, drawdown is expressed as a percentage ranging from 0 (indicating that the investment value in that row is higher than all earlier values) to –100 (indicating a total loss of the original investment). The last step is to find the smallest (most negative) of the values in the third column. This smallest value is the drawdown for the period of data examined.

TABLE 4.4   Sample Spreadsheet Showing the Results of the Calculations of the Drawdown of the Investment Value Data

	Column B	Column C	Column D	Comments
Row 1	Investment Value	Last Maximum	Current Value Divided by Last Maximum Minus 1	The first row has the column headings.
Row 2	100	100	0	Always start at 0 drawdown.
Row 3	300	300	0	The investment is at a new high, so drawdown is 0.
Row 4	500	500	0	The investment is at another new high, so drawdown is 0.
Row 5	400	500	–20%	The investment is 20% off of its last high of 500.

TABLE 4.4 (continued)

	Column B	Column C	Column D	Comments
Row 6	300	500	–40%	The investment is 40% off of its last high of 500.
Row 7	400	500	–20%	
Row 8	600	600	0	The investment is at a new high, so drawdown is back to 0.
Row 9	800	800	0	
Row 10	600	800	–25%	The investment is 25% off of its last high of 800.
Row 11	Maximum Drawdown		Minimum of the Previous Values = –40%	

If you use a spreadsheet to calculate drawdown (which I highly recommend), each cell in the Last Maximum column should have a formula in it to calculate the numerical results that are shown in the example. The first row in the Last Maximum column should repeat the first row in the Investment Value column. All rows in Column C after the first have a conditional statement that performs the following test:

> If the investment value in Column B, Row j (j representing the row number) is larger than the last maximum (in Column C, Row j–1), return the investment value in row j. Otherwise, return the last maximum value from Row j–1. (For example, in Table 4.4, j ranges from 3 to 10. Row 2 is the first row and would not have this formula, and Row 11 is used only to calculate the drawdown from the data in Rows 2–10.)

As an example, consider what would be written into Excel. Investment Value data will be in Column B, Last Maximum data will be in Column C, and the Current Value Divided by the Last Maximum Minus 1 will be in Column D. If the first row of data is Row 2, cell C2 has the formula =B2, which copies the first piece of investment value data. (In Excel, every formula starts with an equal sign to distinguish a formula from a string of text.)

The actual formulas in the cells from an Excel spreadsheet that generated Table 4.4 appear in Table 4.5. Cell C3 has the formula =if(B3 > C2,B3,C2), and cell D3 has the formula =(B3 / C3) − 1. (In Excel, an if statement has three parts—for example, =if(condition, result 1, result 2). If the condition is true, result 1 is placed in the cell where the if formula resides. Otherwise, result 2 is placed in that cell.) Cell C4 has the formula =if(B4 > C3,B4,C3), and cell D4 has the formula =B4 / C4 − 1. Cell D11 calculates the drawdown as =min(D2:D10).

TABLE 4.5   Excel Formulas as They Would Appear in a Spreadsheet to Calculate Drawdowns from the Investment Data Presented in Table 4.4

Column A Date	Column B Investment Value	Column C Calculate Highest Prior Peak Value	Column D Calculate Drawdown for Each Date
Row 2	1	=B2	=B2/C2–1
Row 3	3	=IF(B3>C2,B3,C2)	=B3/C3–1
Row 4	5	=IF(B4>C3,B4,C3)	=B4/C4–1
Row 5	4	=IF(B5>C4,B5,C4)	=B5/C5–1
Row 6	3	=IF(B6>C5,B6,C5)	=B6/C6–1
Row 7	4	=IF(B7>C6,B7,C6)	=B7/C7–1
Row 8	6	=IF(B8>C7,B8,C7)	=B8/C8–1
Row 9	8	=IF(B9>C8,B9,C8)	=B9/C9–1
Row 10	6	=IF(B10>C9,B10,C9)	=B10/C10–1
Row 11	Worst drawdown		=MIN(D2:D10)

Appendix C to Chapter 4: Volatility of Past Returns as a Risk Measure

I prefer to use drawdown as a risk measure because it is so easy to understand visually, and because it is a measure of risk that reflects the investor's real experience of losses when they occur. Nonetheless, for a variety of reasons, most academic investment research and much of the available risk data reports risk as the standard deviation of returns.

The standard deviation is not an intuitive measure to many investors. Basically, the standard deviation of a list of numbers describes how widely spread the numbers range about their average value. A low standard deviation implies a set of numbers that lie close to their average value, whereas a large standard deviation means that the numbers are all over the place.

The reason why the standard deviation can serve as a measure of investment risk is the assumption (which is mostly borne out by historical observation) that an investment with the potential to produce widely varying returns from month to month also has the potential to suffer large losses. Conversely, an investment whose returns have stayed close to a single average value is not likely to generate too unpleasant a surprise. To the extent that these expectations are usually fulfilled, the lower a standard deviation of an investment's past returns, the lower its risk.

Although standard deviation has served well as a measure of risk (and it simplifies the mathematics in academic studies, which is why it was adopted in the first place), it is not a perfect measure. The standard deviation measure of risk indicates that an investment that regularly loses 1 percent each month is less risky than an investment that makes 2 percent per month half the time and loses one-half percent per month the other half of the time. Also, as with any measure of risk, the value of the result depends heavily on the period of data you examine.

As an example, we will calculate the standard deviation of the 12 months of S&P 500 total returns for 2005, which appear in Table 4.6.

TABLE 4.6   Monthly Total Returns for the S&P 500 Index in 2005

Month in 2005	S&P 500 Total Return for That Month (%)
January	–2.44
February	2.1
March	–1.77
April	–1.9
May	3.18
June	0.14
July	3.72
August	–0.91
September	0.81
October	–1.67
November	3.78
December	0.04
Average of 12 months	**0.42**

If you had this set of numbers in a spreadsheet such as Excel, you could use a built-in function called stdev to calculate the standard deviation. The steps are as follows:

1. Find the average of the return data, which in this case is 0.42 percent.

2. For each month, subtract this average from that month's return, and square it. For January, the result would be $(-2.44-0.42)^2$, which is $-2.86\times-2.86=8.1796$. For February, the result would be $(2.1-0.42)^2 =1.68\times1.68=1.8224$, and so on. Do this for each of the 12 months, and add all 12 results together. In this example, the sum comes to 57.48696.

3. Divide this sum by the number of data points minus 1. For this example, this step comes to 57.4896/11, or 5.2263.

4. Take the square root of the result of step 3: $\sqrt{5.2263} = 2.2861$. This is the standard deviation. Because the original data was a percentage, the standard deviation is also a percentage. The result of all this calculation is that the average and standard deviation of monthly returns for the S&P 500 in 2005 was 0.42 percent +/–2.2861 percent. This is actually a low standard deviation compared to the risk levels calculated most of the time for the S&P 500 Index.

Note this technical point. Yahoo Finance and many other sources of standard deviation data report "annualized standard deviation." This is simply the monthly standard deviation, calculated as described in this appendix, multiplied by $\sqrt{12}$, or 3.464. So, for example, using the procedure described would result in a 60-month standard deviation of 4.3 percent for the ETF that tracks the S&P 500 Index (ticker symbol SPY). Yahoo Finance reports the five-year standard deviation of SPY as 14.9 percent, which is 4.3 percent × 3.464.

There is no reliable way to estimate what your worst loss might be from knowledge of a standard deviation. Market history suggests that drawdown risk is likely to be significantly more than five standard deviations (based on monthly data). The best you can do with standard deviation data is to compare the potential risk levels of different investments.

Let us use standard deviation to ask whether stocks appear safer now than they did in the past. The standard deviation for the S&P 500 Index for the 60-month period 2001–2005 was 4.3 percent. The first observation is that 2005 was a quiet year, with just more than half the volatility of the past five years. My interpretation of that finding is that 2005 is not an instructive year for investors looking to gauge the amount of risk they face from their investments in large U.S. company stocks.

In December 1999 (three months from the peak of the stock market bubble), the standard deviation of the previous 60 months' returns for the S&P 500 was 4.03 percent, or slightly less than the most recent 60-month risk level. With the wisdom of hindsight, December 31, 1999 was not a good time to buy U.S. stocks if you intended to hold them for five years. Yet most investors would not project that stocks are riskier in 2006 than they turned out to be at the start of 2000. The moral of the story is that risk measures are only as good as the data used to make them. An accurate risk assessment requires looking to previous market disasters for guidance rather than automatically using a fixed window of time (such as three or five years, which are commonly seen).

Endnotes

1 A handful of mutual funds have managers who break the mold by daring not to track closely with a benchmark. Although many such funds have been excellent investments, you need to understand the limitations in using benchmarks to make projections about how such funds might behave in the future.

2 The data in Figure 4.10 represents monthly total returns taken from the 12/31/2005 edition of the Steele Mutual Fund Expert Database.

5

HOW WELL ARE YOUR INVESTMENTS REALLY DOING? RISK-ADJUSTED PERFORMANCE

Now that you understand the importance of investment risk and how to measure it, you are equipped to compare the performance of different investments, taking both risk and reward into account. Investment reward is easy to understand. It is simply the historical compounded annual rate of return. Appendix 5A describes in detail the formula to calculate this using the length of the period you are studying and the values of the investment at the beginning and end of that period. This chapter considers two different measures of risk-adjusted performance. The first, a ratio between investment returns and drawdown is, in my opinion, more intuitive. The second, the Sharpe ratio, is widely used among academics and quantitative portfolio analysts.

The First Risk-Adjusted Performance Measure—Annual Gain-to-Drawdown Ratio

The simplest risk-adjusted performance measure is the ratio of compounded annual gain to drawdown. (For the rest of this chapter, we will use the abbreviation GPA, short for gain per annum, to denote the compounded annual growth rate. A negative GPA indicates a loss in value over the period studied.) The higher this ratio, the better.

Figure 5.1 shows an example of how to calculate the GPA-to-drawdown ratio. The data in this figure represents the hypothetical growth of $1 invested in the Dow Jones Utility Average from 12/31/1992–2/28/2006. During this period, the GPA (including dividends) was 9.7 percent per year. Figure 5.1 shows that there were two major drawdowns: 27 percent in 1993–1994 and 49 percent in 2000–2002. To calculate the GPA-to-drawdown ratio, you use only the largest drawdown during the period. In this example, the GPA-to-drawdown ratio is 9.7 percent divided by 49 percent, which is 0.2.

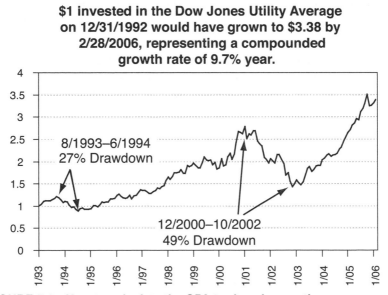

$1 invested in the Dow Jones Utility Average on 12/31/1992 would have grown to $3.38 by 2/28/2006, representing a compounded growth rate of 9.7% year.

FIGURE 5.1   How to calculate the GPA-to-drawdown ratio.

The importance of risk-adjusted performance measurements is that they can reduce the evaluation of the relative performances of two different investments into an apples-to-apples comparison. Figure 5.2 shows an example of this using the Dow Jones Industrial Average and the Dow Jones Utility Average from 1998–2006. (Note that this is a shorter time period than covered in Figure 5.1.) Visual inspection of the 1998–2006 history shown in Figure 5.2 shows that the Dow Jones Utility Average had a larger drawdown than the Dow Jones Industrial Average during the 2000–2002 market decline, but it had larger overall gains for the period. In other words, utilities were both more profitable and riskier than industrials. Table 5.1 shows the numerical GPA and drawdown data for both indexes that correspond to the chart in Figure 5.2. The table shows that, as judged by the GPA-to-drawdown ratio, the Dow Jones Industrial Average was a slightly better investment during this period. (The data in Figure 5.2 and Table 5.1, taken from the 2/28/2006 edition of the Steele Mutual Fund Expert database, includes the effects of reinvesting dividends but takes into account neither taxes nor transaction costs.)

TABLE 5.1   Risk and Total Return Data for the Dow Jones Industrial Average and the Dow Jones Utility Average, January 1998–February 2006 (98 Months)

Index	Compounded Annual Growth Rate	Maximum Drawdown	GPA-to-Drawdown Ratio
Dow Jones Industrial Average	6.1%	31%	0.20
Dow Jones Utility Average	9.2%	49%	0.19

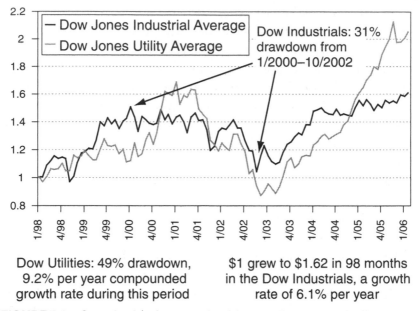

Dow Utilities: 49% drawdown, $1 grew to $1.62 in 98 months
9.2% per year compounded   in the Dow Industrials, a growth
growth rate during this period   rate of 6.1% per year

FIGURE 5.2   Growth of $1 invested in either the Dow Jones Utility Average or the Dow Jones Industrial Average from 12/31/1997 through 2/28/2006.

One reason why you might find this measurement useful is its intuitive interpretation: Comparing GPA and drawdown tells you how many years of average performance are required to recover from the worst historical loss in the period studied. For example, in 2000–2003, the drawdown of the S&P 500 was 45 percent. The long-term average return of large U.S. stocks has been approximately 11 percent per year (although I expect that during the decade ahead, the return will be closer to 8 percent per year). Therefore, the GPA-to-drawdown ratio has been approximately 1:4, or 0.25. This means that an investor should expect to require four years to recover from a severe bear market. Regarding the 2000–2003 bear market, this estimate appears to be on track. However, the recovery from the 1973–1974 bear market was significantly quicker than expected: The length of the drawdown was 45 months (see Table 5.2), but of this 45 months, the market spent 21 months falling and required only 24 months to recover.

Another Risk-Adjusted Performance Measure—The Sharpe Ratio

A less intuitive but more widely used measure of risk-adjusted performance is called the Sharpe ratio. The performance measure used in the Sharpe ratio is not simply the average return, as discussed in the preceding section. Rather, Sharpe ratio calculations use something called the excess return. The *excess return* is the amount of profit above what was earned from a risk-free investment. (See Figure 5.3.)

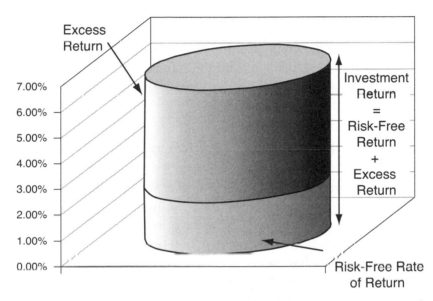

FIGURE 5.3   The relationship among risk-free return, excess return, and total investment return.

In practice, the figure used for the risk-free return is that available from 90-day Treasury bills. For example, if your investment returned 8 percent per year on average for the past ten years, and if Treasury bills returned an average of 3.6 percent per year during the same period, your excess investment return is:

$$8\%\text{–}3.6\% = 4.4\%$$

The use of an excess return as a performance measure makes sense. If you were able to get a risk-free return of 4 percent per year from a money market fund or bank CD, has your investment really "performed" if it delivered the same return while exposing you to investment risk?

The risk measure used in the Sharpe ratio is the standard deviation of monthly returns of the investment you are evaluating. The calculation of standard deviations is described in Appendix 4C.

The Sharpe ratio, a reward-to-risk ratio, is:

(average excess return)/(standard deviation of investment returns)

Returning to the example, if the excess return of your investment averaged 4.4 percent per year, and the standard deviation of returns was 13.2 percent per year, the Sharpe ratio would be as follows:

4.4%/13.2% = 0.33

The calculation of the Sharpe ratio in Excel is detailed in Appendix 5B.

It is important to recognize that the Sharpe ratio in general depends on the frequency of the data you use. Consider an investment with a 6 percent per year average annual return (not compounded) and a standard deviation of 13.9 percent per year. Assume the risk-free return has averaged 3.6 percent per year. If you use this annual data, the Sharpe ratio is calculated as follows:

(6%–3.6%)/13.9% = 0.173

Now consider the same investment, but this time with monthly information. An average annual return of 6 percent is the same as a monthly return of 0.5 percent (not compounded). Similarly, an annual excess return of 2.4 percent equals a monthly excess return of 0.2 percent. That was easy, but what should the monthly standard deviation be?

In general, standard deviation is proportional to the square root of the time period.[1] Suppose that I expose myself to a certain amount of risk (as measured by standard deviation of returns) by holding an investment for one month. What happens to my risk if I extend my holding period to four months? The risk is proportional to the square root of the time period, so my risk only doubles even though my holding period quadrupled. Because one year is 12 months, the standard deviation of the annual returns should be $\sqrt{12}$ × (standard deviation of one-month returns). ($\sqrt{12}$ = 3.464). Because the standard deviation of annual returns was 13.9 percent, the one-month standard deviation should be as follows:

$$13.9\%/3.464 = 4.01$$

Let's go back to the Sharpe ratio calculation. The monthly average excess return is 0.2 percent, and the monthly standard deviation is 4.01. The Sharpe ratio using monthly data becomes this:

$$0.2/4.01 = 0.050$$

This is different from the value of 0.173 calculated using annual data. The implication is that when you use the Sharpe ratio to compare different investments, you must be sure that the calculations among all the investments were performed consistently:

> The periods during which performance was measured
> must be the same.

> The frequency of the data (monthly, quarterly, and so on)
> must be the same.

The advantage of using the Sharpe ratio as a risk-adjusted performance measure (compared to the GPA/drawdown ratio) is that with Sharpe ratios, it is possible to calculate the risk-adjusted performance of a whole portfolio knowing only the average returns and standard deviations of each component, along with the correlations between every pair of investments in the portfolio. As a result of this relative simplicity, it is possible to find the portfolio with the best risk-adjusted historical performance using only a relatively small number of calculations.

In contrast, when you are using GPA/drawdown, no shortcut is available. The only way to find the portfolio with the best risk-adjusted historical performance is to repeat the GPA and drawdown calculations for each portfolio you want to consider and then select the one that turned out best.

Risk-Adjusted Performance Review

The 1996–2005 (ten-year) period was a crucible for most styles of stock market investing. That makes it potentially informative to use this period to compare the overall risk-versus-reward balance that has been available from different strategies. Although financial markets were turbulent in 2007–2008, investments such as emerging markets and small caps had worse experiences in 1997–1998, which is why it will be most useful for you to examine more than just five years of history (when available) so that you can include all the market's history since the start of 1997.

Table 5.2 presents the GPA and drawdown from 12/31/1995–12/31/2005 for all the benchmarks whose risks were listed in Chapter 4, "Investment Risk: A Visit to the Dark Side," as well as the risk-adjusted performance measures GPA/drawdown and the Sharpe ratio. During the period, REITs were the most profitable, investment-grade bonds were the safest, technology was the riskiest, investment-grade bonds had the best (highest) GPA/drawdown ratio, and REITs had the best (highest) Sharpe ratio. The calculations in Table 5.2 are based on monthly total return data.

TABLE 5.2   Historical Profit, Risk, and Risk-Adjusted Performance Measures for Different Investment Styles You Can Implement with ETFs, Calculated from 1996–2005

Benchmark	GPA (Percent per Year)	Drawdown (Percent)	GPA-to-Drawdown Ratio	120-Month Sharpe Ratio
Lehman Aggregate Bond Index	6.2%	–3.6%	1.73	0.19
Merrill Lynch U.S. Treasury Master	5.9%	–4.8%	1.23	0.14
NAREIT Equity REIT Index	14.5%	–23.7%	0.61	0.23
Average U.S. Small-Cap Value Equity Fund	13.4%	–27.2%	0.49	0.19
Russell 2000 Value Index	13.1%	–26.7%	0.49	0.18

TABLE 5.2 *(continued)*

Benchmark	GPA (Percent per Year)	Drawdown (Percent)	GPA-to-Drawdown Ratio	120-Month Sharpe Ratio
Russell 1000 Value Index	10.9%	−27.7%	0.40	0.16
Average U.S. Small-Cap Blend Equity Fund	10.6%	−29.6%	0.36	0.13
Average U.S. Large-Cap Value Equity Fund	9.2%	−29.1%	0.32	0.13
Russell 2000 Index (U.S. Small-Caps)	9.3%	−35.1%	0.26	0.11
Dow Jones Utility Average	10.4%	−48.5%	0.21	0.13
Wilshire 5000 Index (Total U.S. Stock Market)	9.2%	−44.1%	0.21	0.12
Average U.S. Small-Cap Growth Fund	9.9%	−53.8%	0.18	0.10
Average Emerging Markets Equity Fund	8.7%	−50.5%	0.17	0.09
S&P 500 Index (U.S. Large-Cap)	7.3%	−46.3%	0.16	0.09
Average International Equity Fund	7.0%	−48.9%	0.14	0.08
Average U.S. Large-Cap Growth Fund	7.3%	−55.1%	0.13	0.08
Russell 1000 Growth Index	6.7%	−61.9%	0.11	0.07
Average U.S. Technology Mutual Fund	8.0%	−82.3%	0.10	0.08
Russell 2000 Growth Index	4.7%	−62.6%	0.07	0.05

Conclusion

It is crucial that you understand the concept of risk-adjusted performance, because it is the most effective criterion for the investor to use in deciding where and how much to invest. The basic idea is to take a measure of profitability, such as average annual return or compounded annual return, and divide that by a risk measure. (You do not necessarily need to master the precise mathematics of calculating standard deviations.)

As with any examination of investment performance, it is important to make sure that you have chosen a sufficiently rich period of investment history in your evaluation. Your long-term investment plan will likely fail if you select your investments based on its performance only during a period devoid of major market declines.

Appendix A to Chapter 5—Calculation of the Compounded Annual Rate of Return

To derive the formula to calculate the compounded rate of return, let us start with the formula to calculate the growth of an investment if you already know the rate of return:

$$\text{Final value} = (\text{initial value}) \times (1 + \text{rate of compounded growth})^n$$

which is read as the final value equals the initial value times (1+growth rate) to the nth power. n is the number of time periods, which must be in the same time unit as the growth rate. So, for example, if your growth rate is 0.5 percent per month, n is the number of months. If your growth rate is 6 percent per year, n is the number of years. n can be a fraction.

What does this "n^{th} power" stuff mean? If you make 6 percent per year on your money for three years, and you start with $100, after year 1, you will have $106. To figure out what you would have after two years, you multiply your ending balance from year 1, $106, by 1.06:

$$\$106 \times 1.06 = \$112.36$$

To figure out what you will have after the third year, you multiply your ending balance from year 2, $112.36, by 1.06 again:

$$\$112.36 \times 1.06 = \$119.10 \text{ (rounded to nearest cent)}$$

The $(1+\text{compounded rate of return})^n$ is simply mathematical shorthand to describe this compounding process.

If you take the preceding equation and divide both sides by the initial value of the investment, you are left with:

$$\text{final value/initial value} = (1+\text{rate of compounded growth})^n$$

Next, you need to take the nth root of each side, giving

$$\sqrt[n]{\frac{\text{final value}}{\text{initial value}}} = 1+\text{rate of compounded growth}$$

Finally, subtract 1 from each side of the equation to isolate the compounded growth rate:

$$\text{Compounded rate of growth} = \sqrt[n]{\frac{\text{final value}}{\text{initial value}}} - 1 \qquad \text{(formula 1)}$$

Suppose that your data is monthly, but you want to know the annualized rate of growth. In this case, the number of periods is not n, the number of months, but n/12, the number of years. Similarly, if you have n weeks of data, the number of years to use in formula 1 is n/52. Be careful with daily data. Most sources of data give you closing prices only for days when the market is open. Therefore, if you have n days' worth of data only on market days, the number of years is only n/253 because there are (on average) 253 trading days per year, or about 21 trading days per month.

If you use Excel, the function that calculates the compounded growth rate per period, implementing formula 1, is:

$$=\text{power(final value/initial value, 1/n)}-1$$

If you have weekly data but want to calculate the annualized rate of growth, the compounded growth rate per year is found in Excel by the following:

$$=\text{power(final value/initial value, 52/n)}-1$$

For daily data, substitute the 253 for 52, and for monthly data, substitute 12 for 52 in this formula.

This formula is useful because some data sources provide beginning and ending values. For example, MSN Investor has interactive charting where you can get the numeric value of an index or ETF by pointing to the point on the chart that corresponds to the date you want. Yahoo Finance gives "adjusted close" data in spreadsheet format that you can export to Excel. It provides a source of total return data you can use to calculate compounded growth rates between any two dates you want. Although I have found both of these websites to be excellent resources, there have been frequent omissions in the historical dividend or distribution data they provide, so make sure to double-check this information. The price data from these websites has, in my experience, been very accurate.

Appendix B to Chapter 5—Calculation of the Sharpe Ratio

To analyze the historical risk-adjusted performance of a potential investment, you need to have historical return data for both the investment and the risk-free return that you could have obtained. I use the 90-day Treasury bill return as the risk-free rate of return. Space the return data at consistent intervals, such as monthly, quarterly, or annually. Although the example in the book uses annual data to fit the spreadsheet on a single page, I used monthly data for these calculations. Quarterly data would work, too, and might be more economical to obtain than monthly data.

Earlier in this chapter, you saw that the formula for the Sharpe ratio of an investment is

$$\frac{\text{average investment return per period–average risk-free rate per period}}{\text{standard deviation of investment returns}}$$

This section shows you how to calculate the Sharpe ratio in an Excel spreadsheet. Figure 5.4 contains a spreadsheet with the historical annual total returns for the S&P 500 Index and 90-day Treasury bills in Columns B and C. This annual data occupies Rows 1–30. In terms of Excel spreadsheet cell formulas:

- The average investment return per period is average(B1:B30) for the S&P 500 and average(C1:C30) for 90-day Treasury bills. These formulas appear in cells B32 and C32, respectively. The numeric result that would appear in cell B32 if you set up your own spreadsheet with this data would be 13.8 percent. In C32, the result would be 6.3 percent.

- The standard deviation of annual investment returns for the S&P 500 Index is calculated according to the formula in cell B33, stdev(B1:B30). The numerical result is 15.7 percent.

- Therefore, the Sharpe ratio of the S&P 500 from 1976–2005 is calculated in Excel as:

$$\frac{(\text{average}(B1:B30)-\text{average}(C1:C30))}{\text{stdev}(B1:B30)}$$

Because each of the averages and the standard deviation appear in cells B32, C32, and B33, the Sharpe ratio = (B32–C32)/B33. This formula appears in cell B34 in Figure 5.4. The numeric result is 0.48.

You can find Sharpe ratios for mutual funds online, so we need to discuss a couple of points before you can safely apply such data. First, make sure when you compare the Sharpe ratios of different investments that the data intervals are the same, as is the period reported. Calculate both ratios that you are comparing from monthly data or quarterly data. (Despite my use of annual data here to save space, I generally do not recommend using such infrequent data for your own analysis because many significant intrayear events such as the market crash of 1987 might be obscured in annual data. It's better to use 300 monthly returns than 25 annual returns.)

Second, the historical period of time covered in any performance reports should be the same when you are comparing two investments. For this reason, data on performance since inception for mutual funds is frequently useless, unless you are willing to go to the trouble of isolating the performance of comparison investments during precisely the same months. It's better to use 1, 3, 5, and 10-year performance histories that are easily compared to one another (as long as they are reported at the same time).

Column	A	B	C
		Total Returns (%)	
Row Number	Year	S&P 500 with Dividends	90-Day T-Bill
1	1976	23.9	5.0
2	1977	−7.2	5.4
3	1978	6.6	7.4
4	1979	18.6	10.5
5	1980	32.5	12.1
6	1981	−4.9	15.0
7	1982	21.6	11.4
8	1983	22.6	9.0
9	1984	6.3	10.0
10	1985	31.7	7.8
11	1986	18.7	6.2
12	1987	5.3	5.9
13	1988	16.6	6.9
14	1989	31.6	8.2
15	1990	−3.1	7.8
16	1991	30.4	5.6
17	1992	7.6	3.5
18	1993	10.1	3.0
19	1994	1.3	4.4
20	1995	37.5	5.7
21	1996	23.0	5.2
22	1997	33.4	5.2
23	1998	28.6	4.9
24	1999	21.0	4.8
25	2000	−9.1	6.0
26	2001	−11.9	3.5
27	2002	−22.1	1.6
28	2003	28.7	1.0
29	2004	10.9	1.4
30	2005	4.9	3.3
31			
32	Average Returns	=average(b1:b30)	=average(c1:c30)
33	Standard Deviation of Returns	=stdev(b1:b30)	
34	Sharpe Ratio	=(b32-c32)/b33	

FIGURE 5.4 Historical annual total returns for the S&P 500 Index and 90-day Treasury bills.

Although gain/loss data for mutual funds is readily available, risk data is not. To implement a Sharpe ratio calculation, you can obtain free monthly total return data from http://finance.yahoo.com, as follows:

- Enter the ticker symbol of the fund you want.
- Select Historical Prices from the menu of options on the left of the screen. The Close column is the mutual fund closing price as reported. The Adjusted Close column represents mutual fund total return (including dividend and capital gains distributions), back-adjusted so that the most current "adjusted close" agrees with the actual reported close.
- At the bottom of the page is a Download to Spreadsheet link that will generate an Excel file with the data. Copy the data and paste it into a file on your own computer.

Changes in the adjusted close data are intended to represent the fund's total return. As with any mutual fund database, distributions that the fund might have made are frequently missed. This is especially the case the further back in history your data download goes. One way to verify the accuracy of the download is to calculate a total return for the fund and see if it agrees with total return data that the mutual fund has provided. Before you use downloaded data on your own, verify its accuracy.

Endnote

1 Technically, this is true only if the investment results during separate periods do not influence each other, and if the likelihood of getting any particular investment return is the same from one period to the next. In fact, this is an oversimplification, but one that does not reduce the usefulness of risk-adjusted performance in evaluating investments for an individual investor.

6

DIVERSIFICATION: THE ONLY FREE LUNCH ON WALL STREET

If you have ever received professional financial advice, you are likely to have heard that diversification is good. Unfortunately, the individual investor almost never gets to see what difference diversification has made—or might be likely to make—in the future. In this chapter, you will see that diversification can be good—in the sense of improving the balance between risk and reward. But diversification in your investments is often more difficult to achieve than you might think. If you are investing in ETFs, most of which are well diversified to begin with, diversifying among multiple ETFs is likely to incrementally improve the risk-adjusted performance of your investments. However, diversification cannot turn straw into gold. On the other hand, if your investments consist of individual company stocks, diversifying can greatly increase the safety of your portfolio.

Reduce Risk, Not Profits, with Diversification

Diversification is not the only way to increase safety. You could, for example, simply allocate a large proportion of your investments to short-term bonds or money market funds as a safety measure. The problem with such a strategy is that for most of us, the returns available from these safe investments are not sufficient to bring us to our long-term financial goals.

The purpose of diversifying is to increase safety without decreasing returns. Figure 6.1 shows an example of how this has worked from 1997–2005 for three different stock market investments: the S&P 500 Index (large U.S. companies), the average small-cap value fund, and the average real estate investment trust (REIT) fund (monthly total returns as reported in the Steele Mutual Fund Expert database of May 31, 2005). The long-term compounded annual returns from these investments have been fairly similar from 5/31/1980–12/31/2005: 12.9 percent for the S&P 500, including dividends, 13.3 percent per year for the average small-cap value fund, and 13.0 percent for the average REIT fund.

However, during the turbulent period from 1997–2005, each of these sectors experienced severe declines at different times. Figure 6.1 shows that, as a result, in 2002 the diversified portfolio (40 percent S&P 500, 40 percent REITs, and 20 percent small-cap value) lost less than any of its separate components.

From 1998–1999, REITs and small-cap value funds lagged most other areas of the stock market, including the S&P 500. Many investors in these areas became discouraged, because it seemed that everyone but them was making money in stocks. Investors during this period clearly would have benefited by having exposure to the broader U.S. stock market in the form of an S&P 500 Index fund (such as SPY).

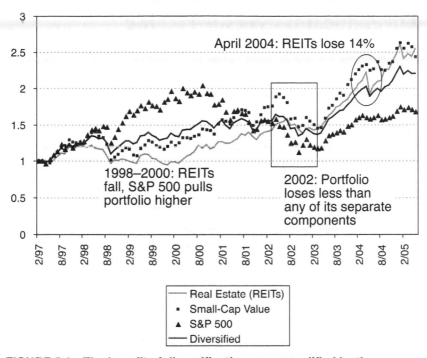

FIGURE 6.1 The benefit of diversification, as exemplified by the performance of a portfolio of REITs, S&P 500, and small-cap stocks compared to their separate components, 1997–2005.

The tables turned starting in 2000. Real estate stocks started what has turned out to be a seven-year bull market. Small-cap value funds, already hit in 1998–1999, hardly suffered ill effects during the bear market of 2000–2003, with the exception of 2002.

In 2002, every area of the stock market suffered a major correction. However, the sell-off in REITs did not coincide exactly with declines in the S&P 500 or in small-cap value funds. As a result, a portfolio diversified among all three areas had less drawdown in 2002 than did any of its individual components. Figure 6.1 illustrates these developments.

Diversification Versus Picking Only the Best

You might ask why anyone should bother diversifying instead of putting all his capital to work in only the most attractive investments, as Warren Buffett does. Buffett has been distinguished by his gift for picking stocks, but his talent seems to be the exception rather than the rule. The undistinguished performance of most equity mutual funds, whose managers are paid for picking stocks, does not suggest that picking the best stocks is easy for them, let alone for individuals who have day jobs. Moreover, Buffett has an unlimited time horizon for his investments because he is not making significant annual withdrawals to meet living expenses. The average individual investor simply cannot afford to weather a 44 percent drawdown, as Buffett's Berkshire Hathaway stock experienced from June 1998–February 2000. (Virtually all of Buffett's wealth is represented in his shares of Berkshire Hathaway, the company he runs. When someone speaks of Buffett's investment performance, he is really referring to the performance of stocks purchased by Berkshire Hathaway under Buffett's direction.)

If you have the time and ability to screen a large number of stocks and to select those with exceptional potential, you might want to give stock picking a try. However, the risks of such an approach are significant, as is the time commitment required. For most individual investors, stock picking is not likely to be more rewarding than investing in ETFs.

One other circumstance where it could pay for individual investors to buy significant amounts in particular companies is when the investor has special insight into the company or industry by virtue of his work in the field. (Be careful not to violate insider trading rules, however.) For example, a physician might have experience that allows him to evaluate a drug company's prospects independently of stock market analysts. In this case, his opinion of the stock might differ from the market's, and the physician-investor might have a reasonable chance of being ahead of the pack. But even then, the typical investor cannot afford the consequences of risking too much on any one insight in case he turns out to be wrong (or if he is ultimately proven correct, but only after years of waiting and suffering a major drawdown).

How to Determine What Should Be in the Optimal Portfolio

Procedures to determine the precise "best" portfolio mix remain the subject of debate. The main difficulty is that future investment performance is unknowable. Portfolio construction then becomes a matter of trying to extrapolate from past performance without exposing your investments to excessive risk in the event that future performance differs from past results.

I recommend the following commonsense process:

1. Identify the range of investments available to you.
2. Use historical performance during a full market cycle that includes both a bull and bear market period for each investment. I used monthly total return data as reported in the Steele Mutual Fund Expert database for the research presented in this book. Morningstar is another potential source of such data. These databases require a paid subscription.
3. Find the risk-adjusted performance for each investment option during the period.
4. Generally speaking, those investment options that have the best historical risk-adjusted performance should be most heavily weighted in your portfolio.
5. Use a spreadsheet program such as Excel to calculate a portfolio's risk-adjusted performance. In Excel, it is easy to try a variety of portfolio weights and calculate how changing the weight of each component affects the portfolio's risk and return.

Example—Determining a Good Mix of Stocks and Bonds

The spreadsheet in Figure 6.2 shows annual stock and bond total return data from 1976–2005 (source: Steele Mutual Fund Expert database of 9/30/2005). Stock market returns in column B are represented by the total return of the S&P 500 Index. Bond market returns in column C are represented by the Lehman Aggregate Bond Index total return, which represents the performance of all U.S. investment-grade bonds. Also shown are the annual total returns from 90-day Treasury bills (column D), which represent the rate of return available from risk-free investments. Column F displays the returns from a portfolio composed of a mix of stocks and bonds without leverage. The fraction of the combined portfolio that is in bonds (represented by the total return of the Lehman Aggregate Bond Index) appears in cell F32. The portfolio is constructed so that all assets that are not in bonds are in stocks. (That is, the fraction of stocks is 100 percent–cell F32.)

Row 33 contains the measure of risk-adjusted performance called the Sharpe ratio. (See Appendix 5B, "Calculation of the Sharpe Ratio.") One possible goal in determining the proper mix of stocks and bonds is to maximize the Sharpe ratio. The best balance between risk and reward would have been obtained with 56 percent bonds and 44 percent stocks (rebalanced annually). The specific formulas in this spreadsheet are listed in Appendix 5B. The indication that holding both stocks and bonds is superior to holding either one separately is that the Sharpe ratio of the stock/bond portfolio is significantly higher than the Sharpe ratio for either stocks or bonds separately.

Column	A	B	C	D	E	F
Row Number	Year	S&P 500 with Dividends	Lehman Aggregate	90-Day T-Bill		Portfolio Spx/Bonds
1	1976	23.9	15.6	5.0		19.3
2	1977	−7.2	3.0	5.4		−1.4
3	1978	6.6	1.4	7.4		3.7
4	1979	18.6	1.9	10.5		9.3
5	1980	32.5	2.7	12.1		15.8
6	1981	−4.9	6.3	15.0		1.3
7	1982	21.6	32.6	11.4		27.7
8	1983	22.6	8.4	9.0		14.6
9	1984	6.3	15.2	10.0		11.2
10	1985	31.7	22.1	7.8		26.3
11	1986	18.7	15.3	6.2		16.8
12	1987	5.3	2.8	5.9		3.9
13	1988	16.6	7.9	6.9		11.7
14	1989	31.6	14.5	8.2		22.1
15	1990	−3.1	9.0	7.8		3.6
16	1991	30.4	16.0	5.6		22.3
17	1992	7.6	7.4	3.5		7.5
18	1993	10.1	9.8	3.0		9.9
19	1994	1.3	−2.9	4.4		−1.1
20	1995	37.5	18.5	5.7		26.9
21	1996	23.0	3.6	5.2		12.1
22	1997	33.4	9.7	5.2		20.1
23	1998	28.6	8.7	4.9		17.4
24	1999	21.0	−0.8	4.8		8.8
25	2000	−9.1	11.6	6.0		2.5
26	2001	−11.9	8.4	3.5		−0.5
27	2002	−22.1	10.3	1.6		−4.0
28	2003	28.7	4.1	1.0		14.9
29	2004	10.9	4.3	1.4		7.2
30	2005	4.9	2.4	3.3		3.5
31						
32	Fraction of Portfolio in Bonds					56%
33	Sharpe Ratio	0.48	0.37			0.54
34	Average Return	13.8	9.0	6.3		11.1
35	Standard Deviation of Returns	15.7	7.5	3.3		9.0

FIGURE 6.2   Excel spreadsheet with annual total returns (percent) for the S&P 500 (large U.S. stocks), the Lehman Aggregate Bond Index (investment-grade U.S. bonds), 90-day Treasury bills (cash), and the optimal stock/bond portfolio.

Interpretation of the Sharpe Ratio

What exactly does it mean for you that the optimum mix of stocks and bonds would have improved your performance from a Sharpe ratio of .48 (stocks only) to 0.54 (56 percent bonds/44 percent stocks)? One way of interpreting this is to compare the stock/bond optimal portfolio to the portfolio with the same risk but composed of only stocks and cash (Treasury bills). In the Sharpe ratio framework, risk is measured by the standard deviation of the investment returns. So, in the specific spreadsheet used as an example here, the risk of each investment option is the standard deviation of the returns that appear in rows 1–30 of the spreadsheet in Figure 6.2.

It turns out that a mix of 56 percent stocks/44 percent cash has the same historical risk as the mix of 44 percent stocks/56 percent bonds. However, the returns of the stock/cash portfolio averaged 10.4 percent per year, less than the 11.1 percent per year for the optimal mix of stocks and bonds. The difference of 0.7 percent per year represents additional profit potential without additional historical risk.

How about the investor who wants to be conservative by holding bonds as his only risky asset? The historical risk of a 100 percent bond portfolio (standard deviation of annual returns=7.5 percent per year) has been the same as the historical risk of a portfolio composed of 82 percent bonds and 18 percent stocks. However, the 18 percent stock/82 percent bond portfolio returned 9.8 percent per year during the past 30 years, whereas the bond-only portfolio returned just 9.0 percent per year. In this example, diversification to include both stocks and bonds added 0.8 percent per year in additional profit potential without additional historical risk, compared to holding only bonds.

The Uncertainty of Future Investment Returns

The major caveat in making investment decisions for yourself based on this type of analysis is that future results will probably not exactly repeat the past. Interest rate and stock market conditions from 1976–2005 were, for the most part, exceptionally favorable for both stock and bond investors.

Figure 6.3 shows that the nearly two decade bull market of the 1980s and 1990s (which has shaped many investors' expectations) is historically exceptional. In contrast, the current decade is on track to be the worst decade for stocks since the 1930s.[1] Favorable conditions such as investors enjoyed during the 1990s are unlikely to repeat themselves before 2010, if that soon. What will transpire over the longer term, in the next 30 years, is anybody's guess. Most likely, as in past decades, we will have a prolonged investment boom in addition to periods lasting several years when profits are harder to come by. (See Figure 6.3.)

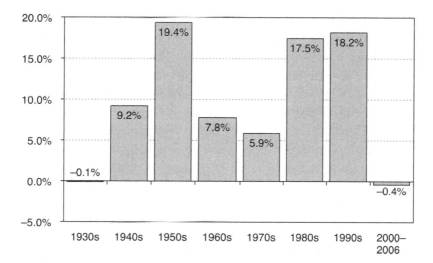

FIGURE 6.3   Annual total returns by decade from large-company stocks for 1930–2006.

Source: *Stocks, Bonds, Bills, Inflation* by Ibbotson Staff, Michael W. Barad (ed.).

As a consequence, the optimal portfolio in the future is unknowable, but it likely will be different from 56 percent bonds/44 percent stocks. Although we cannot know just how different, I fully expect the qualitative conclusion to remain valid: Investors are better off (from the perspective of balancing risk and reward) including both stocks and bonds in their portfolios compared to holding only one or the other.

It is a matter of judgment what mix of stocks and bonds you should hold for yourself. It depends on many factors, including your age, rate of savings, ability to tolerate risk emotionally, and anticipated future needs for your money. My own experience has suggested that all but the most aggressive investors should have approximately 25 percent of their portfolios in bonds, and all but the most conservative investors should have at least 25 percent of their portfolios in stocks.

According to academic theory, the observation that there has been an optimal mix of stocks and bonds implies that even investors who have different risk and return objectives should maintain this same, optimal mix in their portfolios. Investors who desire greater safety than this portfolio affords, rather than increasing the proportion of bonds compared to stocks, should allocate some of their assets to cash. More aggressive investors, rather than allocating more assets to stocks, should theoretically borrow at the risk-free rate and purchase the optimal portfolio with leverage.

In practice, conservative investors should dilute the optimal stock/bond portfolio with enough cash to bring the risk level down to acceptable levels for them. Aggressive individual investors, however, cannot borrow at the risk-free rate in the real world. As a result, the best course of action to meet their return goals might be to deviate from the optimal portfolio mix by increasing the proportion of stocks. Even so, the results shown on the spreadsheet in Figure 6.2 clearly demonstrate that historically, almost any investor would have benefited from holding both stocks and bonds, rather than only one or the other. Although it is not possible to predict the future, it seems prudent to me to assume that this will continue to be the case over the long term in the future.

ETF and mutual fund investors have the option of investing in more than just the S&P 500 and in U.S. investment-grade bonds. Chapter 7, "The One-Decision Portfolio," builds on this initial discussion by exploring how you should choose from the wide variety of ETFs that are available. It also shows how you can combine ETFs (or mutual funds) into a one-decision portfolio for long-term holding that represents a successful mix of different stock, bond, and real estate investments.

Conclusion

The goal of diversification is to improve the balance between risk and return in your investment results. Historically, diversifying to include more than just a single type of investment (such as U.S. stocks, U.S. investment-grade bonds, and REITs) has achieved this goal. The specific example of combining the S&P 500 and U.S. investment grade bonds, when examined in detail, demonstrates the superior historical performance of a combination of stocks and bonds compared to either one separately, even for conservative investors who might expect to be told to invest entirely in bonds. Although the particular mix of investments that will perform best in the future is likely to be different from the exact mix that performed best in the past, diversification between stocks and bonds should improve your results in the future as in the past. The next chapter presents a long-term, one-decision portfolio that takes advantage of diversification between stocks, bonds, REITs, and cash to produce attractive returns at surprisingly low risk (historically).

Endnote

1 Ibbotson Staff and Michael W. Barad, ed. *Stocks, Bonds, Bills, and Inflation 2005 Yearbook.* Chicago: Ibbotson Associates, 2005.

7

THE ONE-DECISION
PORTFOLIO

In the previous chapter, you saw examples from investment history that showed that with an appropriately selected portfolio, the balance between risk and reward for the portfolio as a whole could be better than the risk/reward balance of any of the individual investments within it. In other words, with proper diversification, the whole can be greater than the sum of its parts. This chapter describes a specific application of the principle of diversification by giving you an investment recipe that in the past has generated attractive returns at low risk. I have called it the *one-decision portfolio*, because after you adopt the asset allocation described in this chapter, all that is required from you in the future is a few minutes' work once each year to maintain the specified program. The goal here is to offer you the best possible investment that requires only a minimal time commitment. In particular, the strategy presented in this chapter does not require that you follow the market except to check on the value of a handful of holdings once each year.

A Risk-Reducing Investment Mix

Back in Chapter 6, "Diversification: The Only Free Lunch on Wall Street," Figure 6.1 showed how three different areas of the stock market suffered significant losses at some points during 1997 to 2005, but at different times. As a result, a portfolio consisting of 40 percent S&P 500, 40 percent real estate investment trusts (REITs), and 20 percent small-cap value had less drawdown than did any of its individual constituents. This mix of investments serves as the equity portion of the one-decision portfolio.

As a general rule, diversification works best when you include a mix of different investments whose price movements have not usually tended to coincide with each other. (In the jargon, such investments are said to be *uncorrelated*.) These three areas—REITs, small-cap value, and the S&P 500—have historically had a relatively low correlation with each other. In contrast, most other broad subsets of the stock market have tended to be more highly correlated. As a result, diversification among these areas has historically been effective at reducing risk, particularly during the volatile 1997 to 2004 market period.

Diversification using just these three areas of the stock market has been so effective at reducing risk, especially for long-term investors, that even if you take no other idea away from this chapter, you will have learned something potentially valuable. In the interest of highlighting this risk-reducing investment mix, it is repeated here:

- 40 percent S&P 500
- 40 percent diversified REITs
- 20 percent diversified small-cap value

It is important to recognize that even a well-diversified portfolio of stocks can be subject to significant market risk. For example, during the stock market crash of October 1987, all three of these areas (as well as most others) suffered significant simultaneous losses, as shown in Figure 7.1. Events such as the 1987 crash have historically been rare, but there is no way for you to protect yourself from such catastrophes while you are committed to an investment philosophy that maintains assets in the market at all times. Note that in the 1990 bear market, diversification would have spared you from bearing the full brunt of the losses in small-cap value stocks (represented in Figure 7.1 by the Russell 2000 Value Index).

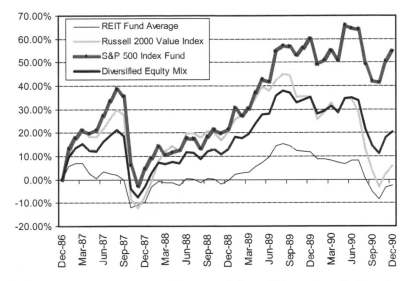

FIGURE 7.1   The percentage changes of three different equity investment areas 12/31/1986 to 12/31/1990.

Stock market risk is too high for most individual investors to bear with their entire savings. The one-decision portfolio addresses this risk by incorporating a significant allocation to bonds and cash. However, if you are willing to expend the effort to track your stock holdings at regular intervals and move some or all of your assets from equities into cash at propitious times, it might be possible for you to devise your own risk reduction strategy.

When I developed this portfolio in the late 1990s, I was searching for a mix of assets that would minimize the (historical) risks of suffering a losing calendar year. Clearly, holding all your assets in just a money market fund or bank CDs would accomplish this safety goal, but at the sacrifice of missing out on the large gains that have been available from equities since 1980.

A mix of assets that has been far safer than stocks alone and far more profitable than bonds alone is 50 percent in bonds/cash and 50 percent in equity funds. The equity portion of the portfolio is simply the blend described earlier: 40 percent S&P 500, 40 percent REITs, and 20 percent small-cap value. The income part of the one-decision portfolio is 60 percent cash/40 percent intermediate-term investment-grade bonds. Putting all this together results in the following overall one-decision investment mix:

- 20 percent S&P 500
- 20 percent REITs
- 10 percent small-cap value
- 20 percent investment-grade bonds
- 30 percent cash (90-day U.S. Treasury bills)

Figure 7.2 shows how the income part and the stock part blend together to form the overall one-decision portfolio. For those of you who are unfamiliar with the bond terminology *investment-grade bonds*, a brief overview of bond investing is provided in the appendix at the end of this chapter.

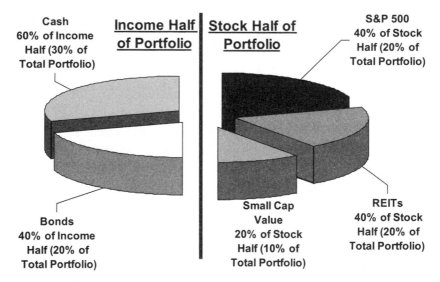

FIGURE 7.2 Pie chart showing the separate components of the one-decision portfolio.

Indexes Used to Test the One-Decision Portfolio

To demonstrate the performance of the one-decision portfolio, it is necessary to select a representative benchmark for each of its constituents. The data used is monthly total returns that extend from 5/31/1980 to 1/31/2008, a span of more than 27 years. As a proxy for the S&P 500 Index total return, I used the total return history for the Vanguard S&P 500 Index Fund (VFINX) because this investment was available throughout the historical period. REITs are represented by the U.S. Equity REIT mutual fund average from the Mutual Fund Expert database.[1] Because it has the longest available history compared to other small-cap value benchmarks (back to 1979), the Russell 2000 Value Index represents small-cap value stocks. The Lehman Aggregate Bond Index, which consists of all outstanding investment-grade bonds of all maturities in the United States, represents the bond portion of the portfolio. Ninety-day Treasury bills represent the cash portion of the portfolio.

Performance History for the One-Decision Portfolio

Table 7.1 shows the returns of the one-decision portfolio and each of its components by calendar year. (Taxes and transaction costs are not accounted for in these results.) The important points to note from the table are that the one-decision portfolio suffered only three losing years (1990, 2002, and 2007) in the entire history shown, and that losses during each of these years were very small (1.5 percent, 2.3 percent, and 0.03 percent, respectively). In contrast, the S&P 500 had five losing years during the same period. The worst year, 2002, saw a loss of more than 22 percent.

Only Treasury bills have been safer when judged by the likelihood of having a losing year. (However, as you will see in the table, when risk is judged by drawdown, both bonds and Treasury bills were safer but less profitable than the one-decision portfolio, as you would expect.)

TABLE 7.1   Calendar Year Total Returns for the One-Decision Portfolio, Both with 30 Percent Cash Position and without Cash

Calendar Year	One-Decision Portfolio Total Return	One-Decision Portfolio without Cash
1981	8.8%	6.1%
1982	21.3%	25.5%
1983	14.8%	17.3%
1984	11.9%	12.5%
1985	22.0%	28.4%
1986	13.6%	16.8%
1987	1.6%	–0.6%
1988	11.8%	13.9%
1989	15.2%	18.3%
1990	–1.5%	–5.4%
1991	21.6%	28.9%
1992	10.2%	13.2%
1993	10.7%	14.0%
1994	1.2%	–0.2%
1995	18.1%	23.8%
1996	15.5%	20.2%
1997	17.7%	23.3%
1998	4.5%	4.1%
1999	4.8%	4.8%
2000	9.8%	11.4%
2001	4.0%	4.0%
2002	–2.3%	–4.1%
2003	17.8%	25.7%
2004	11.8%	16.5%
2005	5.4%	6.2%
2006	14.2%	18.5%
2007	0%	–2.2%

Figure 7.3 shows the compounded annual gains for each of the separate components of the one-decision portfolio and for the overall portfolio from 5/31/1980 to 1/31/2008 (27 2/3 years). The equity components of the portfolio (40 percent S&P 500, 40 percent REITs, and 20 percent small-cap value) gained 13.2 percent per year, while the

income components (60 percent Treasury bills, 40 percent investment-grade bonds) gained 7.1 percent per year. The one-decision portfolio generated a compounded annual return of 10.3 percent per year which, as expected, is between the returns generated by its stock and bond components. During this very profitable period, the one-decision portfolio returned 2.9 percent per year less than its equity components, and 3.2 percent per year more than its income components.

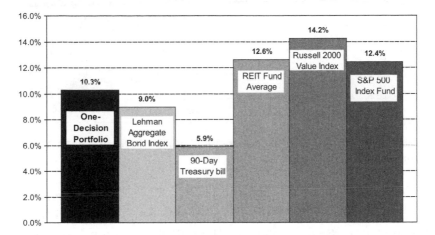

FIGURE 7.3   Compounded annual returns for the one-decision portfolio and for each of its separate components, May 1980–January 2008.

The benefit of the one-decision portfolio becomes apparent when you consider the tremendous reduction in risk that would have occurred historically if you had invested in the one-decision portfolio compared to only its equity components. The drawdown of the one-decision portfolio was 11.2 percent, which is barely worse than the 9 percent drawdown that you would have incurred through an investment entirely in investment-grade bonds. The extra 2.2 percent in risk (increase in drawdown from 9.0 percent from bonds alone to 11.2 percent in the one-decision portfolio) is a small price to pay for an increase of 3.5 percent per year in investment return. Figure 7.4 shows the drawdowns of the one-decision portfolio compared to the drawdowns of each of its constituents. Note that Treasury bills had no losing months during the period covered (5/31/1980 to 1/31/2008), demonstrating that they were a riskless investment.

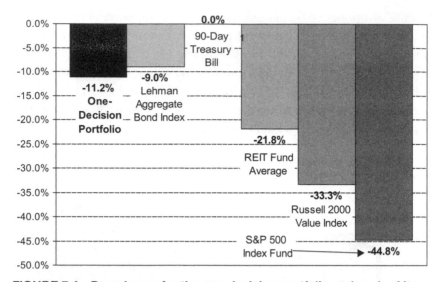

FIGURE 7.4 **Drawdowns for the one-decision portfolio and each of its constituents.**

The risk-adjusted performance of the one-decision portfolio exceeded that of every one of its constituents, as measured by the Sharpe ratio. (See Chapter 5, "How Well Are Your Investments Really Doing? Risk-Adjusted Performance," for more discussion on the Sharpe ratio.) This is the best measure of the benefit of diversification. Figure 7.5 shows the risk-adjusted performance (Sharpe ratio) of the entire portfolio compared to that of its components.

In this figure, Sharpe ratios are calculated using the 332 months of total return data from June 1980 to January 2008. The higher the Sharpe ratio, the better the risk-adjusted performance of an investment. Even though the one-decision portfolio was less profitable than any of its equity components (shown in Figure 7.3) and riskier than either of its income components (shown in Figure 7.4), the data in Figure 7.5 shows that the balance between risk and reward is best for the portfolio as a whole.

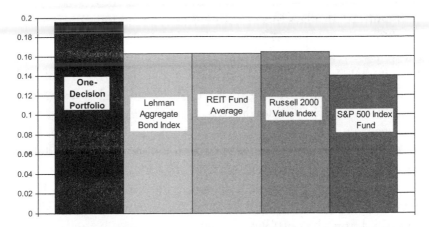

FIGURE 7.5 Risk-adjusted performance of the entire one-decision portfolio versus each of its components, 1980 to 2008.

The One-Decision Portfolio for Less Conservative Investors

You might feel that having half of your investments in bonds and cash at all times is too conservative. Not to worry. It is easy to adapt the one-decision portfolio to meet the needs of less conservative investors. Recall that changing (or eliminating) a cash position does not affect the risk-adjusted performance of a portfolio (as measured by the Sharpe ratio). Simply eliminate the 30 percent cash position while retaining the same proportions for the other investment categories. The result will be a more growth-oriented portfolio that still offers improved risk-adjusted performance compared to any of its separate constituents. For such an investor, the portfolio would look like this:

- 14.2 percent (1/7) small-cap value
- 28.6 percent (2/7) S&P 500
- 28.6 percent (2/7) REITs
- 28.6 percent (2/7) investment-grade bonds

Figure 7.6 displays this investment portfolio graphically. This figure differs from Figure 7.2 because it doesn't have a cash position. The year-by-year performance for this modified portfolio appears in the right column of Table 7.1. Of the 27 years covered in that table without cash, there were five years of losses. Although 5 losing years out of 27 is not trivial, calendar year losses have been modest when they occurred, with an average loss of 2.5 percent and the worst loss of 5.4 percent. Eliminating cash from the portfolio would have increased the compounded annual return to 12.1 percent per year (versus 10.3 percent for the complete one-decision portfolio). Drawdown increased from 11.2 percent to 16.4 percent when cash was eliminated from the portfolio.

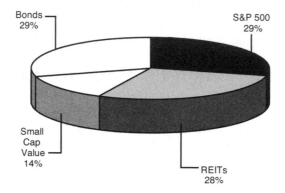

FIGURE 7.6   Pie chart showing the one-decision investment allocation for less conservative investors.

ETFs You Can Use to Create Your Own One-Decision Portfolio

Some ETFs closely track each of the constituents in the one-decision portfolio, and these are summarized in Table 7.2. No ETF is available that closely resembles a money market fund. Rather, if you are going to maintain a cash position in your portfolio, you should look for the highest yielding money market fund or bank CD. With the exception of the historical results for the S&P 500 (where I used data for the

Vanguard S&P 500 Index Fund), none of the other index data takes into account the annual expenses in maintaining an ETF. As a result, even a closely tracking ETF is expected to underperform its benchmark by the amount of its expense ratio. Table 7.2 also lists the expense ratios of these ETFs so that you can estimate the impact of using ETFs (compared to using theoretical index investments). If you use the ETFs in Table 7.2 to implement the one-decision portfolio, your overall investment return will be 0.16 percent per year behind that of the underlying benchmarks due to the ETFs' expense ratios.

TABLE 7.2   ETFs That Most Closely Match the Components of the One-Decision Portfolio, and Their Expense Ratios

Index/Benchmark	ETF That Most Closely Tracks the Benchmark	ETF Expense Ratio
S&P 500	S&P 500 Depository Receipts (SPY)	0.12%
	iShares S&P 500 Index Fund (IVV)	0.09%
REIT Mutual Fund Average	iShares Cohen and Steers Realty Majors Index Fund (ICF)	0.35%
Russell 2000 Value Index	iShares Russell 2000 Value Index Fund (IWN)	0.25%
Lehman Aggregate Bond Index	Shares Lehman Aggregate iBond Index Fund (AGG)	0.2%
	Vanguard Total Bond Market ETF (BND)	0.11%

As discussed in Chapter 2, "The Multifaceted Stock Market: A Guide to Different Investment Styles," and Chapter 12, "It's a Jungle Out There: Selecting from Among Different ETFs with Similar Investment Objectives," some investment objectives are represented by more than one ETF. As a result, you could implement the one-decision portfolio in numerous ways. In particular, I recommend using the StreetTracks Dow Jones U.S. Small-Cap Value Fund, ticker DSV, as the small-cap value holding. It has had a slightly better risk-adjusted performance than has the Russell 2000 Value Index Fund (IWN) during the one- and three-year periods ending April 2008.

Rebalancing

Suppose at the start of the year that you place your assets into a one-decision portfolio in the exact proportions. What will your investments look like at the end of the year? In general, your investments will deviate from the prescribed portfolio because each of the components will have grown at a different rate. If the S&P 500 rose faster than REITs, you would end the year with extra assets in the S&P 500 compared to the amount you would have in REITs. Similarly, if bonds and cash both lagged stocks, the income portion of your portfolio would be lower at the end of the year than it was at the start.

To restore the original balance in your portfolio, you have to sell off part of the investments that performed more strongly than the overall portfolio and place additional capital into those areas that did not earn as much as the entire portfolio. This process of trimming your stake in the winners and adding to your stake in the laggards is called *rebalancing*, because your goal in so doing is to restore the balance in your portfolio.

When maintaining the one-decision portfolio, I recommend rebalancing after holding for one year and one day, rather than on the same date each year. This way, any gains you realize are taxed at the more favorable long-term capital gains rate.[2]

The future taxation of dividends remains an unresolved political issue at this writing (2008). Based on current tax law dividends from the small-cap value and S&P 500 should be taxed at the favorable "qualified dividend" tax rate, whereas dividends from REITs and interest from bonds and Treasury bills are taxed at the high ordinary dividend rate.

There is nothing you can do about the taxation of REIT dividends. However, you can substitute municipal bond investments for the income portion of the portfolio if you are in a high enough tax bracket. The Vanguard Tax-Exempt Money Market Fund and the several single-state tax-exempt money markets that Vanguard offers are likely to be excellent alternatives to Treasury bills for high-income investors.

Intermediate-term municipal bonds represent a less obvious improvement over the more diversified and highly liquid iShares Lehman Aggregate Bond Index Fund (AGG). Before investing in municipal bonds, you should carefully compare the potential after-tax and after-expense returns with what you could get from taxable bonds. Many municipal bond mutual funds have such high expenses that they negate the potential tax advantages, particularly in the current climate of historically low interest rates.

There is always a concern about whether ETFs will accurately reflect the performance of their benchmark indexes. In the past, tracking error has been a practical issue only over short periods (intraday or intraweek), and even then only on rare occasions. For long-term holding, tracking error is likely to be minimal.

Why Are Only U.S. Investments Included in the One-Decision Portfolio?

Many advisors recommend holding some international equity investments along with the sorts of holdings outlined earlier, all of which are based in the United States. In particular, emerging market equity funds (stocks from developing countries in South America, Asia, and Africa, and many in the formerly Communist states of Eastern Europe) have enjoyed a low correlation with the U.S. stock market, which could make them candidates for a diversified, static portfolio.

I have excluded emerging market stocks from the analysis in this chapter for two reasons. First, only since early 2003 has the performance of emerging market stocks been strong enough to warrant attention from individual investors. The period from 1990 to 2003 was marked by strong gains on three occasions (1993, 1995 to 1997, and 1998 to 1999), each of which was wiped out by subsequent declines in the emerging market area. Indeed, from the start of 1990 through the end of 2002 (13 years), the average emerging market equity mutual fund returned only 3 percent per year, compounded. Second, much less historical data is available regarding broadly diversified emerging market equity investments than for the better-established asset classes in the one-decision portfolio.

Emerging markets represent only a small fraction (13 percent) of the total dollar value of the world's stock markets. The bulk of international stock market wealth is concentrated in Western Europe (approximately 26 percent of world market total) and Japan (approximately 8 percent of world market total). Stocks from other developed countries, as a group, are best held when their long-term trends are favorable vis-à-vis our own market, rather than at all times. A method for recognizing when this is likely to be the case is presented in Chapter 10, "When Is It Safe to Drink the Water? International Investing." Also, *Beating the Market, 3 Months at a Time* (Gerald Appel and Marvin Appel, FT Press, 2008) presents a timing model for selecting which area of the international marketplace is likely to perform most strongly.

Conclusion

The right mix of stock and bond investments has generated attractive returns at modest risk since 1980 without requiring active oversight of your investment except to rebalance at the end of each year. Because so little ongoing effort is required, I have called this mix the one-decision portfolio. It is especially appropriate for conservative investors.

The one-decision portfolio places half of your assets in stocks (S&P 500, REITs, and small-cap value) and half in income investments (risk-free cash and intermediate-term bonds). The one-decision portfolio consists of 20 percent S&P 500 Index, 20 percent diversified REITs, 10 percent diversified small-cap value stocks, 20 percent diversified intermediate-term investment-grade bonds, and 30 percent Treasury bills (or money market or bank CDs).

Less conservative investors can omit the cash position, while leaving all four other investment categories in the same proportion. The resulting portfolio consists of 28.6 percent S&P 500 Index, 28.5 percent REITs, 14.3 percent small-cap value stocks, and 28.6 percent bonds.

ETFs are available to gain exposure to each of these areas, except for cash. Particular selections include these:

- S&P 500 Depository Receipts (SPY) for the S&P 500
- IShares Cohen & Steers Realty Majors Index Fund (ICF) for REITs

- StreetTracks Dow Jones U.S. Small-Cap Value Index Fund (DSV) for small-cap value stocks
- iShares Lehman Aggregate Bond Index Fund (AGG) for intermediate-term investment-grade bonds

Appendix to Chapter 7—A Brief Discussion of the Bond Market

Unlike the case for stocks, the selection of available bond ETFs is fairly limited. Just as a number of different investment styles exist within the universe of stocks, so, too, can the bond market universe be broken down into distinct pieces based on two characteristics of each bond: the length of time until the bond matures, and the credit rating of the bond issuer.

A *bond* is simply a loan that you, the bond or bond fund buyer, make to the bond issuer. Bonds are usually sold in units of $1,000. For every $1,000, there is a specified interest payment that you, the bond investor, receive every six months. As an example, if you own a $1,000 bond that makes two payments of $30 per year, you are being paid an interest rate of 6 percent per year. ($30 payments received twice per year equals $60 in interest received per year. $60 is 6 percent of the face value of $1,000 of the bond.) On the specified maturity date, you receive your $1,000 back from the bond issuer.

Credit Risk

The same considerations apply to bonds as would apply to you when you take out personal loans. If you have a bad credit history, it will be harder for you to get a loan than if you had a good history. Moreover, as a high-risk borrower, you will have to pay a higher rate of interest. Similarly, bonds issued by companies or governments with perceived credit problems pay higher interest rates than bonds issued by borrowers with a low perceived risk of default. *Investment-grade bonds* are those issued by generally solid borrowers. Historically, even the riskiest investment-grade bonds have had an annual average default rate of less than 1 in 400. (A *default* is a failure of a bond issuer to make a scheduled interest or principal payment for more than 30 days.)

All currently available bond ETFs hold portfolios of investment-grade bonds. Apart from investment-grade bonds (which account for approximately 90 percent of all bonds outstanding in the United States), there are *high-yield bonds*, also called *junk bonds*. These pay higher interest, but in the past, they have had a higher rate of default.

Interest Rate Risk

The other defining characteristic is the maturity of a bond. Just as a 30-year mortgage generally carries a higher rate than a 10-year mortgage, longer-term bonds generally pay higher interest than shorter-term bonds. At first impression, you might assume that the best strategy for an individual investor would be to buy the longest-term bond available in pursuit of the highest yield. That is generally unwise, however, because higher bonds also have higher price risks.

If you buy a 30-year bond paying 5 percent for $1,000, and immediately thereafter interest rates rise to 6 percent, you are potentially stuck for the next 30 years receiving a below-market yield on your bond. If you try to sell your bond before its maturity, nobody will pay you the full face value of $1,000 per bond because your bond is paying only $50 per year (5 percent of $1,000), whereas other bonds are paying the prevailing 6 percent interest rate, or $60 per year. As a result, you have to sell your bond at less than its face value to compete. In this example, when interest rates rose, the total return of your long-term bond would be less than the interest payment of $50 per year because your bond lost some of its value.

Suppose that instead of a 30-year bond, you bought a 2-year bond paying 5 percent per year. If interest rates rise to 6 percent, your bond would again lose value. However, the loss would not be as severe as the 30-year bond because you are in this case stuck receiving a below-market yield only for the next two years, rather than for the next 30. It is precisely because of the size of potential price declines when interest rates rise that long-term bonds are riskier than short-term bonds.

The safest possible investment for U.S. investors is considered to be a U.S. Treasury bill, with 90 days chosen as the typical maturity. With so short a time until maturity, the risk of a falling price when interest rates rise is extremely small. Indeed, Treasury bills have not had a losing month, U.S. Treasury bills (or any other Treasury debts) also have no credit risk, because the federal government can always print enough money to pay off its debts as a last resort, at least in theory.

Short-term bonds have little price risk, but under normal bond market conditions, they pay relatively low yields. The longest-term bonds (30 years) usually pay the best yields, but their prices are so volatile that they are undesirable for most individual investors.[3] For individuals, the best balance between the risk of rising interest rates and the reward for holding longer-term bonds is generally found in the intermediate-term range, which is to say, maturities of five to ten years.

Figure 7.7 displays the different levels of interest rate risk for hypothetical bonds of different maturities. All three are assumed to be worth 100 and to have a yield of 6 percent when the prevailing interest rate is 6 percent. Note that a change in rates from 6 percent to 7 percent causes practically no decline in the value of the short-term bond and causes the largest price decline in the value of the long-term bond. Similarly, a drop in interest rates from 6 percent to 5 percent causes practically no increase in the value of the short-term bond and causes the greatest increase in the value of the long-term bond.

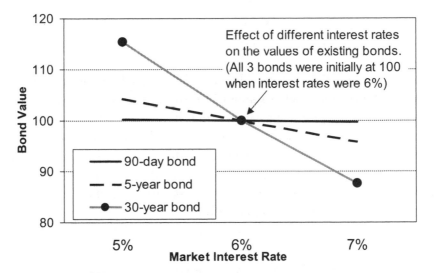

FIGURE 7.7   Effect of a 1 percent change in interest rate on the value of a short-term (90-day), intermediate-term (5-year), and long-term (30-year) bond.

Intermediate-Term Bond ETFs

The Lehman Aggregate Bond Index represents all investment-grade bonds in the United States. As such, it contains short-term bonds (maturity in two years or less), long-term bonds (maturity in more than ten years), and intermediate-term bonds. Despite the diversity of bond maturities, the average maturity in the Lehman Aggregate Bond Index is approximately seven years. As a result, the ETF that tracks this index, the iShares Lehman Aggregate Bond Index Fund (AGG), behaves like an intermediate-term investment-grade bond fund.

Since the publication of the first edition of *Investing with Exchange-Traded Funds Made Easy*, iShares has launched several new bond ETFs. The most attractive one for long-term holding is the iShares Lehman Intermediate Credit ETF (CIU), which holds investment-grade corporate bonds that have an average maturity of five years. Although CIU was launched only recently (January 2007), the underlying benchmark has an excellent history of low risk. In May 2008, CIU yielded approximately 0.6 percent per year more than AGG and is currently a more attractive bond selection. However, during periods when corporate bonds are lagging other areas of the bond market, you will do better with AGG. If you are not going to follow the bond market, make AGG your default selection.

Two other intermediate-term investment-grade bond ETFs are available from iShares: the Lehman 7–10 Year Treasury Index Fund (ticker symbol IEF) and the iShares Goldman Sachs $ InvesTop Corporate Bond Fund (ticker symbol LQD), the latter of which holds a selection of the most heavily traded investment-grade corporate bonds. LQD, the corporate bond ETF, yields more than the broad bond market ETF (AGG), but the short-term price risk has been far higher with LQD than with the more diversified AGG. As a result, I have selected the broader bond ETF, AGG, to use in the ETF implementation of the one-decision portfolio.

Endnotes

1 The data through February, 2006 was taken from that month's edition of the Mutual Fund Expert database as in the first edition of *Investing with Exchange-Traded Funds Made Easy*. Data from March, 2006 to January, 2008 was taken from the January, 2008 edition of the Mutual Fund Expert database.

2 In addition to tax considerations, rebalancing causes you to incur transaction costs. In general, rebalancing the one-decision portfolio incurs four transactions. Depending on the size of your portfolio and the amount you pay per transaction, these costs can be significant, especially if your portfolio is under less than $20,000. Some investors could opt to reduce the frequency of rebalancing transactions by acting at the end of a year only if one of their holdings deviates by a specified amount from the target allocation, rather than automatically rebalancing every year. For example, you might not rebalance any portfolio component of your portfolio until its weight deviates by more than 10% percent of the target amount. (In this case, if your cash allocation has fallen from the desired 30% percent to a level of less than 27% percent of the total portfolio, that would trigger a year-end rebalancing.)

3 During early 2006, interest rates on long-term Treasury bonds were at times actually lower than the rates paid on two-year Treasury bonds. This unusual situation is called a *yield curve inversion* and is discussed in detail in Chapter 11, "What Bonds Can Tell You about Stocks: How to Use Interest Rates."

8

WHEN TO LIVE LARGE: AN ASSET ALLOCATION MODEL FOR SMALL- VERSUS LARGE-CAP ETFs

The 1998 to 2005 period witnessed huge discrepancies between the performance of large and small-cap stocks.[1] In 1998, for example, large-cap stocks (Russell 1000 Index) gained 27 percent, whereas small-caps (Russell 2000 Index) lost 3 percent. However, starting at the end of 1998 and continuing through the first quarter of 2006, the tables turned. During this latter period, large-cap stocks have gained 23 percent, whereas small-caps nearly doubled. (The total return of the Russell 2000 Index was 99 percent from 1/1/1999 to 3/31/2006.) This example is historically extreme but not unique. There have been great rewards for investors who have made good decisions about when to switch from large-caps to small-caps and back.

Unfortunately, neither ETF sponsors nor the managers of most mutual funds will decide for you when you are likely to be better off in small-caps or in large-caps. As a result, long-term investors who do not shift assets between small- and large-cap stocks at opportune times might be leaving a great deal of money on the table.

This chapter presents a simple but historically powerful technique for deciding when market trends favor small-caps and when they favor large-caps. The method uses data from large- and small-cap benchmarks whose behavior is closely tracked by available ETFs. However, even mutual fund investors can benefit from the market projections that require just a few minutes of work once a year to formulate.

Why Market Capitalization Matters

In *Small Cap Dynamics*,[2] analyst Satya Pradhuman lists four features of the economic climate that have historically favored small company stocks as a group compared to large-cap stocks. Even though the universe of small-cap stocks represents a wide range of industries, these factors seem to have influenced the relative performance of small-cap stocks overall.

- **Strong economic growth**—A growing economy disproportionately benefits small companies (and their stocks). When the economy is expanding, small companies are capable of more rapid growth than large ones as new business opportunities present themselves. Conversely, when the economy falters, small companies are vulnerable to shrinking faster and face a greater risk of failure.

- **Strong corporate profit growth**—Just as small companies respond more acutely to changes in the rate economic growth than do large ones, so, too, are they more sensitive to changes in the overall level of business profitability. For example, an improvement in pricing power or a deceleration in the growth of labor costs is thought to have a greater positive impact on the profitability of small businesses than on large ones.

- **Easy credit conditions**—Small companies benefit during periods of high business confidence in which lenders do not demand as great a premium for making loans to small companies, compared to the rates on loans to large companies. When banks are stingy about making loans (this usually occurs after they have been burned), small companies have a harder time getting credit compared to large ones. During such periods of risk aversion by lenders, the adage applies that to get a loan, you have to prove to the bank that your financial condition is sound enough for you not to need one.[3]

- **Geopolitical stability**—In theory, according to Pradhuman, investors should favor large-caps as a defensive maneuver during periods of geopolitical instability. When the world is stable, investors feel secure enough to invest more in riskier but potentially faster growing, enterprises. This pattern has not been observed recently, however. Since 9/11/2001, small-caps proved stronger than large-caps until the end of 2006 despite the upheavals that were occurring around the world during that time.

These four conditions that influence the relative performance of small-caps versus large-caps typically remain in effect for long periods. As a result, cycles that favor large- versus small-cap stocks have the potential to last for years at a stretch, and indeed, they have done so historically, as shown in Figure 8.1. Notice also that in any given year, the disparity between returns from large- and small-cap funds can be quite large, and that during much of the 46 years shown, trends favoring either large- or small-caps have lasted for several years at a time. (All the mutual fund and index data in this chapter came from the Mutual Fund Expert database. No account was made for taxes or transaction costs.)

The fact that market cycles favoring small- versus large-caps or vice versa have lasted as long as they have gives you the opportunity to recognize the prevailing trend in time to profit from it. The remainder of the chapter shows you a simple asset allocation model that would have allowed you to achieve the goal of increasing your investment return through timely switches between large- and small-cap stocks.

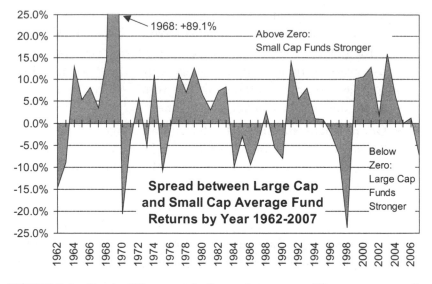

FIGURE 8.1   Yearly differences in the performance of the average small-cap blend and large-cap blend mutual funds, 1962 to 2007.

Trading Rules

The asset allocation model that determines whether to be in small- or large-cap ETFs operates based on the premise that major trends favoring one or the other will continue to persist for years at a time, as they have in the past. The model consists of one simple rule: Invest for the coming year in whichever of the two alternatives returned more in the previous year.

We have already seen in Chapter 2, "The Multifaceted Stock Market: A Guide to Different Investment Styles," that there is now a variety of small-cap benchmarks with ETFs that track them, and we do not want to get lost in the maze of alternatives. Rather, for the purposes of deciding whether small-caps as a group are more promising than large-caps, we have to bite the bullet and select a single benchmark to represent small-cap stocks and another to represent large-caps. After we have made that decision, we will see how to choose which group of stocks has the better prospects.

The logical choices of benchmarks to use when analyzing an asset allocation strategy are those with the longest history. That brings us to the Russell 2000 Index, which was the first small-cap stock benchmark, launched in 1979. This chapter uses the Russell 1000 Index as the large-cap benchmark.[4] With this pair of benchmarks in hand, you take the following steps to select in which of these two groups of stocks to invest:

1. On the last trading day of the year, calculate the total returns for each of these indexes.
2. Take whichever of the two returned more as your investment selection for the coming year.

For example, if on December 31 you determine that the Russell 2000 Index did better during the past 12 months, the asset allocation strategy calls for you to hold small-caps during the next 12 months. On the other hand, if the Russell 1000 Index returned more by year's end, you should invest in large-caps for the coming year.

Results

Table 8.1 shows the year-by-year total returns for the Russell 1000 and 2000 Indexes and the results of the investment that would have been chosen based on selecting whichever of these two indexes was more profitable the year before. The shaded box in each row represents the investment that would have been selected for that year according to the model presented in this chapter. If the market capitalization selected (shaded box) actually had a higher return than the one not selected, the trade is termed "successful" in the right-hand column. If the shaded box had a lower return than the box not shaded, the trade is deemed "unsuccessful."

The Russell Indexes first appeared at the start of 1979, so there would have been no way to use these benchmarks to choose between large- and small-caps until after they had been around for a full year. Therefore, data from 1979 first allowed the hypothetical investor to implement this strategy at the start of 1980. The lower section of Table 8.1 shows the compounded annual gain and maximum drawdowns for the Russell 1000 Index, the Russell 2000 Index, and the asset allocation strategy based on the annual data presented in the upper section of that table.

TABLE 8.1 Hypothetical Investment Results Based on Selecting Whichever of the Russell 2000 Index (Small-Caps) or the Russell 1000 Index (Large-Caps) Returned More in the Prior Year

Year	Russell 1000 Index Total Return (Large-Caps)	Russell 2000 Index Total Return (Small-Caps)	Comment
1979	22.3%	43.1%	Not applicable
1980	31.9%	38.6%	**Successful**
1981	–5.1%	2.0%	**Successful**
1982	20.3%	24.9%	**Successful**
1983	22.1%	29.2%	**Successful**
1984	4.7%	–7.3%	Unsuccessful
1985	32.3%	31.1%	**Successful**
1986	17.9%	5.7%	**Successful**
1987	2.9%	–8.8%	**Successful**
1988	17.2%	25.0%	Unsuccessful
1989	30.4%	16.3%	Unsuccessful
1990	–4.2%	–19.5%	**Successful**
1991	33.1%	46.0%	Unsuccessful
1992	8.9%	18.4%	**Successful**
1993	10.2%	18.9%	**Successful**
1994	0.4%	–1.8%	Unsuccessful
1995	37.8%	28.5%	**Successful**
1996	22.4%	16.5%	**Successful**
1997	32.8%	22.4%	**Successful**
1998	27.0%	–2.6%	**Successful**
1999	20.9%	21.3%	Unsuccessful
2000	–7.8%	–3.0%	**Successful**
2001	–12.5%	2.5%	**Successful**
2002	–21.7%	–20.5%	**Successful**
2003	29.9%	47.3%	**Successful**
2004	11.4%	18.3%	**Successful**
2005	6.3%	4.6%	Unsuccessful

TABLE 8.1   (*continued*)

Year	Russell 1000 Index Total Return (Large-Caps)	Russell 2000 Index Total Return (Small-Caps)	Comment
2006	15.5%	18.4%	Unsuccessful
2007	5.8%	–1.6%	Unsuccessful

Summary of Results 1980–2007

	Russell 1000 Index	Russell 2000 Index	Active Strategy
Compounded annual gain	12.9%	11.8%	14.7%
Maximum drawdown	–45%	–36%	–35%

As shown in the lower section of Table 8.1, switching would have increased your returns by 1.8 percent per year over the Russell 1000 Index and by 2.9 percent per year over the Russell 2000 Index. Moreover, drawdown risk was the same with the active switching strategy as what the investor would have experienced in the safer of the two indexes, which in this case has been the Russell 2000 Index. Figure 8.2 shows the growth of $1,000 invested in the Russell 1000 Index, in the Russell 2000 Index, or in the switching strategy.

You can see that the added return, compounded over 28 years, can make a big difference in the final value of your investments. A hypothetical $1,000 investment in the Russell 1000 Index (large-cap stocks) would have grown to $29,668 during the 28-year period presented here. A hypothetical investment in the Russell 2000 Index (small-cap stocks) would have returned a bit less, growing to $22,910. Switching between the Russell 1000 and Russell 2000 Indexes as in accordance with the strategy presented here would have increased your initial investment of $1,000, to the far greater figure of $45,888. The added return, compounded over 28 years, would have resulted in your accumulating more than 50 percent more than you would have if you had the foresight to select the more profitable Russell 1000 Index and stayed with it during the entire period.

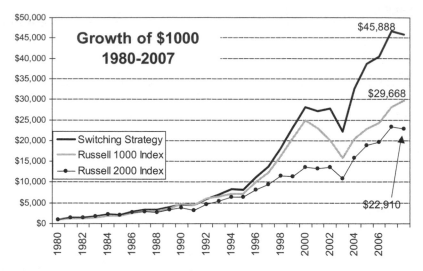

FIGURE 8.2   Growth of $1000 invested in the Russell 1000 Index, in the Russell 2000 Index, or in the switching strategy between these small- and large-cap benchmarks.

Real-World Implementation with ETFs

Even though the hypothetical past performance results presented in this chapter use the total returns of the actual benchmark indexes, as a practical matter, individual investors will not have access to this information on the last day of the year. However, you will be able to get a good idea of the total return of the two ETFs that track these benchmarks from information available online: the iShares Russell 2000 Index Fund (IWM) and the iShares Russell 1000 Index fund (IWB).

Recall that the total return from an ETF is its change in price plus distributions paid to shareholders. These distributions represent dividends paid by the stocks in an index but also include realized capital gains that occur when a stock is removed from the underlying ETF benchmark and replaced by another. When the composition of an index changes, the corresponding ETF must sell all shares in stocks that were removed from the index, realizing capital gains or losses. As with mutual funds, capital gains must be distributed to ETF shareholders so that the government can levy the resulting taxes. (In contrast, the total return of a market index does not include capital gains distributions, only dividends from underlying stocks, in addition to price changes.) ETFs are usually tax efficient, meaning that the capital gains distributions are expected to be relatively minor. Nonetheless, it is important to take account of all distributions when you're evaluating the performance of ETFs.

The first step in calculating the total return of an ETF is to find the price at the beginning and end of the period you want to study. Fortunately, ETF price information is relatively easy to obtain by going to http://finance.yahoo.com.

Distribution information requires a little more work to acquire, but it, too, is readily available on the Internet. The Yahoo Finance website also offers distribution history. When you are at http://yahoo.finance.com, enter the ticker symbol of the ETF whose distribution history you seek in the box next to the "GET QUOTES" button. After you hit Enter or click that button, the next screen that comes up will be a delayed quote for the ETF you entered. At the left of that screen will be a column of selections under the heading "More on [ticker symbol]". One of those selections will be "Historical Prices." When you scroll down the screens that contain the historical prices, the distributions should also be listed. Just to be safe, you should also consult the website of the company that sponsors the ETF, which is likely to contain the distribution history of the ETF.

In the case of the two ETFs used here, we can turn to the iShares website (www.ishares.com/home.htm), which reports all distributions previously made for the ETFs they sponsor. Table 8.2 shows the distributions for IWM (small-cap) and IWB (large-cap) made in 2007. The amounts shown in Table 8.2 represent the sum of dividend, short-term capital gains, and long-term capital gains distributions. The ex-date is the date on which the share price of the ETF drops by the amount distributed. The Appendix to Chapter 8 explains more about ETF distributions, in particular, what factors determine how much the distributions are and how they are treated for tax purposes. The numbers from Table 8.2 for which we need to calculate the calendar year total returns are the total distributions for 2007 for IWM and IWB.

TABLE 8.2   Distributions per Share for the iShares Russell 2000 Index ETF (IWM) and the iShares Russell 1000 Index ETF (IWB)

2007 Distributions for IWM (Small-Cap ETF)		2007 Distributions for IWB (Large-Cap ETF)	
Ex-Date	Amount	Ex-Date	Amount
12/27/2007	$0.267	12/27/2007	$0.355
9/25/2007	$0.195	9/25/2007	$0.341
6/28/2007	$0.159	6/28/2007	$0.315
3/23/2007	$0.154	3/23/2007	$0.324
2007 total	$ 0.775	2007 total	$1.335

Table 8.3 shows how to use this information from Table 8.2 to calculate the total returns of the two ETFs. In Table 8.2, the price change for 2007 (in $ per share) is added to the total distributions paid in 2007 (also in $ per share) to get the total return in $ per share for the two ETFs. The percentage total return for 2007 is calculated as the total gains (price change plus distributions) divided by the share price at the start of the year. In this example, IWB (large-cap) outperformed IWM (small-cap) in 2007, so the large-cap ETF was selected for 2008.

The data in Table 8.3 also demonstrates that ETF total returns are close to but not exactly the same as those of their underlying benchmarks. This turns out not to be a problem because, as a general rule, the difference between an ETF's performance and those of its benchmark is typically quite small for ETFs that are actively traded, such as IWM and IWB.

TABLE 8.3   Calculation of Total Return for IWM and IWB in 2005

Information Used to Calculate 2007 Total Returns	IWM Small-Cap	IWB Large-Cap
12/29/2006 closing price	$78.03	$76.84
12/31/2007 closing price	$75.90	$79.60
Price change in 2007 ($)	−$2.13	$2.76
Distributions received in 2007 ($) per share (from Table 8.2)	$0.775	$1.325
Total return in 2007 ($/share)	−$1.355	$4.085

Information Used to Calculate 2005 Total Returns	IWM Small-Cap	IWB Large-Cap
Total ETF return in 2007 **(% of 12/29/2006 price)**	**–1.74%**	**5.32%**
Total return of underlying benchmark indexes in 2007	–1.55%	5.77%

Conclusion

As we first saw in Chapter 2, there have been significant differences in the performance of stocks in small versus large companies. Even though small companies have returned more than large ones over the long term (since 1926), there have been periods typically lasting several years at a time when large-cap stocks as a group have done better than small-caps, and vice versa.

This chapter has described a simple yet historically successful way to capitalize on the shifting trends that favor either small- or large-cap stocks during different periods. Simply by staying with the group that returned more in the prior year, you would have made the better selection for the coming year some 70 percent of the time. The result would have been a greater investment return than that achieved by either small- or large-caps separately, without an increase in risk.

The most current projection from the small-cap/large-cap asset allocation model is that large-cap stocks are favored for 2008. Although small-caps might lead large-caps during isolated periods, I expect the long-term trend to favor large-caps for 2008 and for several years after that. A review of the fundamental economic factors that favor small-caps that are listed at the start of this chapter shows that not a single one is in effect as of early 2008.

- The U.S. dollar is weak (at all-time lows since floating exchange rates were established in 1971).
- Corporate earnings growth is not strong because there is a good chance (as of early 2008) that the U.S. economy will slide into recession.

- Borrowers are cautious about extending credit after being burned by exposure to subprime mortgage–backed and other asset-backed bonds.
- The geopolitical situation is stable for now but certainly not favorable.

However, the point is again emphasized that you do not need to accept this projection or to have a crystal ball of your own. Simply utilizing the model presented here should, if historical patterns repeat themselves, keep you on the right side of major trends favoring either large- or small-cap ETFs.

Appendix to Chapter 8—ETF Distributions and Taxes

ETFs resemble mutual funds in that they generally distribute to shareholders all realized gains and dividend income from the underlying stocks they hold. Let us first take a moment to see why ETFs are required to make taxable distributions.

Suppose hypothetically that you buy SPY at $131 per share. Based on the current 2.18 percent dividend yield of the basket of stocks that comprise the S&P 500, you would expect to collect approximately $2.75 per year in dividends (2.1 percent, which equals the 2.18 percent dividend yield of the S&P 500 less the 0.08 percent per year expense ratio of SPY). The dividends from the stocks are not paid to you separately as a shareholder of SPY. Rather, they are deposited with the ETF custodian. The fair value (also called IOPV, see Chapter 1, "Exchange-Traded Mutual Funds: Now Individuals Can Invest Like the Big Players") of your ETF share increases to reflect all dividends accumulated in this way.

In contrast, if an investor owned the individual stocks that make up the S&P 500, he would receive a stream of dividend checks throughout the year. All of these would be taxable payments to the investor, and would be reported to the Internal Revenue Service (IRS).

At first glance, it would appear that you as an ETF shareholder would have a tax advantage compared to an investor in individual stocks. Your dividends would result in an increase in ETF share price that you would not realize until you sold the ETF. The investor who holds individual shares would be taxed on dividends received whether or not he sells the underlying shares of stock.

Similarly, if you hold an ETF that sells shares of underlying stock at a profit, that profit will already have been accounted for in the share price of the ETF. As an ETF shareholder, there would be no activity in your own account to reflect any transactions that occurred in the underlying holdings of your ETF. In contrast, an investor in individual stocks *does* have a brokerage record of every sale of stock, and the proceeds of every sale are reported directly to the IRS.

To level the playing field, the IRS requires ETFs and mutual funds to make taxable distributions to their shareholders so that they will pay taxes similar to someone who held the underlying individual stocks directly. Distributions are taxable to you whether or not you actually sell your ETF shares. It is important to recognize that the amount of a distribution does not affect your investment return from an ETF or mutual fund. The distribution is merely a mechanism that allows the government to assess taxes.

ETF (and mutual fund) distributions reflect the tax consequences of the transactions in the underlying shares of individual stocks. If an ETF received dividends of 1.5 percent on its shareholdings, you would receive a distribution equal to 1.5 percent of the ETF share price and a report from your broker letting you know that this distribution should be treated the same as if you received stock dividends. If an ETF sold a stock at a long-term gain, you would receive a corresponding distribution to be taxed as a long-term capital gain.

Because a distribution does not reflect the creation of new wealth, the amount distributed has to come from somewhere. The source of taxable distributions is the underlying assets of the ETF. Therefore, the amount paid to you as a taxable distribution must reduce the fair value of the ETF shares. As a result, ETF share prices drop by the amount distributed.

Here is an example. Suppose that you buy an ETF for $10 per share and that, after six months, it rises to $11 per share. If you do not sell, you have an unrealized gain of $1 per share and, so far, no taxes to pay. Toward the end of the calendar year, the ETF makes a qualified dividend distribution of $0.15 per share and a long-term capital gains distribution of $0.35 per share. Because these distributions total $0.50 per share, the ETF fair value must drop by $0.50 per share. Typically, the share price of the ETF drops by the same amount. The date on which the ETF share price drops to reflect taxable distributions is called the *ex-date*. (The date on which you receive the distributions in your brokerage account is later than the ex-date.)

As a result of these occurrences, you, as an ETF shareholder for six months, will owe long-term capital gains taxes on $0.35 per share and income taxes on $0.15 per share. In this case, the distribution worked to your advantage because $0.35 per share of your investment gain has been realized as a long-term gain even though you have held the ETF for only six months.

However, if you happened to buy the ETF just a few days before the distribution and had not realized gains, you would still owe the same taxes. The only way to recoup your tax liability would be to sell the ETF shares. The drop in share price resulting from the distribution would then be realized as a loss to offset the "profit" assigned to you (but which you never really earned) as a shareholder of the ETF on the ex-date.

The moral of the story is to be careful when buying mutual funds or ETFs near the end of the year, lest you end up paying taxes on a distribution that reflects profits you never enjoyed. If you are purchasing funds or ETFs in the fourth quarter of the year, try to find out from the ETF or fund sponsor when distributions will be paid and how much is expected to be distributed.

1 Recall from Chapter 2 that small-cap stocks are defined as having a total market value of $2 billion or less for all outstanding shares at the current share price. Large-cap stocks are defined as companies whose outstanding shares have a total market value of at least $10 billion.

2 Satya D. Pradhuman. *Small Cap Dynamics* (Princeton, New Jersey: Bloomberg Press, 2000).

3 Bankers' risk aversion is measured in numerous ways, including surveys of lend-ing officers. One simple proxy for bankers' optimism described in Small Cap Dynamics is the difference between the prime interest rate and the rate of inter-est available from Treasury debt. The prime rate is the amount of interest that banks charge business borrowers. When bankers are confident enough in busi-ness to lend at rates close to Treasuries (which have no risk of default), the envi-ronment is favorable for small-caps. When bankers are insecure, the gap between the prime rate and Treasury yields widens, as banks charge more for their exposure to the risk of default.

4 The S&P 500 Index is a better-known large-cap benchmark than the Russell 1000 Index. However, different index providers use different methodologies to select the component stocks in each index. Specifically, the Russell Indexes con-tain all stocks within the desired range of market capitalization. On the other hand, Standard and Poor's has an investment committee select a subset of stocks from within each range of market capitalization for its indexes based on at least partially subjective criteria. Using two indexes from the same family results in a cleaner comparison.

9

Boring Bargains or Hot Prospects? Choosing between Growth and Value ETFs

Every time you can figure out an additional way to differentiate winners from losers in the stock market, you are creating investment opportunity for yourself. You learned in Chapter 8, "When to Live Large: An Asset Allocation Model for Small- versus Large-Cap ETFs," that making the correct choice between large and small-cap ETFs was one way to earn an advantage over the broad stock market. This chapter examines another way to divide the universe of ETFs and pick the stronger group, this time between growth and value. The expenditure of the modest effort required to distinguish better times to be in growth from the better times to be in value can improve your returns tremendously, especially in the realm of small-cap ETFs.

Chapter 2, "The Multifaceted Stock Market: A Guide to Different Investment Styles," introduced you to the notions of growth and value stocks. Briefly, a value stock appears to be a better bargain than the average stock. When you purchase a share of common stock, you are purchasing a fraction of the current profits, assets, dividends, and sales of the underlying company. Similarly, when you purchase an

ETF, you are purchasing a share of the profits, assets, sales, and dividends that underlie the basket of stocks in the ETF.

An ETF that holds a basket of stocks selected because they are cheaper than the average stock (by some criterion) is called a *value ETF*. Similarly, growth ETFs hold baskets of stocks that as a group are more expensive than the market because they are thought to enjoy brighter-than-average prospects.

Although the general concept of growth and value ETFs is easy to understand qualitatively, no universally accepted criteria define precisely what is considered to be a growth or value stock. The lack of consensus has given rise to multiple growth and value ETFs, each of which is based on its own methodology. Chapter 12, "It's a Jungle Out There: Selecting from among Different ETFs with Similar Investment Objectives," discusses some of the different rules that have been used for ETFs and describes how you should approach the challenge of selecting from among competing alternatives. In addition to the strategies embraced by different index providers, individual portfolio managers have adopted their own particular rules to identify growth and value stocks.

Fortunately, you as an individual investor do not need to decide on your own how to classify any particular stock as growth or value. Even though different methodologies are used to construct various growth or value indexes, all growth stock indexes and all value stock indexes have certain features in common.

First, certain industry groups are disproportionately represented in most growth or value indexes. The largest industry sectors represented among value stocks include financial services, integrated oil companies, and utilities. The largest sectors among growth stocks include technology, health care, and consumer goods/services.[1]

Second, growth indexes have tended to rise faster than value indexes during periods of overall stock market appreciation, whereas value indexes have usually suffered smaller losses than growth indexes during periods of overall market decline.[2]

Third, value indexes and the ETFs that track them have generally been less volatile than growth indexes and ETFs.

Even though the universes of growth or value stocks contain multiple industry groups, certain changes in the economic climate have caused these diverse collections of stocks to move in relative unison. (This behavior is analogous to the phenomenon you saw in Chapter 8, wherein environmental factors including easy credit and rapid growth have tended to favor small-cap stocks as a group, across a variety of industries.) For example, three economic factors have favored value stocks over growth stocks historically:[3]

- Sharply rising commodity prices
- A strong U.S. dollar
- Accelerating economic growth

These three conditions that have favored value are connected. An accelerating economy increases the demand for commodities, thereby driving prices higher. Strengthening economic expansion also increases the demand for credit and spurs the Federal Reserve to curb potential inflation, both of which result in higher interest rates. The reality or prospect of higher interest rates attracts capital from abroad, strengthening the U.S. dollar.

At first glance, it appears paradoxical that an environment of an overheating economy would favor value stocks over growth stocks. It turns out that companies whose earnings are relatively undependable tend to be represented among value stocks. Such stocks, particularly industrial companies, suffer disproportionately when the economy slows down. The vulnerability of these companies' earnings to the state of the economy represents a source of potential investment risk; therefore, the stocks need to sell more cheaply to attract investor capital. Other value areas such as integrated oil stocks or utilities simply make more money as energy prices rise.

In contrast, companies in areas such as health care or low-priced consumer goods are relatively recession proof. The potential stability of their earnings attracts higher prices relative to the broad market. Such companies figure prominently among growth stocks. Technology companies do not fit this pattern of being immune to the economic cycle—they suffer when the economy slows down and benefit when it heats up. However, as major exporters, a strong U.S. dollar makes technology companies less competitive abroad, thereby reducing their sales or profits. They are also hurt when commodity prices rise, because increased raw materials costs can force business and household customers to cut their spending on new technology.

Regardless of the underlying economic explanation, the fact remains that growth and value stocks have tended to move as groups and, like small- and large-caps, have undergone periods when one was considerably stronger than the other. ETFs allow you to take advantage of long-term disparities in the performance of growth or value stocks when they occur.

The Concept of Relative Strength

It is useful when making a decision about what to buy or sell to be able to tell at a glance which of two investments is currently stronger than the other. You can accomplish this by plotting the *relative strength* between two investments, which is simply a graph of the value of one investment divided by the value of the other.[4]

The relative strength chart in Figure 9.1 can show you which of two investments is stronger. If you calculate the relative strength between A and B as A divided by B, then whenever the relative strength is rising, A is stronger. Investment A being stronger can mean either that A is growing faster than B or that A is falling more slowly than B.[5] The relative strength chart alone does not tell you whether an investment is making or losing money.

Figure 9.1 contains five regions (labeled in the lower half of the figure) that illustrate how the relative strength chart (value of investment A divided by value of investment B) behaves under different scenarios.

- **Region 1**—A and B grow at the same rate, so the relative strength chart is flat.
- **Region 2**—A grows faster than B, so the relative strength rises.
- **Region 3**—B grows faster than A, so the relative strength falls.
- **Region 4**—A falls more slowly than B, so the relative strength rises.
- **Region 5**—A falls more quickly than B, so the relative strength falls.

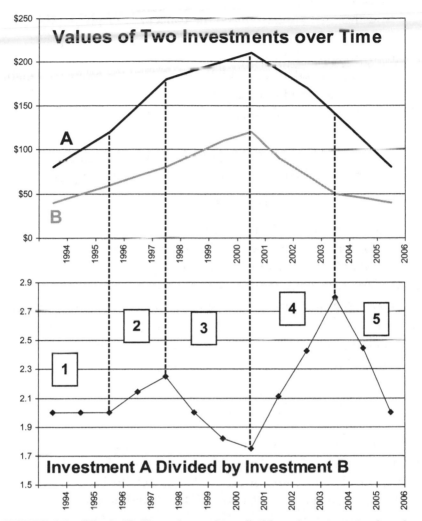

FIGURE 9.1 (Top half): The values of two fictitious investments, A and B, from 1994 to 2006.

(Bottom half): Relative strength between investment A and B, which is a graph of the value of A divided by the value of B at each point in time.

Note that the rate of growth or decline in an investment is the percentage change per year (or per month, and so on). When we say that the relative strength between two stocks is flat, it means that the percentage changes in their prices are the same, not that the dollar amount of a change is the same. A $10 per share change in the price of a $100 stock represents a different rate of change than a $10 per share change in the price of a $50 stock.

Now that we have introduced the concept of displaying the relative strength between two investments as the ratio of their prices, we are ready to apply this tool to the evaluation of whether the market climate favors growth or value ETFs. The use of the relative strength ratio is also reinforced in Chapter 10, "When Is it Safe to Drink the Water? International Investing."

History of Relative Strength Changes between Growth and Value

As has been the case with large-caps and small-caps, value stocks have been stronger than growth stocks during some periods, and vice versa during others. The disparities between growth and value have been particularly large within the small-cap universe.

Figure 9.2 shows the growth of the averages of small-cap growth mutual funds and small-cap value mutual funds from 1967 to 2006. Also shown in Figure 9.2 (below the chart of investment growth and with aligned time axes) is the following ratio:

$$\frac{\text{Small-cap growth fund average}}{\text{Small-cap value fund average}}$$

When the ratio is constructed this way (small-cap growth in the numerator is rising), small-cap growth is stronger. When this ratio is falling, small-cap value is stronger. The results in Figure 9.2 (from Mutual Fund Expert, 3/31/2006 and 4/30/2008) do not reflect taxes or transaction costs.

During some periods (such as 1992 to 1995), the relative strength chart in Figure 9.2 was flat, meaning that it did not matter whether an investor had chosen to be in small-cap growth or in small-cap value. On the other hand, the differences between these two groups were very large on several occasions. The arrows labeled A–D in the lower half of Figure 9.2 indicate major long-term relative strength trends, which are also described in Table 9.1.

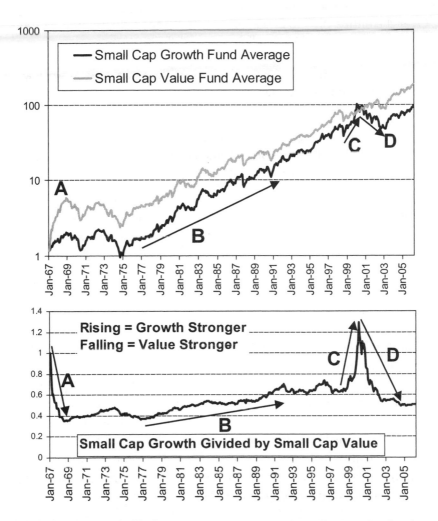

FIGURE 9.2   (Top half): Growth of the average of small-cap value funds and small-cap growth funds, 1/1/1967 to 4/30/2008.

(Bottom half): Hypothetical value of an investment in the average small-cap growth fund divided by the value of an investment in the average small-cap value fund, when both started with a value of 1.0 on 1/1/1967.

- **A**—(1967 to 1968) Small-cap value much stronger than growth
- **B**—(1977 to 1991) Small-cap growth stronger than value
- **C**—(1998 to 2000) Small-cap growth much stronger than value
- **D**—(2000 to 2004) Small-cap value much stronger than growth

Over the entire 1967 to 2008 period, small-cap value funds as a group have been stronger than small-cap growth funds.

TABLE 9.1   Four Historical Periods When Small-Cap Growth and Value Had Very Disparate Performances

Date Range	Average Small-Cap Growth Fund Performance	Average Small-Cap Value Fund Performance	Comment
A: 1/1967 to 6/1968	72%	396%	Small-cap value stronger
B: 2/1977 to 12/1991	1062%	512%	Small-cap growth stronger
C: 5/1998 to 2/2000	104%	–1%	Small-cap growth stronger
D: 2/2000 to 8/2004	–35%	69%	Small-cap value stronger
Entire period 1967 to 2008	11.0%/year	12.9%/year	Small-cap value stronger

Figure 9.2 displayed historical results for *small*-cap growth and value fund averages. Figure 9.3 shows the growth of a hypothetical investment in the average *large*-cap growth and value mutual fund from 1966 to 2006 (top half) and the value of the large-cap growth fund average divided by the value of the average large-cap value fund (bottom half). With the relative strength plotted as growth/value, growth is stronger when the relative strength ratio is rising, whereas value is stronger when the ratio is falling. Five periods when major long-term trends favored one style over the other are labeled in Figure 9.3 and described in more detail in Table 9.2.

- **A**—(1972 to 1977) Large-cap value is stronger than growth.
- **B**—(1977 to 1983) Large-cap growth is stronger than value.
- **C**—(1983 to 1988) Large-cap value is stronger than growth.
- **D**—(1997 to 2000) Large-cap growth is stronger than value.
- **E**—(2000 to 2005) Large-cap value is stronger than growth.

Until 1997, the spreads between the performance of the average large-cap growth mutual fund and the average large-cap value mutual fund were not nearly as wide as for the small-cap value and growth funds. However, the market bubble of the late 1990s swept large-cap growth stocks higher and left value behind. Starting in 2000, the situation reversed itself, with large-cap value holding up better than large-cap growth from 2000 to 2002 and then gaining more from 2003 to 2005. However, from 2005 through mid-2008, the performances of growth and value mutual funds have been similar.

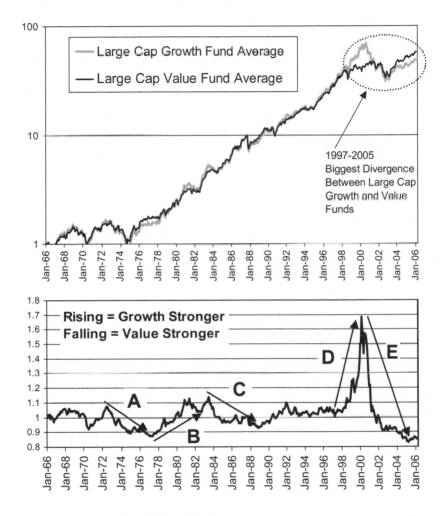

FIGURE 9.3 (Top half): Growth of the average of large-cap value funds and large-cap growth funds, 1/1/1966 to 3/31/2006 (data from Steele Mutual Fund Expert).

(Bottom half): Hypothetical value of an investment in the average large-cap growth fund divided by the value of an investment in the large-cap value fund, when both started with a value of 1.0 on 1/1/1966.

Table 9.2 shows the extent of the largest trends that favored large-cap growth over value or vice versa from 1966 to 2006. The periods of time labeled A through E in the table correspond to the labels A through E in Figure 9.3. The data in Table 9.2 confirms the visual impression of Figure 9.3 that, for most of market history, there has been no major difference between the profitability of large-cap growth and large-cap value. Keep in mind, however, that in addition to being slightly more profitable than large-cap growth (average performance advantage of 0.4 percent per year), large-cap value was also 20 percent less volatile over that 40-year period. In particular, large-cap value was significantly safer during the 2000 to 2003 bear market. Consequently, the use of an asset allocation model to limit your exposure to growth stocks to only those periods when growth is favored has the potential to improve the balance of reward versus risk that you can achieve.

TABLE 9.2   Five Historical Periods When the Average Large-Cap Growth and Large-Cap Value Mutual Funds Had Disparate Performances

Date Range	Average Large-Cap Growth Fund Performance	Average Large-Cap Value Fund Performance	Comment
A: 6/1972–4/1977	–7%	13%	Large-cap value stronger
B: 4/1977–6/1983	255%	172%	Large-cap growth stronger
C: 6-1983–11/1988	58%	95%	Large-cap value stronger
D: 3/1997–2/2000	128%	36%	Large-cap growth stronger
E: 2/2000–4/2005	–34%	33%	Large-cap value stronger
Entire period 1966–2008	9.8%/year	10.2%/year	Large-cap value slightly stronger

Recognizing the Emergence of a New Trend Using the Relative Strength Ratio

One strategy for deciding when to switch from growth to value or vice versa is to update the relative strength chart. When the chart changes directions, allow a suitable delay to verify that a new long-term trend has begun, and then jump on board somewhat after the fact. It might sound like you would have to rely on completely subjective criteria to decide when to rebalance your investments, but in fact there is a relatively simple rule that can take the guesswork out of this decision.

What is the simple rule for rebalancing? Will Rogers advised that the strategy for investing was to "buy some good stock and hold it till it goes up, then sell it. If it don't go up, don't buy it."[6] Fortunately, the strategy of jumping on board after a new trend has begun does not require the ability to forecast the future that Will Rogers described. Rather, there is a specific criterion that determines when a new trend has begun. The rest of this section describes the rule.

Growth versus Value Rule

A disparity of 10 percent in relative performance between growth and value defines the current long-term trend.

The point at which you start to measure relative performance is at a minimum or a maximum in the relative strength chart. In understanding this concept, a picture really is worth a thousand words. We will revisit Figure 9.1 to see how to recognize new relative strength trends on its stylized data. Figure 9.4 displays the same fictitious data as in Figure 9.1, but with additional comments regarding recognizing new trends. The bulleted list that follows describes the interpretation of the relative strength ratio in each region of Figure 9.4.

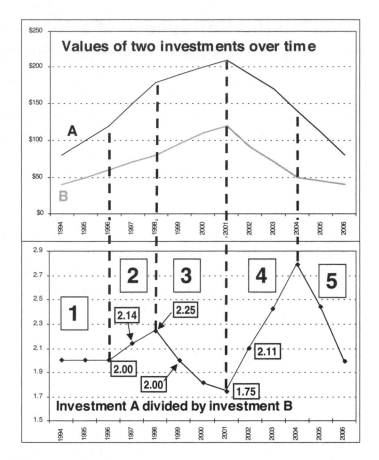

FIGURE 9.4   **Recognizing new relative strength trends after the fact.**

- Region 1 in Figure 9.4 has no trend. The relative strength chart is flat, and its starting value is 2.0.

  A 10 percent change in relative performance between investments A and B would be reflected in a 10 percent change in this value of 2.0—that is, to below 1.8 or to above 2.2. (The 1.8 and 2.2 threshold levels are not shown in Figure 9.4. Because the relative strength chart reflects A divided by B, a rising ratio A/B means that A is stronger, whereas a falling ratio indicates that B is stronger. Using the 10 percent threshold, we would say that a fall in the ratio A/B to 1.8 or below signifies a new trend favoring B, or that a rise in the ratio A/B signifies a new trend favoring A.

- In region 2, A is stronger than B (because the ratio A/B is rising).

  However, to identify a long-term trend favoring A, we require more than just the ratio A/B to be rising. It must have risen at least 10 percent off of its last low point for the new trend to be recognized. The initial low level for the relative strength ratio is 2.0, so a new trend favoring A over B would require the ratio to increase by at least 10 percent over 2.0, which is above 2.2. This does not occur over 1997, because the ratio at that point is only 2.14 (as indicated in the figure). It is only in 1998 that the new trend favoring A over B is recognized according to the 10 percent rule. In 1998, the ratio A/B reached a value of 2.25 (which is labeled in Figure 9.4).

- In region 3 of Figure 9.4, the ratio A/B has turned downward, meaning that B is stronger than A.

  In fact, the 10 percent rule has not served us well with this fictitious data, because it told us to buy investment A at its peak relative performance, when the ratio of A/B was 2.25. Remember: We do not switch from A to B at the first decline in the ratio A/B. Rather, we wait for a full 10 percent decline—in this case to 2.025 or lower. (2.025 is 10 percent less than 2.25.)

- In 1999, the ratio of A/B has fallen to 2.0, initiating a new trend favoring B over A.

  Because this is below the level of 2.025 that is required to recognize a new trend in favor of B, at 1999 we would have switched from investment A into investment B. We would continue to enjoy the trend favoring investment B until the end of region 3 (2001), when the ratio A/B bottoms out at 1.75.

- A new trend favoring A over B is recognized in 2002.

  In 2001, the ratio A/B begins to turn up, showing that A has become stronger than B again. However, we do not act on this observation until the ratio A/B increases by 10 percent off of this last minimum level of 1.75, meaning that we wait until the ratio A/B gets above 1.925. (1.925 is 10 percent more than 1.75.) This next occurs in 2002. The trend favoring A over B lasts until the end of region 4—that is, until 2004.

The natural question is why we should bother waiting for a 10 percent change in direction in the relative strength ratio rather than acting on the first change in direction. The answer is that real investment data has a significant amount of random movement from one month to the next. Random price fluctuations that are not part of a longer-term trend are called *noise* (a concept borrowed from engineering). With real historical investment data, most changes in direction do not begin new longer-term trends. If you were to take a new position following every month-to-month change in direction, you would almost certainly make many unprofitable trades and achieve poor results.

If the purpose of waiting for 10 percent reversals is to avoid reacting to market noise, you might wonder why you shouldn't wait even longer, say for 20 percent, before acknowledging a new trend. The answer here is that a new trend might be nearly over if you wait too long before acting on it. In this type of active asset allocation strategy, investors who wait too long are apt to find themselves buying at the top and selling at the bottom, exactly the reverse of what they want to do.

The 10 percent threshold level is a compromise between the costs of reacting to investment noise and the cost of acting too late to profit from a change in trend. The advantage of utilizing this strategy is the potential to place your investments on the right side of major trends before they have gotten too far underway. Note that this 10 percent level is not necessarily applicable to every comparison you might want to make between all possible pairs of different investments. Research is required to determine what threshold levels have been historically successful for different types of investments. (For example, in Chapter 10, we will use a 15 percent level to distinguish whether U.S. or foreign stocks are favored.)

As with any active asset allocation strategy, some of the decisions you make will turn out less favorably than had you done nothing. The long-term track record will be presented in the next section, and you will be able to see for yourself that, despite the occurrence of unsuccessful trades, the use of the growth/value model here would have improved your investment results.

The opposite objection could also be made: In waiting for a 10 percent reversal to occur before changing your investment allocation, you are guaranteed to miss the best opportunities to act. If there were a foolproof way to spot market tops and bottoms at the instant they were occurring, every investor would be a billionaire. In the real world, your returns will always be less than they could have been with the benefit of hindsight. The goal is to improve your returns compared to what the rest of the stock market (in the aggregate) is returning. Baron Rothschild explained his success in investing, "I never buy at the bottom, and I always sell too soon."[7] We are not exactly in tune with Baron Rothschild here, because in utilizing the relative strength ratio, you will always sell a little late rather than too soon.

One final comment: Although I have found the method used in Chapter 10 and Chapter 11 to be successful and easy to implement, it is not the only way to identify new market trends. The book *Technical Analysis: Power Tools for the Active Investor* by Gerald Appel (Prentice Hall, 2005) presents additional approaches to this important investment challenge.

In the historical studies presented in the next section, the 10 percent level has worked for both small- and large-cap benchmarks as a criterion for deciding when to switch from growth to value or vice versa.

Results with Small-Cap Value versus Growth

The goal of this asset allocation model is to distinguish the periods when value ETFs will return more from the periods when growth ETFs will be more profitable. The model is judged to have succeeded if, during a period when value ETFs were expected to outperform, they in fact did so. Similarly, the model would be judged to have succeeded if, during a period when growth ETFs were expected to be more profitable, they in fact were.

Table 9.3a displays the Russell 2000 Value and Growth Indexes during different periods from 1979 to 2008 when *growth was favored over value* according to the model presented in this chapter. (The Russell 2000 Value and Growth Indexes are, respectively, the small-cap value and small-cap growth benchmarks with the longest available history.) Table 9.3b displays the performance of the same two benchmarks but it differs from Table 9.3a in that the results in Table 9.3b are for the period when *value was favored over growth*. The shaded boxes contain the results for whichever of the two choices returned more. Trades are labeled as Successful when the style that the model selected actually performed better. (Results are hypothetical and do not take into account taxes or transaction costs.)

Table 9.3a: Performance of the Russell 2000 (Small-Cap) Value and Growth Indexes during Periods When the Model Favored Small-Cap Growth over Small-Cap Value

a) Periods When the Model Favored Small-Cap Growth Over Small-Cap Value

Start Date	End Date	Russell 2000 Growth Index Total Return	Russell 2000 Value Index Total Return	Comment
1/1/79	2/28/81	121%	77%	Successful
1/31/83	9/30/83	19%	30%	Unsuccessful
5/31/90	4/30/92	17%	23%	Unsuccessful
6/30/95	7/31/96	11%	15%	Unsuccessful
11/30/98	3/31/00	71%	5%	Successful
9/30/07	5/31/2008	–5%	–8%	Successful, open trade
Compounded result of above:[8]		**456%**	**219%**	Successful

Table 9.3b: Performance of the Russell 2000 (Small-Cap) Value and Growth Indexes during Periods When the Model Favored Small-Cap Value over Small-Cap Growth

b) Periods When the Model Favored Small-Cap Value Over Small-Cap Growth

Start Date	End Date	Russell 2000 Growth Index Total Return	Russell 2000 Value Index Total Return	Comment
2/28/81	1/31/83	24%	50%	Successful
9/30/83	5/31/90	41%	94%	Successful
4/30/92	6/30/95	43%	60%	Successful
7/31/96	11/30/98	19%	41%	Successful
3/31/00	9/30/07	–2%	168%	Successful
Compounded results of above:		**191%**	**1667%**	Successful

During the entire 1979 to 2008 period, small-cap value was far more profitable than small-cap growth. In this setting, where value was much stronger, any position in growth started at a disadvantage (with the wisdom of hindsight). For this reason, the success record for periods when the model selected growth has only been 50 percent (with the most recent successful trade still open). Nonetheless, during unsuccessful selections of growth over value, the disparities between growth and value were relatively small. In contrast, during the two periods when the selections of small-cap growth over value were successful, growth was much stronger than value. As a result, the amounts lost by following the model during its unsuccessful trades were far smaller than the amounts gained by following the model during its successful trades. Overall, following all five attempts to select growth would have been significantly more profitable than staying in value all the time.

Since value was so much stronger than growth during the entire 1979 to 2008 period, it is not surprising that periods when the model selected value did indeed turn out to be times when value returned more than growth.

The big question that arises when reviewing this data is whether it is ever worth investing in small-cap growth given the tremendous performance of small-cap value during this extended period of more than 29 years. My own interpretation is that if you were constrained to choosing only one small-cap investment (perhaps for reasons of small account size or large transaction costs), you should choose either small-cap blend or small-cap value. Small-cap growth appears historically to have been an inferior long-term holding compared to either small-cap value or growth.

Nonetheless, do not be too complacent about the future performance of small-cap value ETFs. In particular, the relative safety of small-cap value since the last market peak in March 2000 is not historically typical. The losses suffered by small-cap value mutual funds during the 2000 to 2003 bear market were far smaller than their losses during previous bear markets such as 1973 to 1974 or the 1987 market crash. In fact, after such a large performance disparity in favor of small-cap value, it is especially important to be alert for the emergence of a new trend.

Results with Large Cap Value versus Large Cap Growth

The disparities between the performance of large-cap value and large-cap growth have been smaller than what we saw to be the case with small-caps. Table 9.4a shows how the large-cap benchmarks, the Russell 1000 Growth Index and the Russell 1000 Value Index, performed during periods when growth was favored over value. Table 9.4b shows how these benchmarks performed during the periods when value was favored over growth. As in Tables 9.3a and b, the returns from whichever selection returned more appear in shaded boxes, and if the better return (shaded box) was in the investment that the model selected, the trade is labeled Successful.

Table 9.4a: Performance of the Russell 1000 (Large-Cap) Value and Growth Indexes during Periods When the Model Favored Small-Cap Growth over Small-Cap Value

a) Periods When the Model Favored Large-Cap Growth Over Large-Cap Value

Start Date	End Date	Russell 1000 Growth Index Total Return	Russell 1000 Value Index Total Return	Comment
1/1/79	4/30/81	63%	57%	Successful
6/30/86	9/30/86	–12%	–2%	Unsuccessful
11/30/89	6/30/92	35%	23%	Successful
7/31/95	5/31/99	152%	134%	Successful
9/30/99	5/31/00	21%	6%	Successful
6/30/00	9/30/00	–5%	8%	Unsuccessful
10/31/07	5/31/2008	–3%	–10%	Successful, Open trade
Compounded results of above:		442%	355%	Successful

Table 9.4b: Performance of the Russell 1000 (Large-Cap) Value and Growth Indexes during Periods When the Model Favored Small-Cap Value over Small-Cap Growth

b) Periods When the Model Favored Large-Cap Value Over Large-Cap Growth

Start Date	End Date	Russell 1000 Growth Index Total Return	Russell 1000 Value Index Total Return	Comment
4/30/81	6/30/86	117%	155%	Successful
9/30/86	11/30/89	64%	57%	Unsuccessful
6/30/92	7/31/95	48%	54%	Successful
5/31/99	9/30/99	3%	–7%	Unsuccessful
5/31/00	6/30/00	8%	–5%	Unsuccessful
9/30/00	10/31/07	–17%	74%	Successful
Compounded results of above:		385%	849%	Successful

Real-World Implementation with ETFs

The first step in implementing a program of switching between growth and value is to gather monthly total return data (as described in Chapter 8). Some of the historical illustrations that have appeared in this chapter have used mutual fund performance averages because these have a much longer history than do the widely used ETFs or their benchmark indexes. However, we could have applied the growth/value asset allocation strategy to various Russell Indexes with profitable results. Moving forward, however, you can use ETF total returns to perform the necessary calculations.

As was the case in the small-cap/large-cap asset allocation model described in Chapter 8, the ETFs that track the various Russell Indexes are also convenient sources of information for the growth/value model. You need to follow two ETFs to implement the growth/value model with small-caps:

- iShares Russell 2000 Value Index Fund (IWN)
- iShares Russell 2000 Growth Index Fund (IWO)

Similarly, the two ETFs that you need to track to utilize the growth/value model on large-caps are as follows:

- iShares Russell 1000 Value Index Fund (IWD)
- iShares Russell 1000 Growth Index Fund (IWF)

As of March 2008, the models have you in growth for both large- and small-cap ETFs. The most recent peak in the relative strength ratio of growth/value occurred on December 31, 2007 for large-caps. That means that to track the evolution of the model, you can follow the growth (or shrinkage) of $1,000 hypothetically invested in both IWD and IWF on December 31, 2007. Following are the steps to carry forward the required calculations from that start date for large-cap value and growth ETFs.

1. Use data such as that available at http://finance.yahoo.com/ to calculate the growth of $1,000 invested in IWD and in IWF including distributions.

2. Divide the value of the IWF (large-cap growth) investment by the value of the IWD (large-cap value) investment to get the relative strength ratio.

3. Update this calculation as of the last market close of each month.

The calculations to determine whether small-cap growth is favored over small-cap value (or vice versa) are analogous, the difference being that you would use the total returns of the iShares Russell 2000 Growth ETF (IWO) and the iShares Russell 2000 Value ETF (IWN) starting on December 31, 2007. If you do not want to perform the calculations on your own, you can visit www.appelasset.com for a link to an Excel spreadsheet with the updated results.

One last comment: I have performed the historical tests on the oldest benchmarks, which are the Russell Indexes. Although it is not possible to guarantee which ETFs will prove to be superior in the future, there is no reason why you could not utilize the strategy in this chapter to track the relative strength between other pairs of growth and value ETFs. Although the iShares ETFs generally have the lowest bid-ask spreads and the best associated options (important considerations for my money management clients), as an individual investor, you might consider taking advantage of Vanguard's ETFs, which generally have slightly lower expense ratios than iShares'.

Conclusion

Chapter 9 has introduced the concept of the *relative strength chart*, which is simply a graph of how the ratio of the prices of two investments changes over time. We have seen how to use this tool to compare monthly data from growth and value benchmarks to determine which style is in favor according to long-term trends. A 10 percent spread between the performance of a growth ETF and a value ETF indicates the direction of the prevailing trend, which remains in place until the occurrence of a new 10 percent spread in the reverse direction. We will revisit the use of relative strength in Chapter 10, where the problem will be in deciding between domestic and foreign stock ETFs.

The long-term trend that had favored value over growth ETFs from 2000 ended in late 2007. It is tempting to speculate that growth stocks are now due for a long reign of superior relative strength, especially given the troubles that began to hit financial companies during the summer of 2007 and which are continuing as of June 2008. However, an examination of the underlying valuations of growth and value indexes does not support the notion that the value stocks have become overpriced relative to growth stocks. Rather, as of June, 2008, the relationship between growth and value stocks (in terms of their price/earnings ratios overall) is close to long-term averages. Also, large oil companies figure prominently among value stock indexes, and they will likely continue to outperform the broad market, helping value stock indexes keep up.

Over the next several years (starting in 2008), my expectation is that the market will see a better balance between the performance of growth and value indexes than was seen from 1997 to 2007. If anything, growth stocks could enjoy a slight advantage. As of June 2008, the trend favors growth over value among both large- and small-caps.

1   Consumer goods/services companies that are generally considered growth stocks include PepsiCo or Wal-Mart. Integrated oil companies that are part of value indexes are the large companies that operate in all aspects of energy production and sales (drilling, refining, sales), such as ExxonMobil, ChevronTexaco, and ConocoPhillips.

2   Note, however, that during the 2003 to 2007 market advance, value outperformed growth—an exception to the rule that during rising markets, growth usually outperforms value.

3   Ned Davis Research, charts AA73A, AA68, and AA78, data through 4/30/2006.

4   Do not confuse this definition of relative strength with the "Relative strength indicator." The latter is a tool in technical analysis that is used to evaluate a single investment, not to compare two different investments as we are doing here.

5   If you chose to calculate relative strength as B/A, this ratio would be rising whenever B is stronger. When the investment in the numerator is stronger, the relative strength ratio would be rising, and vice versa.

6   Ted Goodman (ed), *The Forbes Book of Business Quotations* (New York: Black Dog and Leventhal Publishers, Inc., 1997).

7   http://marketplacemoney.publicradio.org/archive/old_features/chris971227.htm.

8   Just as a reminder of how compound return was calculated here: Final account value = (initial value)$\times$(1+return1)$\times$(1+return2)$\times$(1+return3)$\times$(1+return4)$\times$(1+return5). The initial value can be any number above zero without affecting the calculation of investment return, so it is easiest to assume an initial value of 1.0. Then the final value is (1+1.21)$\times$(1+0.19)$\times$(1+0.17)$\times$(1+0.11)$\times$(1+0.71)$\times$(1–0.05)=5.55. This means that the initial value of 1.0 increased to 5.55, representing a gain of 455%. The data listed in the table have been rounded to two significant digits. However, unrounded data was used to calculate the reported overall compounded gain of 456%.

10

WHEN IS IT SAFE TO DRINK THE WATER? INTERNATIONAL INVESTING

Investing abroad has become popular in recent years because foreign stock markets have in many cases been stronger than our own. This has especially been the case when our own currency has been weak, as it has been from 2003 to 2008.

A certain inherent logic is involved in looking abroad for investments rather than limiting yourself to just the United States. The more choices available to you, the better results you can obtain.

However, investing abroad also has inherent obstacles. Currency risk is added onto whatever local stock market risk exists. This currency risk has no offsetting expectation of reward. Currencies have gone up and down, often without establishing a trend even over the long term. This is evident from the history of the U.S. dollar since exchange rates were allowed to float in 1971. (See Figure 10.1.)

FIGURE 10.1   U.S. Dollar Index monthly, 1971 to 2008.

The U.S. Dollar Index has had wide swings up and down since 1971, but during the entire interval (July 30, 1970 to February 29, 2008) the average change in the value of the U.S. currency has been only –1.3 percent per year. In contrast, the compounded annual gains for the S&P 500 during the same period have averaged 11.9 percent per year (including dividends).

If you assume that the U.S. dollar will continue to depreciate at an annual rate of 1.3 percent per year, which is hardly assured, you might expect a 1.3 percent per year edge to guarantee the future superiority of foreign stocks over the long term. However, further disadvantages exist beyond just the assumption of currency risks. Transaction costs are typically higher abroad than they are for managers who buy on U.S. exchanges. Active international managers have additional overhead as well in analyzing foreign stocks because U.S. accounting standards are not universal. You must expend effort to understand other countries' rules for financial reporting, not to mention the burden of translating foreign shareholder reports. Dividends received from foreign companies are often subject to foreign or U.S. withholding taxes. In taxable accounts, individual investors might be able to recoup some or all of the taxes that a foreign government withholds from U.S. investors' profits. In retirement accounts, these forfeitures are unrecoverable.

ETFs representing foreign stocks also have handicaps. If they are limited to foreign companies whose shares are listed in the United States (called *American Depository Receipts*, or *ADRs*), their investment choices are artificially narrow, which could reduce performance.

If the ETF holds shares traded abroad in different time zones, the ETF costs more to trade. You might recall the discussion about arbitrage in Chapter 1, "Exchange-Traded Mutual Funds: Now Individuals Can Invest Like the Big Players." One source of liquidity (that is, low bid-ask spread) in domestic ETFs is the ability of the securities dealer or specialist to buy or sell the actual basket of stocks necessary to offset your ETF order at the time he fills your order. As a result, the specialist's market position does not change during the day as a result of filling your order.

Specialists do not have this option available to them when the ETF contains underlying stocks traded on exchanges in different time zones from ours. When foreign markets are closed, a specialist cannot offset your ETF order with a transaction involving the underlying stocks. If the specialist sells you shares of an international stock ETF, his position in that ETF is reduced. That is fine with him if the market falls, but if the market rises, he will have missed out. Even worse, if you sell shares of an ETF to a specialist and the market falls, he will have actually lost money as a result of filling your trade.

To compensate themselves for assuming these added risks, specialists in international stock ETFs generally demand a higher bid-ask spread than they do for ETFs that hold domestic stocks. Just as currency risk is an irremediable added cost of investing abroad, so, too, is the problem of untradable underlying stocks an unavoidable added cost that the specialist or market maker charges you in return for liquidity on demand. The bid-ask spreads of some of the more broadly diversified foreign ETFs appear in Table 10.1. Although in most cases these are less liquid than domestic equity ETFs, there is more than sufficient liquidity during normal market conditions to allow individual investors to take advantage of these ETFs to gain market exposure abroad.

TABLE 10.1   Representative Bid-Ask Spreads on Selected International Equity ETFs in May 2008

ETF Name	Ticker Symbol	Bid Price ($)	Ask Price ($)	Bid-Ask Spread as % of Midpoint	Size of Market (Shares in 100s)[1]
iShares MSCI EAFE Index Fund	EFA	76.09	76.10	0.01%	4×27
iShares MSCI Pacific ex-Japan Index Fund	EPP	149.21	149.27	0.04%	1×1
iShares MSCI Emerging Markets Index Fund	EEM	147.14	147.16	0.01%	9×6
iShares S&P Europe 350 Index Fund	IEV	109.68	109.74	0.05%	2×2
iShares Latin America 40 Fund	ILF	292.44	292.68	0.08%	1×1
iShares MSCI Japan Index Fund	EWJ	13.28	13.29	0.08%	1,376×1,139

The addition of currency risk and the added transaction and management costs of foreign investments mean that an investor in shares abroad starts with a handicap of higher risk compared to a domestic investor. Investing abroad is a bit like betting on a horse carrying a 200-pound jockey. It might pay off in the end, but the horse has to be exceptional.

Figure 10.2a shows the hypothetical long-term growth of $1 invested in the S&P 500 Index compared to a broad benchmark of developed-country foreign stocks, the Morgan-Stanley Europe, Australasia, and Far East Index (EAFE). Like the S&P 500, EAFE is free-float weighted, so that the behavior of large companies dominates its action. Because the largest concentration of stock market value (outside of North America) lies in Western Europe, European stocks have the greatest collective weighting in the EAFE index.

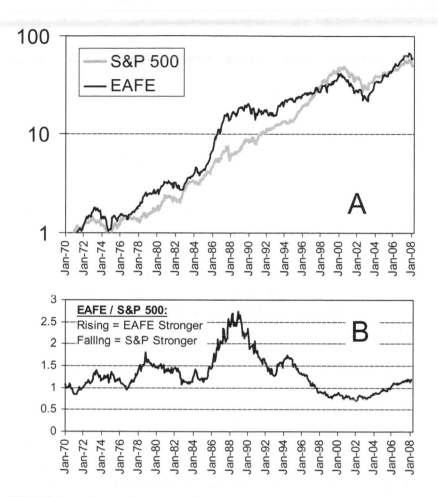

FIGURE 10.2 **Figure 10.2a: Hypothetical growth of $1 invested since the start of 1970 through 2/29/2008 in the EAFE Index and in the S&P 500 Index (log scale).**

Figure 10.2b: EAFE total return divided by S&P 500 total return 1970 through 2/29/2008.

Also shown (see Figure 10.2b) is the relative performance of these two benchmarks, which is the value of the equity in the EAFE investment divided by the equity in the S&P 500 investment (both including dividends but excluding taxes or transaction costs). For example, starting in 1970 with $1 in each, by 2/29/2008 the $1 would have grown to $58.97 in the EAFE and to $49.19 in the S&P 500. (This represents compounded annual gains of 11.3 percent per year for EAFE and 10.8 percent per year for the S&P 500.) The ratio of these two amounts is 58.97/49.19=1.199. Therefore, the rightmost data point in the chart in Figure 10.2b is 1.199. This represents an annual advantage of 0.5 percent per year for foreign stocks over this 38-year period. At the time of the first edition (mid-2006), there had been no advantage for foreign stocks from 1970 to 2006.

When the graph in Figure 10.2b is rising, foreign stocks were outperforming. For example, foreign markets far outperformed our own from 1985 to 1988. Conversely, when the graph in Figure 10.2b is falling, the S&P 500 was outperforming. From 1988 to 1997 (with the exception of 1993), the U.S. market outperformed those in the rest of the world.

The important point to glean from these graphs is that foreign and U.S. stocks have been superior at different times, but since 1970, there has been little consistent advantage in owning foreign stocks continuously. Since June 2002, foreign stocks have been beating the S&P 500. Between 6/30/2002 and 2/29/2008, the cumulative outperformance of foreign stocks has been 43 percent, or 6.5 percent per year. Although this is a big advantage for foreign stocks, history strongly refutes the notion that the stronger performance of foreign stocks will persist indefinitely. More likely, our own stock market will recover lost ground over the coming years.

Currently, U.S. investors can avail themselves of index funds and ETFs that allow them to invest in the S&P 500 at a cost of less than 1/10 percent per year. However, international index funds are a bit less economical. For example, Vanguard's international index funds have expenses that range from 0.22 percent to 0.4 percent, and these figures do not include higher transaction costs. As a result, when expenses are factored in, investors in the United States can very nearly match their benchmark, whereas foreign investors are likely to experience more significant handicaps relative to their benchmarks.

The best way to invest abroad is to take positions only when long term trends are favorable. This chapter discusses a simple but powerful way to accomplish just that, using ETFs that are readily traded at low cost.

How to Identify Whether the Long-Term Trend Favors U.S. or Developed-Country Foreign Stocks

The chart in Figure 10.2b suggests that you can improve your investment performance by taking positions in international stocks only when the long-term trend is favorable. The key is the following observation: Periods when foreign stocks have been stronger than our own have usually lasted for more than one year (graph on Figure 10.2b rising). Periods when the S&P 500 was stronger than foreign markets have also generally lasted for more than a year (graph on Figure 10.2b falling).

This observation suggests the basis for an asset allocation system: When a trend in favor of foreign stocks has begun, jump on board. Conversely, when a trend in favor of U.S. stocks has emerged, reduce or eliminate your exposure to foreign stocks.

You can identify a major trend by a 15 percent disparity in the performance of foreign versus U.S. stocks. Specifically, when the S&P 500 Index lags the EAFE by more than 15 percent, it is time to invest abroad. Conversely, when the EAFE lags the S&P 500 by 15 percent or more, invest in the United States.

The major peaks and valleys that capped off performance gaps of at least 15 percent between S&P 500 and EAFE are shown in Figure 10.3. This is the same data that appears in Figure 10.2b, except that this figure indicates the specific peaks and troughs with vertical lines. Since 1970, 17 trend changes have occurred—an average of less than once every two years.[2]

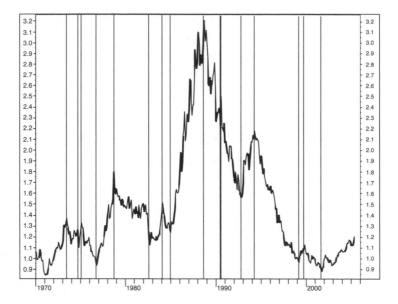

FIGURE 10.3 Value of $1 invested in EAFE divided by value of $1 invested in S&P 500 (ratio of total returns) from 1970 to 2005, with vertical lines showing where trends reversed.

In theory, it would be ideal to enter EAFE at each trough and switch back to the S&P 500 at each peak, but this is not possible. However, you can identify each new trend favoring foreign stocks after it has begun by waiting for a 15 percent rise from a trough in the EAFE/S&P 500 ratio. Similarly, each 15 percent drop from a peak in the EAFE/S&P 500 ratio can define a new trend favoring the S&P 500. At the time a new trend emerges, as defined this way, you should shift your allocation accordingly.

It turns out that price-only data is easier to come by in a timely manner than is total return data (which includes dividends). Moreover, the use of price-only data in hypothetical, historical testing actually produced better results. The trading model that will be described in the rest of this chapter uses price data for the EAFE and S&P 500 Indexes. Both of these are available daily in the *Wall Street Journal*, but to use this asset allocation model on your own, you need to check the newspaper only once each month.

The chart in Figure 10.4 illustrates visually when new trends are recognized (15 percent after the fact). Specifically, two historical price reversals are indicated, the first of which represents an example of an unsuccessful trade and the second of which represents a successful asset allocation that remains in effect as of May 2008.

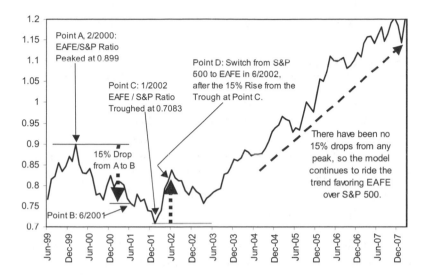

FIGURE 10.4 EAFE price/S&P 500 price, 1999 to 2005, with two 15 percent reversals illustrated.

- **Point A**—Peak value of EAFE/S&P 500, marking the end of a period when the EAFE was stronger and the beginning of a new trend favoring the S&P 500 over EAFE beginning on February 29, 2000. With perfect foresight, one would have switched from the S&P 500 to EAFE at this point. However, using the model from this chapter allowed the new trend in favor of the S&P 500 to be recognized only in hindsight at Point B.

- **Point B**—The new trend favoring the S&P 500 over EAFE began at Point A but is not recognized until 6/30/2001. The ratio of EAFE to S&P 500 was 0.8992 on 2/29/00, but by 6/30/2001, it had fallen by more than 15 percent to 0.756. (The trigger for a new trend would have been any fall in the ratio from 0.899 to 0.764 or below, because 0.764 is 15 percent less than 0.899.) Because the EAFE/S&P 500 ratio has fallen by at least 15 percent off a peak, the model says to switch from EAFE to S&P 500 as of 6/30/2001.

- **Point C**—The S&P 500 leads EAFE until 1/31/2002. The ratio of EAFE to S&P 500 has fallen to 0.708. At Point C, a new trend begins that favors EAFE over S&P 500. However, this new trend will be recognized only in retrospect, at Point D, after a 15 percent or greater rise in the ratio, from 0.708 to 0.814 or higher.
- **Point D**—On 6/30/2002, the ratio of EAFE to S&P 500 tops 0.814 for the first time. Therefore, the new trend favoring EAFE over the S&P 500 is recognized, five months after it began. Because the EAFE/S&P ratio has risen by at least 15 percent off of a trough, the model says to switch from S&P 500 to EAFE on 6/30/2002. Point D is higher than Point B, indicating that the switch from EAFE to S&P on 6/30/2001 was unsuccessful. (That is, the investor would have done better, in retrospect, not to switch to the S&P 500 at Point B.)

The trend favoring EAFE that began on 6/30/2002 has remained in force, because there has been no 15 percent fall in the ratio from any peak since the trend began. Since the time that the model indicated switching to EAFE from S&P 500, EAFE has outperformed the S&P 500 index by more than 43 percent in total return. Therefore, the switch from S&P 500 to EAFE on 6/30/2002 has been successful as of the summer of 2008.

Results of Using the EAFE/S&P 500 Asset Allocation Model[3]

The dates of the trades from such a system are summarized in Tables 10.2a and 10.2b, as are the performance results.

Model Favored EAFE . .		While Model Favored EAFE . . .		
From	To	EAFE Gained	S&P 500 Gained	Comment
July 1971	December 1973	25.0%	9.9%	Successful
February 1975	June 1975	–1.1%	18.3%	Unsuccessful
February 1977	August 1979	66.5%	24.7%	Successful
January 1984	August 1984	–0.9%	4.9%	Unsuccessful
August 1985	May 1989	222.7%	93.8%	Successful
October 1990	March 1991	2.9%	25.3%	Unsuccessful
April 1993	May 1995	22.4%	28.7%	Unsuccessful
February 2000	October 2000	–10.1%	5.4%	Unsuccessful
June 2002	June 2008	107.4%	44.5%	Successful, open position as of 6/30/2008

Table 10.2a: Total returns of the EAFE and S&P 500 Indexes during periods when the model favored EAFE over the S&P 500.

Model Favored EAFE . . .		While Model Favored S&P 500		
From	To	EAFE Gained	S&P 500 Gained	Comment
December 1973	February 1975	3.9%	–11.8%	Unsuccessful
June 1975	February 1977	9.5%	12.1%	Successful
August 1979	January 1984	60.0%	87.7%	Successful
August 1984	August 1985	32.3%	18.2%	Unsuccessful
May 1989	October 1990	–7.2%	–0.5%	Successful
March 1991	April 1993	13.2%	24.9%	Successful
May 1995	February 2000	70.4%	178.5%	Successful
October 2000	June 2002	–22.6%	–29.2%	Unsuccessful

Table 10.2b: Total returns of the EAFE and S&P 500 Indexes during periods when the model favored the S&P 500 over EAFE.

When large trends get underway, this type of switching can add greatly to your investment performance. The trades marked Successful in the preceding tables are those that would have improved your investment performance compared to buying and holding a fixed allocation of foreign and American stocks. The most notable examples from the table occurred from 1985 to 1989 and 2002 to 2008, when international stocks far outperformed U.S. stocks, and from 1995 to 2000, when U.S. stocks were much stronger than foreign stocks. It is the nature of this type of system that gains (or reductions in losses) can be extremely large from using the model instead of buying and holding a fixed allocation if a major imbalance develops between foreign and U.S. stocks.

However, when trends are detected but do not follow through, attempting to follow the trend by switching can cost you in terms of lost performance and increased transaction costs plus taxes. The trades marked Unsuccessful are those that would have reduced your results compared to maintaining a fixed allocation to foreign and American stocks. It is the nature of this type of system that losses (or reductions in profit) from unsuccessful trades are limited in size. However, unsuccessful trades can be frequent.

Table 10.2 shows that the odds of making a successful trade have not been much better than 50:50. (Specifically, nine out of 17 transactions would have improved performance, whereas 8 would have reduced performance compared to buying and holding an equal mix of EAFE and the S&P 500.) The system has nonetheless improved overall performance because the average benefit from successful trades has been much larger than the average cost from unsuccessful trades. Unfortunately, it is impossible to know at the time of a signal which trends will persist and which will prove abortive. As of this writing (June 2008), foreign stocks remain favored over the S&P 500 according to this longer-term trading model.

With all the caveats and with nearly half the trades unsuccessful, how can you tell that the EAFE/S&P 500 asset allocation model improved results overall? For a numerical answer, you would simply need to compound the trade-by-trade results and compare the final total to the historical total returns for EAFE and the S&P 500. That calculation reveals that from 1970 to 2008, switching returned 12.2 percent per year, compared to 11.1 percent per year for the EAFE Index and 10.8 percent for the S&P 500 Index. Risk, although basically similar for all three cases, was higher under the asset allocation model compared to either index separately.

The chart in Figure 10.5 shows the hypothetical growth of each $1 invested according to the asset allocation model, compared to each index separately. Whenever either the S&P 500 or EAFE was significantly stronger than the other, the asset allocation model basically kept up with the stronger index.

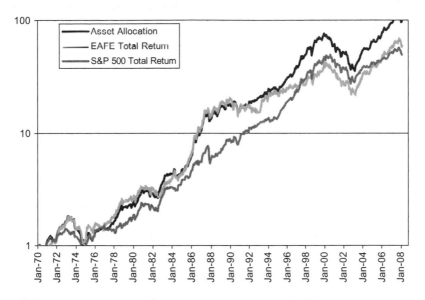

FIGURE 10.5 **Growth of $1 invested at the start of 1970 through 2/29/2008 in the S&P 500 Index, the EAFE Index, or switching between them according to the asset allocation model presented here.**

Emerging Market ETFs—Investing for the Future

Up until now, we have examined only the performance of international investments in developed countries such as Western Europe, Japan, and Australia. These and the other free-market economies account for some 80 percent of the value of stocks listed outside the United States. The remaining 20 percent of non-U.S. stock market value lies in countries with less well-established financial systems, called emerging markets. The largest emerging market countries (by stock market value) are Russia, China, Hong Kong, Brazil, and India.

As a general rule, emerging market stocks have a greater correlation with trends in commodity prices: When commodities are strong, emerging market stocks benefit. Compared to indexes such as EAFE, broad-based emerging market indexes have been roughly twice as risky. In fact, the performance of emerging market stocks over the past 20 years (1988 to 2008) has been inconsistent and very rocky. Figure 10.6 shows the total returns (in U.S. dollars) of the MSCI Emerging Market and World Indexes. (No provision for taxes, transaction costs, or ETF expense ratios has been made in Figure 10.6.)

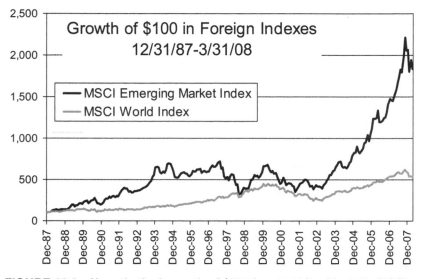

FIGURE 10.6 Hypothetical growth of $100 invested in either the MSCI Emerging Market Index or the MSCI World Index, 12/31/87 to 3/31/08.

Many investors are aware of emerging market stocks because of their strong performance this decade. From the start of September 2001 through the end of October 2007, the MSCI Emerging Market Index returned more than 35 percent per year, compared to just 12.7 percent per year for the MSCI World Index (which includes the United States and all other developed-country stock markets). From October 2007 through June 2008, the Emerging Market Index has lost almost 19 percent, while the World Index has lost 15 percent.

I doubt that emerging market stocks can maintain their torrid rate of growth that they achieved from 2001 to 2007. Indeed, a review of the history in Figure 10.6 shows the potential for emerging market stocks to suffer a prolonged correction, as they did from 1994 to 1998. However, in view of the higher risk in emerging market stocks compared to developed country stocks, it is reasonable to expect higher returns from developing country ETFs over the long term. Moreover, emerging market investments have a second advantage that is likely to persist for years to come: diversification.

Emerging market stocks have been relatively uncorrelated with developed country stocks. As a result, a portfolio of both would actually have had less drawdown than either type of investment separately. Specifically, allocating 25 percent of equity assets into the MSCI Emerging Market Index and the remaining 75 percent into the MSCI World Index would have reduced drawdown and increased returns compared to holding the World Index of developed-country stocks alone. These results are shown in Table 10.3. (No provision is made for taxes, transaction costs, or ETF expense ratios in Table 10.3.) The decrease in risk would be negligible, but the improvement in return (8.7 percent per year to 10.6 percent per year) from diversifying would be significant.

TABLE 10.3   Annual Total Return and Worst Drawdown for Developed and Emerging Market Indexes

12/31/87–3/31/08 (Monthly Data)	MSCI World (Developed Country)	MSCI Emerging Markets	25% Emerging Markets + 75% Developed Country
Annual total return	8.7%	15.5%	10.6%
Worst drawdown	46%	56%	45%

Even though historical results would have warranted allocating 25 percent of your stock market investment to emerging market stocks, such a portfolio would represent a far more aggressive strategy than most financial planners would recommend, particularly since past results are not guaranteed to repeat themselves. A weighting of 12 to 13 percent in emerging markets would be consistent with their representation in the world's pool of publicly traded equities and would be considered neutral. Investors with a time horizon of more than ten years and the tolerance for the risk could utilize the higher weighting. Investors who anticipate needing to access their savings for living expenses in less than ten years should lean toward a smaller representation in emerging market ETFs (approximately 10 percent of total equity investments).

The easiest way to gain long-term exposure to emerging markets using ETFs is to invest in the Vanguard Emerging Market ETF (VWO), which tracks the MSCI Emerging Market Index. The iShares MSCI Emerging Market Index ETF (EEM) tracks that index too, but its expense ratio is much higher than Vanguard's (0.74 percent versus 0.25 percent). On the other hand, active traders or investors looking to utilize option strategies are likely to be better off with the iShares offering (EEM) because of its higher liquidity and lower bid-ask spread. Active investors who want to utilize emerging market ETFs only when they are favored can refer to the international equity ETF allocation strategy in *Beating the Market, 3 Months at a Time* by Gerald Appel and Marvin Appel (FT Press, 2008).

Outlook for International Investing

When I wrote the first edition, I projected that the trend favoring international stocks over U.S. stocks from 2002 to 2006 could reverse imminently. Instead, it continued. International stocks put more distance between themselves and the lagging U.S. market through the end of 2007, and the U.S. dollar slumped to new all-time lows. However, during the first half of 2008, there has been no clear leader between the overall U.S. and foreign markets; both have been exceptionally volatile.

Through 2009, it is likely that the U.S. economy will grow more slowly than the world's average because we have deeper and more painful adjustments to make than most. For example, America's traditional reliance on domestic consumption financed by foreign lenders to fuel economic growth appears unlikely to work anymore. Imports are now too costly, and lenders are chastened by the collapse in mortgage-backed and other asset-backed debt. Moreover, rising home equity is no longer guaranteed. Indeed, Americans' equity in their own homes is less than half those homes' total value, the lowest equity since these records began in 1945.

Evidence of a shift away from domestic consumption is the observation that exports are growing faster than domestic spending, and the size of the trade deficit (relative to total U.S. economic production, called GDP) has shown some signs of contracting despite record high prices for energy imports. An improvement in our balance of trade would be a favorable trend for America's economic security.

The continuation of these economic trends should favor foreign over U.S. stocks. (Within the United States, companies with significant sales or operations abroad should fare better than companies with only domestic exposure.)

Of course, nothing lasts forever. Foreign governments and central banks are not going to sit still for increases in U.S. exports at the expense of their own export industries. The Federal Reserve has fueled the exceptional decline in the U.S. dollar by lowering interest rates in 2007 and 2008 in response to stress in the credit system, while European central banks have not gone along. Once the Fed stops easing or European central banks begin reducing their own rates, the U.S. dollar will gain a source of support that is lacking as of June 2008.

Conclusion

Market history shows that investing abroad has not always improved performance compared to holding domestic stocks. In fact, long-term returns from large company stocks in economically developed foreign countries have been similar to the returns of the S&P 500. Moreover, holding a fixed allocation to developed-country foreign stocks would not have reduced your investment risk historically.

Rather than always keeping a portion of your equity investments in developed-country foreign stocks, a better strategy has been to limit your exposure to such markets to periods when foreign stocks are stronger than American stocks. This has been possible because the major trends that have favored foreign stocks over American stocks, or vice versa, have persisted for years at a time.

Emerging market stocks, unlike foreign stock markets in developed countries, have offered a diversification advantage. That means that holding a fixed allocation of your equity assets in emerging markets might reduce your overall portfolio risk or increase your returns (to the extent that historical patterns repeat themselves).

Many analysts and commentators will attempt to predict when the current trend favoring foreign stocks will end. Some might succeed, and many will fail. However, following the model presented here will remove the guesswork from your asset allocation decision.

1 The size of the market is the number of shares you could sell at the bid and the number you could buy at the ask at any given instant. For example, 4×27 means that you could have sold 400 shares at the bid price or purchased 2,700 shares at the asked price at the moment the data was reported. This type of information changes second by second throughout the trading day.

2 Only 16 vertical lines are visible in the printed Figure 10.3 because the lines on September 1990 and October 1990 are too close together to be distinct. In October 1990, the EAFE Index gained more than 15 percent, whereas the S&P 500 lost 0.4 percent—the biggest single-month disparity in performance between foreign and U.S. stocks in the history of the EAFE.

3 All the model results presented in this chapter are hypothetical and based on monthly index total return data. This data is believed reliable but cannot be guaranteed. Although historical data back to 1970 has been used, individual investors did not have access to index fund investments during most of that period (for the EAFE) with which to implement the strategy presented here. The first S&P 500 available to individual investors was Vanguard's, started in 1976. Results do not include the impact of transaction costs, mutual fund expenses, or taxes. Past results do not predict future performance.

11

What Bonds Can Tell You about Stocks: How to Use Interest Rates

Interest rates are perhaps the most influential factors of stock market performance. However, translating a knowledge of interest rates into a specific plan of action for your equity investments is no simple matter. In a nutshell, two features of the interest rate climate are important to follow as an equity investor:

- Whether interest rates (as a whole) are rising or falling
- Whether it costs more for the U.S. Treasury to take out long-term loans or short-term loans

This chapter describes how the interest rate environment (as reflected in bond market data) affects the stock market. It also explores some simple rules to help you use interest rate data as a warning signal for stocks.

A Basic Introduction to the Bond Market

Bonds are loans. If you are a bond investor, you have in effect lent money to a borrower, the company, or government that issued the bonds you hold. The bond market as a whole is far more complicated than the stock market. Whereas companies issue common stock only once, or at most on few occasions, a single company can take out loans through the bond market many times in its lifetime. Each new bond issue has its own conditions, including interest rate, length of the loan, and possible other terms.

Just as when you apply to a bank for a loan, the interest rate that the bond market charges depends on two things: the length of the loan and its riskiness. (Risk can be reduced either by your having a good credit history or by having excellent collateral with which to guarantee the loan. These same factors operate in the bond market.) Similar to when you take out a mortgage, the longer the term of the loan you want, the higher the interest rate you need to pay. (For a further discussion on why this is usually the case, please refer to the Appendix to Chapter 7, "The One-Decision Portfolio.")

In some circumstances, interest rate changes are irrelevant to the broad stock market. For example, if a company issues a bond when it is financially sound and later issues a second bond of the same term[1] after its financial situation has deteriorated, the interest rates on the two bond issues will not be the same. Specifically, the interest rate that the company must pay will likely be higher when the company is a bad credit risk than when the company is in better shape (assuming that overall interest rates have not changed). This type of change in an interest rate (if it is a relatively isolated occurrence) is not what we need to help us make stock market decisions. When we are trying to identify the best periods for stocks, we are interested only in an apples-to-apples comparison of interest rates.

One way to simplify the bond world is to focus only on U.S. Treasury debt as the segment of the bond market from which to glean interest rate data. Because the Treasury can, in theory, print money to pay off all its debt as a last resort, there is no risk that the federal government will default on its loans. If you look at the interest rate on a

10-year loan to the U.S. Treasury and you note that the rate has changed from 4 percent to 4.8 percent over the past six months, what you are observing reflects purely a change in the interest rate climate, rather than a change in the level of business confidence. For this reason, both of our interest rate indicators use interest rates only on Treasury debt.

Why Rising Interest Rates Have Usually (But Not Always) Been Bad for Stocks

Several notions could explain why periods of rising interest rates have been associated with below-average performance for stocks. One notion is the idea that stocks and bonds compete for investors' capital. If interest rates rise, a certain proportion of investors will become attracted to bonds and will sell off some stocks to free up capital for bond purchases. Such selling depresses the price of stocks.

Another notion is that rising interest rates reduce economic growth, because companies are more reluctant to invest in new ventures or new plant and equipment if their cost of borrowing to finance such engines of growth rises. Stocks are attractive because of their growth prospects; therefore, a climate of rising interest rates is also a climate of greater pessimism for prospects of business growth. In addition, higher interest rates increase the cost of doing business (in many industries), reducing profit potential and, as a result, acting as a drag on stocks.

Until 1995, interest rate indicators had a good record of predicting periods of above-average market risk. However, the relationship between stocks and interest rates became more complicated after 1995. The different phases of the stock/yield relationship from 1994 to 2006 are shown in Figure 11.1.

FIGURE 11.1   Trends in stock prices and interest rates, 1994 to 2006.

The top half of Figure 11.1 shows the S&P 500 Index (daily, price-only), and the bottom half shows the 10-year Treasury Note Yield Index (which is simply the yield in percent times 10). Note that in 1994, interest rates rose sharply and stocks went nowhere. From 1995 to 1998, the overall trend in interest rates was lower, and the trend in stock prices was higher. During this period, the stock market was so strong that it was nearly impervious to periods of rising interest rates such as occurred in 1996 and early 1997.

From 1998 to 2003, fears of deflation[2] and recession[3] reversed the normal relationship between stock prices and interest rates; when stocks were weak, interest rates fell (the stock market decline of July through October 1998 provides an example), and when stocks were strong, interest rates rose. Interest rates became less a driving force for stocks and behaved merely like a symptom of expectations of how the economy and stock market would perform.

The concern was that higher productivity would perpetually depress the prices of both commodities and manufactured goods, dragging down corporate profits and creating an environment of refractory unemployment and anemic economic growth. When prospects for growth improved, the stock market heaved a collective sigh of relief (stocks rose), and interest rates rose as the demand for capital was expected to improve. When prospects for prolonged deflation and recession increased, however, investors fled stocks and rushed to lock in whatever long-term rate was available, no matter how low it seemed. At its nadir in 2003, the 10-year Treasury note paid only 3.1 percent per year, its lowest yield since 1958 and well below its average yield of 6.5 percent in the 1953 to 2006 period.

This scenario actually does resemble what played out in Japan from 1990 to 2005 when prices declined, unemployment rose, and the economy stagnated despite huge government deficit spending in that country and despite interest rates at or near zero. With hindsight in 2008, however, fears of deflation appear naive now that oil and gold (among other commodities) have been breaking record after record.

Since 2003, the relationship between stock prices and interest rates has been inconsistent. On the one hand, from April to June 2003, interest rates collapsed and stocks were strong. When interest rates recovered from June to September 2003, stock prices stalled. This is the historically normal relationship of lower interest rates going hand in hand with rising stock prices. On the other hand, from May 2005 to May 2006, both interest rates and stock prices trended higher, similar to what occurred from 1998 to 2000. Likewise, the market decline that began in October 2007 was accompanied by a drop in 10-year Treasury note yields, both of which hit bottom in March 2008.

Avoiding stocks during periods of rising interest rates would have kept you out of the market crash of 1987 and would have greatly improved your stock market investment performance in the 1970s. However, simple indicators of rising interest rates would not have protected you adequately during the prolonged 2000 to 2003 bear market and might have caused you to miss out on some of the gains of the 1990s bull market. My belief is that indicators of rising interest rates will again prove valuable, now that fears of intractable deflation and recession have evaporated. Nonetheless, the experience of the 2000 to 2003 bear market should make all of us a little uneasy about relying too heavily on just this tool.

An Indicator of Rising Interest Rates

In my research, I have generally found that a six-month time frame for analyzing interest rate trends has produced the most useful tools to gauge the stock market. The first of the two interest rate indicators that will be described in this chapter is simply the six-month change in the yield on 10-year Treasury notes. When this interest rate is higher than it was six months ago, the interest rate environment is unfavorable for stocks. When 10-year yields are lower than they were six months ago, the interest rate climate is favorable for stocks. It's that simple.

From January 1965 to March 2008, the S&P 500 gained 10.1 percent per year with a 45 percent drawdown (monthly total return data). If you had stayed in stocks only when the interest rate climate was favorable (that is, when 10-year Treasury yields were lower than they had been six months previously) and stayed in Treasury bills at other times, your investment return would have increased to 10.9 percent per year and your drawdown would have decreased to 30 percent. Achieving this would have required a total of 42 round-trip switches from stocks to Treasury bills and back, which is an average of just 1 round trip per year.

Figure 11.2 compares the growth of $1 from 1965 to 2008 invested in the S&P 500 (including dividends) for the entire period ("buy and hold") or switching from S&P 500 into 90-day Treasury bills ("S&P 500/cash") during periods when the interest rate environment was unfavorable (as determined by 10-year Treasury yields being higher than six months previously, based on monthly average data from the Federal Reserve). These hypothetical results are based on monthly total return data and do not account for taxes or transaction costs.

An investor would have avoided many significant bear market periods by staying out of stocks when interest rates were climbing, including most of the 1969 to 1970, 1973 to 1974, 1980 to 1982, and 1987 market declines. (These bear markets are circled in Figure 11.2.)

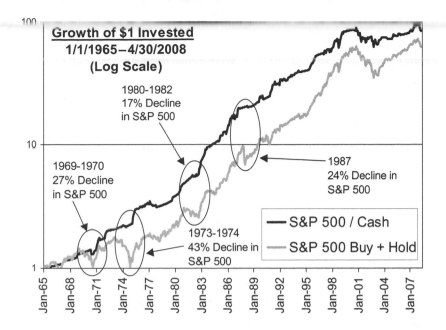

FIGURE 11.2   Long-term growth of $1 (log scale) invested in the S&P 500 continuously from 1/1/1965–4/30/2008 ("buy and hold"), or switched between the S&P 500 and cash as determined by whether interest rates were rising or falling ("S&P 500 / cash").

Starting in 1995, this particular interest rate indicator became less effective. Reliance upon rising interest rates as an indication to exit stocks would have reduced the drawdown suffered during the 2000 to 2003 bear market from 45 percent to 30 percent. This one-third reduction in risk is attractive, but it's not nearly as spectacular as the results obtained in earlier bear markets. Moreover, staying out of the stock market during periods of rising interest rates from 1995 on would have reduced your investment return. However, by adding a second interest rate indicator, you can do even better.

Yield Curve Indicator

Two interest rate climates have been bad for stocks. We have already explained the first: an environment of rising interest rates. The second warning sign is called an *inverted yield curve*. This term describes a bond market in which the interest rate on long-term bonds is lower than the rate on short-term bonds. This section explains why an inverted yield curve has anything to do with the stock market.

Interest Rates and the Implied Economic Forecast

In the Appendix to Chapter 7, I explain that longer-term loans should carry higher interest rates than shorter-term loans. This is true most of the time. It is during the unusual periods when long-term interest rates are *lower* than short-term rates that the stock market has been especially risky. Long-term rates sometimes fall below those of short-term rates from another risk with which bond investors must contend—the risk of inflation.

As a general rule, you want your investments to be worth more in terms of purchasing power in the future than now. Otherwise, you would have no economic rationale to defer consumption to invest in bonds in the first place. For example, if you predict that a house will be worth 20 percent more two years from now but you can earn only 5 percent on your investment, you have a strong incentive to place all available cash into buying a house. The same considerations apply to any nonperishable item that you have a choice of buying now or later.

Therefore, to attract capital, borrowers must be willing to pay more than the projected rate of inflation. If inflation is expected to be high in the future, interest rates will be high now (because the rate locked in now will be in effect at the time of the projected change in inflation). Conversely, if inflation is expected to be low in the future, interest rates will be low now.

As with interest rate risk, inflation risk is greater for long-term loans than for short-term loans. If you are locking in a rate of interest for just three months by purchasing a 90-day Treasury bill, changes in inflation will have at most a small effect on your purchasing power. On the other hand, if you lock into a 30-year rate and inflation increases, the purchasing power of your investment will erode for the next 30 years, at considerable cost to you.

You have already seen that considerations of interest rate risk argue that long-term interest rates should be higher than short-term rates. When that is indeed the case, the yield curve is said to be *normal*. However, inflation expectations can reverse this normal relationship. Suppose that inflation is 4.2 percent (which was the case as of May 31, 2008) but is expected to fall significantly in the year ahead because of a worldwide recession. Would you as a bond investor be willing to lose a bit to inflation in the near term to lock in what you expect to be an above-inflation rate for the long term? At times, when the bond market is sanguine about inflation and is worried about the lack of opportunity to earn attractive rates of return in the future (perhaps because a recession is feared), the answer is yes. During periods such as this, short-term rates can be higher than long-term rates, and the yield curve is said to be *inverted*.

An inverted yield curve is a fairly unusual phenomenon. It has been in effect less than 10 percent of the time since 1962. But when it does occur, it has far more often than not represented bad news for the economy and for the stock market. The next section describes exactly how to calculate the state of the yield curve from publicly available data and presents the track record of this indicator as a sign to stay out of stocks.

The Rules for the Yield Curve Indicator

To construct the yield curve indicator, we need to compare the rate for 90-day loans to the government, called the 90-day *Treasury bill yield*, and the rate for 10-year loans to the government, called the 10-year *Treasury note yield*.[4] As an example, Table 11.1 shows the monthly average data from the Federal Reserve Web site on 90-day Treasury bill (secondary market) and 10-year Treasury note yields (constant maturity) for two different months: April 2007 and April 2008. The data in Table 11.1 shows that between these two dates, both short- and long-term interest rates decreased. However, because short-term rates decreased more than long-term rates, the yield curve went from being inverted (short-term rates higher than long-term rates) to normal (long-term rates higher than short-term rates).

TABLE 11.1   An Example of a Changing Yield Curve 2007-2008

Month	90-Day Treasury Bill Yield (%)	10-Year Treasury Note Yield (%)	Spread (10-Year Minus 90-Day Yield, %)
April 2007	4.87	4.69	-0.18 (inverted yield curve)
April 2008	1.29	3.68	2.39 (normal yield curve)
12-month change	-3.58	-1.01	

What caused the changes in interest rates displayed in Table 11.1? They were the result of the unfolding credit and housing crises. In April 2007, before the extent of the mortgage market's troubles came to light, the Federal Reserve was keeping short-term interest rates relatively high in order to fight the threat of inflation posed by rising commodity prices. However, as weaknesses in the financial system became apparent during the second half of 2007, the Federal Reserve shifted course. Containing the risk of recession and supporting the banking system became the top priority, and in order to achieve these goals, the Federal Reserve began aggressively pushing short-term interest rates lower.

For the purposes of using interest rates as a guide to the stock market environment, we have already examined the importance of rising interest rates. Here we will look at the implications of changes in the spread between short- and long-term rates.

The rules for the yield curve indicator are fairly simple. At the start of each month, you check the Federal Reserve Web site for the monthly data on 90-day Treasury bill yields (secondary market) and on 10-year constant maturity Treasury note yields, both of which are reported in the data release numbered H-15.

Whenever the 10-year yield is higher than the 90-day yield, the yield curve is said to be *normal*, and it is safe to be invested in stocks (at least as far as this indicator is concerned). However, if the 90-day yield exceeds the 10-year yield by any amount, you should exit your equity investments. You do not re-enter the stock market until the Fed's monthly data indicates that the yield curve has returned to normal. Figure 11.3 contains Treasury bill and 10-year Treasury note interest rates from January 2000 through June 2001, providing another past example of how the yield curve has shifted from normal to inverted and back. At the start of 2000, the yield curve was normal, meaning that long-term rates were higher than short term rates. However, in August, the yield curve inverted as short-term rates climbed above long-term rates. The yield curve remained inverted through January 2001. After that, the yield curve normalized as short-term rates fell below long-term rates. If you had been using the yield curve indicator to modify your exposure to stocks, you would have moved from stocks to cash at the end of August 2000, when the yield curve inverted. You would have remained in cash until the end of January 2001, which was the time when the yield curve switched back to normal.

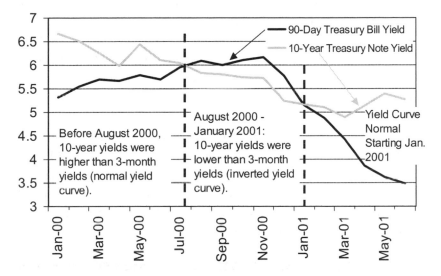

FIGURE 11.3   Short-term (90-day Treasury bill) and long-term (10-year Treasury note) interest rates from 2000 to 2001.

Track Record for the Yield Curve Indicator

Ten periods of yield curve inversion occurred between January 1965 and May 2008. In total, the yield curve has been inverted less than 13 percent of the time during this 43-year period. During these ten yield curve inversions, the S&P 500 gained a total of 2.5 percent, whereas Treasury bills returned 64.6 percent. The compounded annual return of the S&P 500 Index (including dividends) was 10.1 percent per year from 1/1/1965 to 4/40/2008, and the maximum drawdown was 45 percent. An investor who stayed in Treasury bills instead of the S&P 500 during the months when the yield curve was inverted would have earned 11.3 percent per year during the same period, with a maximum drawdown of 39 percent. That is quite an improvement in profitability for the minimal effort required (an average of less than one transaction every two years).

There has been only a 50-50 chance of an actual market decline when the yield curve did invert (five out of ten times). However, declines during yield curve inversions were potentially significant. In contrast, market advances during yield curve inversions were generally modest compared to the returns available from Treasury bills. (Because yield curve inversions are periods when short-term rates are relatively high, Treasury bills have tended to be attractive investments during such times.) Even from 1979 to 1980, when the S&P 500 returned more than 25 percent, Treasury bills returned a respectable 16.5 percent. However, the most recent yield curve inversion (2006 to 2007) bucked historical norms as stocks made far bigger gains than Treasury bills.

Table 11.2 shows the S&P 500 and Treasury bill total returns during the past ten yield curve inversions. In Table 11.2, the yield curve filter is termed Successful if Treasury bills returned more than the S&P 500 during the period when the yield curve was inverted. If stocks returned more than Treasury bills during a period of yield curve inversion, the filter is deemed Unsuccessful.

TABLE 11.2   Performance of the S&P 500 and Treasury Bills during Periods of Yield Curve Inversion from January 1965 to April 2008 Based on Monthly Total Return Data

		During Yield Curve Inversion		
Yield Curve Inverted	Yield Curve Normalized	S&P 500 Total Return	Treasury Bill Total Return	Comment
9/30/66	2/28/67	15.1%	2.4%	Unsuccessful
1/31/69	2/28/69	−4.5%	0.5%	Successful
7/31/69	9/30/69	2.0%	1.1%	Unsuccessful
11/30/69	2/28/70	−3.7%	2.0%	Successful

During Yield Curve Inversion

Yield Curve Inverted	Yield Curve Normalized	S&P 500 Total Return	Treasury Bill Total Return	Comment
6/30/73	7/31/74	–20.8%	8.7%	Successful
8/31/74	10/31/74	3.4%	1.8%	Unsuccessful
12/31/78	5/31/80	25.1%	16.5%	Unsuccessful
11/30/80	9/30/81	–13.8%	12.7%	Successful
8/31/00	1/31/01	–9.6%	2.8%	Successful
8/31/06	5/31/07	19.0%	3.8%	Unsuccessful
All inversions		**+2.5%**	**64.6%**	

The conclusion is that periods of yield curve inversion have been barely profitable but highly risky times in which to own stocks. The main drawback to using overall the yield curve as an indicator is that it rarely inverts. Hypothetical investors who used only the yield curve indicator still would have suffered through significant market declines. For example, relying on the yield curve as the only interest rate tool would have left you exposed to the market crash of October 1987, whereas indicators of rising interest rates would have kept you out of that.

Composite Interest Rate Indicator

In terms of reward versus risk (GPA-to-drawdown ratio), the results obtained using both interest rate indicators have exceeded the buy-and-hold performance of the S&P 500 and exceeded the results of using either interest rate indicator alone. To summarize the rules of the composite interest rate indicator: The investor should be in Treasury bills if the yield curve is inverted or if 10-year Treasury yields are higher than they were six months earlier. Otherwise, the investor should hold the S&P 500. Check these conditions each month using the monthly average data reported in the Federal Reserve release H-15 or the equivalent data.

Table 11.3 compares the results of buying and holding the S&P 500 Index and using the composite interest rate indicator to switch from stocks into Treasury bills during unfavorable periods. The use of the composite interest rate indicator would have resulted in a higher rate of return (the advantage of which would be reduced when transaction costs are factored in). However, the real benefit would have been a reduction in market risk by about half. Figure 11.4 displays the hypothetical growth of $1 invested in both of these strategies from 1965 to 2008. (The data in Figure 11.3 is based on monthly total returns and does not account for taxes and transaction costs.)

TABLE 11.3   **Return and Risk History for a Hypothetical Continuous Investment in the S&P 500 Index ("Buy and Hold") versus a Strategy of Using the Composite Interest Rate Indicator to Switch between the S&P 500 and 3-Month Treasury Bills**

1/1/1965–4/30/2008 (Monthly Total Return Data)	S&P 500 Total Return Buy+Hold	Switching Between S&P 500 and Treasury Bills Using Composite Interest Rate Indicator
Compounded Annual Gain (GPA)	10.1%	11.0%
Maximum Drawdown	45%	23%

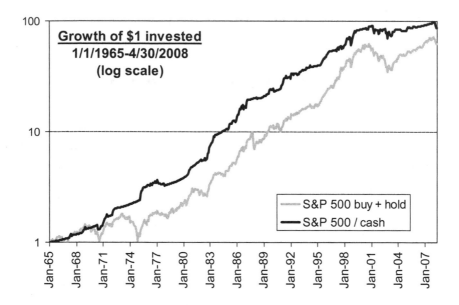

FIGURE 11.4   **Growth of $1 invested from 1/1/1965 to 4/30/2008 in either the S&P 500 throughout the period ("buy + hold") or using the composite interest rate indicator to switch from stocks into Treasury bills.**

Conclusion

Two interest rate conditions have historically been unfavorable for stocks: environments of generally rising interest rates, and periods when long-term interest rates have been lower than short-term interest rates. This chapter has described two simple indicators of these unfavorable conditions that utilize 10-year Treasury note yields and 3-month Treasury bill yields, monthly data for both of which is readily available on the Federal Reserve Web site. Investors who had used both of these indicators as guides for when to stay out of stocks would have greatly reduced their investment risk and slightly improved their returns, compared to investors who had remained invested in the S&P 500 throughout the 43-year period from 1/1/1965 to 4/30/2008.

The caveat regarding these indicators is that from 1995 to 2007, exiting the market during periods of rising interest rates would have reduced return significantly because the stock market did not display its historically typical level of sensitivity to interest rates. (Using interest rate indicators during this period would have cut your investment risk significantly, as during earlier decades.) My own expectation, given the surge in inflationary pressures seen from 2005 to 2008, is that stocks will again respond to changes in interest rates in a manner that will make it profitable to use the interest rate indicators presented here.

---

1 The length of time a borrower has to pay off a loan is called the *term* of the loan, and it is generally expressed in years. In the parlance of the bond market, another expression for the term of the loan is the *maturity*. Do not confuse either of these with the duration of a bond, which also happens to be expressed in years. Duration depends in part on the maturity of a bond, but the two are completely distinct concepts.

Duration is the amount the value of a bond changes in response to a fixed change in interest rates. For example, a bond with a duration of 10 years would lose 10 percent of its value if interest rates rose by 1 percent (such as from 6 percent to 7 percent). Similarly, the value of a bond with a duration of 10 years would increase by 10 percent if interest rates were to fall by 1 percent (such as from 6 percent to 5 percent).

2 *Deflation* is a decline in overall prices that is usually accompanied by falling wages and corporate profits. The last major period of deflation in the United States was during the Great Depression of 1929 to 1939.

3 *Recession* is a period lasting at least six months during which the total production of goods and services has shrunk from its previous peak level on an inflation-adjusted basis.

4 As with the interest rate data used to calculate the historical results of the rising rate indicator earlier in this chapter, the data required for the yield curve indicator is available online from the Federal Reserve Web site, at www.federalreserve.gov/releases/h15/data.htm.

12

IT'S A JUNGLE OUT THERE: SELECTING FROM AMONG DIFFERENT ETFS WITH SIMILAR INVESTMENT OBJECTIVES

One of the most attractive features of ETFs to individual investors is the wide variety of choices. Although the number of selections can seem overwhelming, in some cases competition among different ETFs creates investment opportunity for those who select the best alternatives. In other cases, it is likely to make little difference which of the available alternatives you pick. This chapter reviews some specific examples of investment areas that have multiple ETFs and shows where the proper selection can make a difference for you. The goal is not to comment on every area that has multiple ETFs to choose from. Rather, the goal is to give you a feel for how you might evaluate the available selection for yourself.

The Drawdown Chart—A New Tool

We have already made extensive use of the concept of maximum drawdown (see Chapter 4, "Investment Risk: A Visit to the Dark Side"), which is the largest percentage decline in the value of an investment. Until now, the drawdown statistic has been demonstrated as the extent of the largest decline on a price chart. Here we extend the concept slightly by looking at how drawdown evolves continuously over time. This allows you to discern all periods of investment loss (from previous peaks) and to decide for yourself which declines would have been significant given your own temperament and financial situation. When drawdown is graphed versus time, in the same way that you are familiar with charts of investment value versus time, drawdown represents the extent to which the current value of an investment is below its last peak value.

For example, if you buy a stock at $80 per share and it climbs to $100 per share at the time of your next account statement, you have not experienced a loss, so your drawdown is zero. Now, suppose that by the time of your third statement, the stock has fallen to $90 per share. You are still ahead on your investment, but you have experienced a drawdown of $10 per share, or 10 percent of the peak price of $100 per share.

If your stock subsequently recovers to $95 per share, you are still $5 per share (or 5 percent) below your last peak value of $100 per share, so the latest drawdown is 5 percent. (The maximum drawdown remains 10 percent from before.) Next, your stock surges to $110 per share. $110 per share represents a new peak value, which means that your current drawdown is again zero. Finally, if the stock falls to $105 per share, this is $5 off the high price of $110 per share, so your current drawdown is as follows:

$$\$5/\$110 = 4.55\%$$

Table 12.1 summarizes this series of events and the corresponding drawdown calculations.

**TABLE 12.1   Calculation of Drawdown Based on a Series of Price
Changes in a Stock (Hypothetical)**

Time Period	Stock Price	Drawdown	Comments
First statement	$80	Zero	This is the initial stock purchase; there is no gain or loss yet, so the drawdown is zero.
Second statement	$100	Zero	The stock is at new high value, so the drawdown is zero.
Third statement	$90	10%	The stock is 10% off its previous peak price of $100/share, so the current drawdown is 10%.
Fourth statement	$95	5%	The stock is 5% off its previous peak price of $100/share, so its drawdown is currently –5%. The maximum historical drawdown, which is the preferred risk measure, remains 10% (from the third statement date).
Fifth statement	$110	Zero	The stock is at a new high value, so the current drawdown is again zero.
Sixth statement	$105	4.55%	The stock is $105, which is 4.55% below its last peak price of $110/share, so the newest current drawdown is 4.55%. The maximum historical drawdown remains 10% from the third statement date.

Figure 12.1 shows a different example of the price of a simulated investment and how changes in price correspond to changes in drawdown. The time axes on the two plots in the figure are aligned. (The numbers on the horizontal axis represent time periods, which could be months, years, or statement dates, for example.) The maximum drawdown displayed on the chart in Figure 12.1 is 50 percent, which would be the single risk measurement used to characterize the risk of

this simulated investment. The spreadsheet calculations that you need to perform to generate a drawdown chart are demonstrated in Appendix 4B.

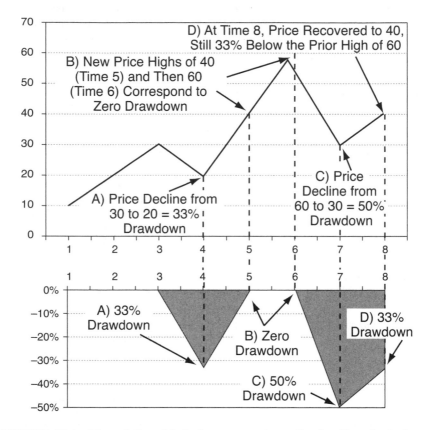

FIGURE 12.1 **The relationship between events on the familiar chart of price versus time (upper plot), and events on a chart of drawdown versus time (lower plot).**

Armed with this new tool for understanding market risk, we will now examine three investment areas that have multiple attractive ETFs with sufficiently long investment histories from which you can choose: small-cap stocks, value stocks, and the utility sector. In each case, we review the price growth and the past risks going back more than five years, a period that encompasses both favorable and falling market climates.

Example 1—Small-Cap ETFs

Literally thousands of small-company stocks exist, and they cover a wide range of market capitalizations. As a result, different small-cap ETFs that attempt to represent the small-cap stock universe with a relatively small number of selections have the potential to perform differently.

The two oldest small-cap ETFs are iShares: the Russell 2000 Index Fund, ticker symbol IWM, and the S&P 600 Small-Cap Index Fund, ticker IJR. These ETFs were launched in mid-2000, although their benchmark indexes began in 1979 (Russell 2000 Index) and 1994 (S&P 600 Index). The underlying benchmarks (Russell 2000 Index and the S&P 600 Index) are constructed differently from each other.

Russell ranks all publicly traded U.S. stocks by market capitalization and then assigns different sections of this list to its various benchmark indexes. The top 1,000 are in the large-cap benchmark, the Russell 1000 Index. The next 2,000 stocks, ranked 1001–3000 in market capitalization, end up in the Russell 2000 Index. Using this methodology, Russell makes its Russell 2000 Index a nearly complete representation of the small-cap stock market in that no attempt is made to filter out any of the stocks in the ranking list. Russell developed this method well before the age of ETFs (in 1979) when presumably little thought was given to the idea that investors might want to trade the entire basket of stocks as a unit.

In contrast, Standard and Poor's selects 600 stocks for its small-cap benchmark. An investment committee chooses these 600 using certain criteria, some of which can be subjective. For example, Standard and Poor's generally excludes stocks in companies that face a significant risk of going out of business. Standard and Poor's also excludes stocks that have excessively low liquidity because they want users of their indexes to be able to assemble the basket of underlying stocks without having too much adverse market impact. Because Standard and Poor's gets to pick and choose which small-cap stocks to include in its index, its investment committee can take into account a desire to assemble a basket of stocks that might be relatively easy to trade as a unit, although that certainly is not their main consideration.

Figure 12.2 charts the price growth (percent change from initial share values) of the ETFs that track the two small-cap benchmarks described earlier (not counting dividends). During the nearly six-year period, IJR has clearly been more profitable than IWM.

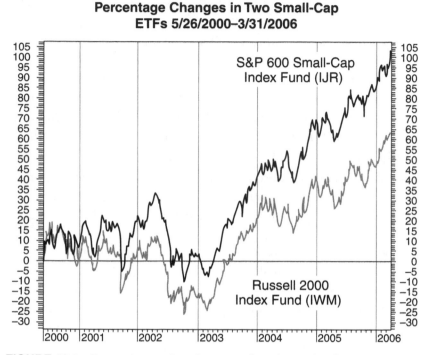

Percentage Changes in Two Small-Cap ETFs 5/26/2000–3/31/2006

FIGURE 12.2   Percentage price changes since inception for two small-cap blend ETFs: the iShares Russell 2000 Index Fund (IWM) and the iShares S&P 600 Index Fund (IJR).

Figure 12.3 displays the drawdowns since inception for both ETFs, showing that IJR has had smaller drawdowns than has IWM. Note that at each of the most significant drawdowns since 2000 (including September 2001, July 2002, October 2002, March 2003, and August 2004), the Russell 2000 Index Fund (IWM) fell further from its prior peak than did the S&P 600 Index Fund (IJR). The conclusion is that IJR has consistently been safer than IWM.

However, IJR has not been more profitable than IWM every year. IJR was more profitable (or lost less) than IWM in 2001, 2002, 2004, and 2005. IWM was more profitable than IJR in 2003 and 2006.

These results are summarized in Table 12.2. No fundamental principle dictates which of these two benchmarks should *a priori* be the better investment. Since inception, IJR has been both more profitable and less risky than IWM. For that reason, I recommend IJR as the better long-term investment.

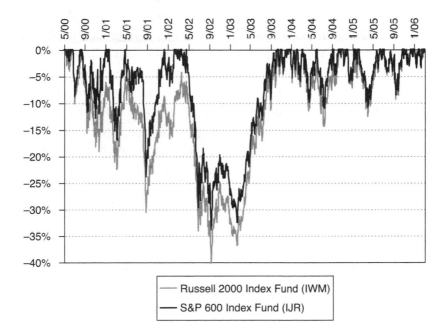

FIGURE 12.3   Drawdowns for the iShares Russell 2000 Index Fund (IWM) and the iShares S&P 600 Index Fund (IJR) based on daily price data.

TABLE 12.2   Annual Total Returns for Two Small-Cap Blend ETFs: The iShares Russell 2000 Index Fund (IWM) and the iShares S&P 600 Index Fund (IJR)*

Year	IWM Total Return	IJR Total Return
2001	1.97%	6.34%
2002	−20.51%	−14.73%
2003	46.94%	38.59%
2004	18.15%	22.45%
2005	4.46%	7.50%
2006	18.17%	14.94%

*Source: Mutual Fund Expert

Example 2—Growth Versus Value ETFs

In theory, investors who believe in fundamental analysis should consider themselves value investors, because the only reason to buy a stock is the belief that it will perform better than the available alternatives. This can occur only if the market has collectively undervalued the stock. Not surprisingly, with so many fundamental analysts looking for bargains, no consensus has emerged regarding what constitutes a "value" stock. Reflecting the breadth of opinion in the marketplace, numerous ETFs are available that represent different methodologies for defining value and growth. At times, some of these notions of value have produced divergent investment results.

The first and simplest definition of value has been the ratio of share price to underlying book value per share, which is called the *price-to-book ratio*.[1] Book value is the worth of a company's assets as reported in its financial statements. All else being equal, a lower price-to-book-value ratio represents a better bargain than a higher price-to-book-value ratio.

Until the end of 2005, the iShares ETFs that track the value and growth subsets of various Standard and Poor's indexes (that is, the S&P 500, the S&P 400 Midcap, and the S&P 600 Small-Cap) used only the price-to-book ratio to classify stocks from the parent indexes as belonging to their growth or value subsets. To constitute the S&P 500 Value Index (ticker SVX), for example, each of the components of the S&P 500 Index is ranked by its price-to-book ratio, starting with the lowest (cheapest). Stocks from this ranking were assigned to the S&P Value Index, moving down the list, until half of the total market capitalization was assigned to the value index. S&P 500 stocks representing the remaining half of its market capitalization become the S&P 500 Growth Index (ticker symbol SGX).

This method had two salient idiosyncrasies. First, it basically defined *growth* as the absence of value rather than as a potentially desirable attribute of a stock. Just because a stock is more expensive than the overall market (in terms of its price-to-book ratio) does not necessarily mean that the underlying company has above-average growth prospects. To the extent that companies with expensive stocks (that is, stocks trading at high price-to-book ratios) do not have bright growth prospects, a growth index selected only on the basis of price-to-book might not be a suitable benchmark for the performance of growth stock pickers.

The second problem with constructing indexes using only the price-to-book ratio is that certain companies have had unusual relationships between their share prices and book values, producing some strange classifications. For example, the formerly high-flying technology stock JDS Uniphase (JDSU) ended up in the S&P 500 Value Index after the technology bubble burst in 2000 even though it has not had a profitable year since 1996. (Most value managers would insist that a "value stock" represent a profitable business before investing in it.) Stocks such as JDSU hindered the performance of the S&P 500 Value Index ETF (IVE) during the 2000–2002 period, when other value stock investments were shining. (Conversely, the S&P Growth Index ETF, ticker IVW, did relatively better than other large-cap growth investments, displaying the flip side of the same quirks in its index construction.) To reduce the likelihood of such anomalies in the future, Standard and Poor's changed its methods for calculating the growth and value index subsets of its S&P 500, S&P 400 Midcap, and S&P 600 Small-Cap indexes in September 2005. Now, value and growth indexes that Standard & Poor's constructs (and the ETFs that track them) use a more complicated methodology than simply dividing stocks based on their price-to-book value ratios.

In fact, many indexes place the same stocks in both growth and value indexes at different weights, depending on what percentage of a stock's attributes meets growth stock criteria and what percentage meets value stock criteria. For example, ExxonMobil (XOM) is in both the S&P 500 Growth Index ETF (IVW) and the S&P 500 Value Index (IVE) because the index provider felt that XOM had characteristics of both growth and value stocks. (Like growth stocks, XOM has enjoyed strong earnings expansion, but at the same time, like value stocks, it has a below-market price-to-earnings ratio.)

Table 12.3 shows how the S&P 500 Value and Growth Index ETFs weight XOM in their portfolios. Based on its proprietary analysis, the index provider (Citigroup) determined that XOM is 36 percent a value stock and 64 percent a growth stock. Therefore, 36 percent of the total $349 billion market capitalization of XOM (that is, $126 billion) is used to calculate the S&P 500 Value Index, and

64 percent of the $349 billion market capitalization of XOM (that is, $224 billion) is used to calculate the S&P 500 Growth Index. (The data in Table 12.3 comes from www.ishares.com.)

TABLE 12.3   Allocation of XOM into the S&P 500/Citigroup Value Index and the S&P 500/Citigroup Growth Index

	Total Market Capitalization as of 12/31/2005	% of Index That XOM Represents	Market Cap ($) of XOM in Index	% of XOM Market Cap in Each Index
S&P 500	$11.26 trillion	3.18%	$349 billion	100%
S&P 500 Value Index	$5.58 trillion	2.26%	$126 billion	36%
S&P 500 Growth Index	$5.73 trillion	3.91%	$224 billion	64%

Within the S&P 500/Citigroup Value Index, XOM is treated as a stock with $126 billion in market capitalization. Adding together the market capitalizations of all stocks assigned to the S&P 500/Citigroup Value Index generates its total market capitalization of $5.58 trillion, of which 2.26 percent (that is, $126 billion) resulted from the contribution of XOM.

As with XOM, it need not be the case that the entire market capitalization of stocks in the S&P 500 Value Index is used to calculate the data for that index. For a significant number of issues (including XOM), only part of the actual market capitalization is used in constructing the S&P 500 Value Index, with the remainder attributed to the S&P 500 Growth Index. In fact, the S&P 500 Value Index has 354 stocks, and the S&P 500 Growth Index has 298 stocks. The total number of stocks in the S&P 500 Value Index plus the number in the S&P 500 Growth Index totals 652. However, because the total universe of stocks from which these two indexes are selected has only 500 stocks altogether, 152 issues must appear in both the value and growth indexes. On the other hand, the Russell Index methodology places XOM only in its Russell 1000 Value Index ETF (ticker IWD) and not in its Russell 1000 Growth Index ETF (ticker IWF).

Did any of this make a difference to an individual investor? The jury is still out on the new methods that Standard and Poor's has been using since late 2005. However, before the changes went into effect, performance differences were significant. Figure 12.4 shows that since inception, the iShares Russell 1000 Value Index Fund (IWD) has had lower drawdown and has been more profitable than the iShares S&P 500 Value Index Fund (IVE). The risk and profit statistics derived from the data in Figure 12.4 are summarized in Table 12.4.

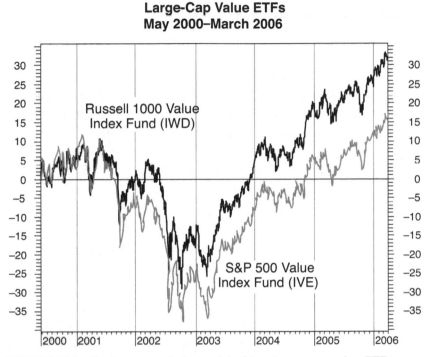

FIGURE 12.4 Performance (price only) of two large-cap value ETFs since inception (5/26/2000–3/31/2006).

TABLE 12.4 Risk and Profit Summary for Two Large-Cap Value ETFs. Results Are Based on Daily Price Data for IVE and IWD from 5/26/2000–3/31/2006

Large-Cap Value ETF	Compounded Gain per Annum	Maximum Drawdown	GPA/ Drawdown
S&P 500 Value Index Fund (IVE)	2.6%	–37%	0.07
Russell 1000 Value Index Fund (IWD)	4.8%	–27%	0.18

Example 3—Utility Sector ETFs

The first three diversified U.S. utility ETFs were the Select Utility Sector SPDR (XLU), the iShares Dow Jones U.S. Utility Index Fund (IDU), and the Utilities HOLDR (UTH). Even though there are three different utility ETFs, not one of them is designed to track the best-known benchmark for the utility sector, which is the Dow Jones Utility Average.

As in the previous examples from this chapter, the various utility sector ETFs are constructed using a different methodology, and they have had assorted performances. XLU consists of the 32 utility stocks within the S&P 500 Index. The component stocks in the XLU are weighted by market capitalization. IDU tracks the Dow Jones U.S. Utilities Index. As with XLU, the stocks in IDU are capitalization-weighted, but IDU has 73 issues. Even though each of these ETFs is different, each has a number of its top holdings in common, such as Exelon, Duke Energy Corp., and Dominion.

We will spend some time on the third utility ETF, the Utilities HOLDR (UTH), because as you will see later, it has been the best-performing of the three utility ETFs. Also, HOLDRs (issued by Merrill Lynch) differ from any of the other ETFs that have been discussed in this book up until now, and it is important to understand their limitations and advantages before you invest in any of them. (HOLDRs represent numerous sectors, including some narrow sub-sectors of the technology universe, such as Internet architecture and B2B Internet businesses.)

The Utilities HOLDR (UTH) was launched in 2000 with a basket of 20 stocks. Unlike other ETFs, HOLDRs have no index provider to update the constituents of this initial basket of stocks. The stocks in UTH will change only following events that would affect long-term investors holding stocks in individual companies, such as stock splits, mergers, spin-offs, or bankruptcy. Over the very long term, this could become a disadvantage to investors in UTH if its portfolio evolves into a poorly diversified investment or into one that is no longer representative of the utility sector. Investors in

UTH should monitor this in future years. For now (2008), however, UTH has the potential advantage of a low expense ratio (eight cents per share per year, which at the current price of more than $120 per share is less than 0.08 percent, compared to 0.6 percent for IDU and 0.25 percent for XLU). Despite its low expense ratio, UTH actually paid out fewer dividends (trailing 12 months through 6/30/2008) than have the other utilities' ETFs. This could be a concern to investors who are looking to utility stocks to provide a source of income, as was traditionally the objective of many investors in the sector.

There are two other bits of useful information about UTH. First, you can buy only multiples of 100 shares, meaning that at current prices, the minimum investment in UTH that you can make is $12,000. This restriction might place UTH beyond the reach of some individual investors. Second, of the three utilities' ETFs, UTH most closely tracks the Dow Jones Utility Average. This might be relevant to active investors and technical analysts who are looking for a way to trade based on that average, which has a long history.[2]

The different utility ETFs have had very similar levels of risk but different investment returns during the 2000–2006 period, as shown in Figure 12.5. The figure shows that of the three utility sector ETFs, UTH had both the highest total return and the highest drawdown over the entire period. Table 12.5 summarizes the numerical results, which favor UTH on a risk-adjusted basis.[3] Although there is no guarantee that future performance will repeat past results, based on the history shown, UTH appears to be the superior investment subject to the caveats just described.

In general, stock dividends are fairly low, so comparing similar ETFs using price-only data (which is easier to obtain online) should not pose a problem. However, in the case of a sector such as utilities or REITs, where dividend yields have historically been well above those of the overall market and the source of most of the historical long-term return, it is important to use total return data (that is, investment results including the effects of both price changes and dividend payouts).

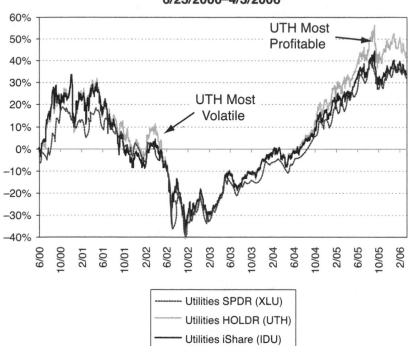

FIGURE 12.5   Percentage total return for three utility-sector ETFs (6/23/2000–4/3/2006).

TABLE 12.5   Risk and Profit Summary for Three Utility ETFs, Based on Daily Total Return Data from 6/23/2000–4/3/2006

Utility ETF	Compounded Gain per Annum	Maximum Drawdown	GPA/ Drawdown
Utility HOLDR (UTH)	6.2%	–56%	0.11
Utility SPDR (XLU)	4.8%	–52%	0.09
Dow Jones U.S. Utility Sector Fund (IDU)	5.2%	–54%	0.10

Conclusion

This chapter has presented three examples of how you might select the optimum ETF when more than one is available to meet your investment objective. Discrepancies between different indexes are more likely to arise in the absence of a uniform definition of how to classify the stocks in a category. People generally agree about large-cap stocks, for example; therefore, the large-cap blend ETFs (those that track the Russell 1000 Index and the S&P 500) have performed similarly. On the other hand, the definition of a value or a growth stock is subject to considerable subjective interpretation, as is the subset of small-company stocks that could be selected to represent the small-cap universe. For these reasons, you should pay particular attention to all available alternatives in small-cap, sector and growth, or value ETFs before committing your capital to any one choice.

The important point to take home from this chapter is that an evaluation of past risk-adjusted performance is the foundation of comparison shopping between similar ETFs. It is vital to analyze data covering a full cycle that includes periods when the market was advancing *and* declining. The examples here have used the GPA-to-drawdown ratio, calculated using daily data. However, you might find that other specific methods and data (such as the Sharpe ratio or monthly data) better match your own practices or available resources.

You should consider other criteria besides risk-adjusted performance. In the late 1990s, when ETFs were relatively new, bid-ask spreads were far more onerous than they are now. Particularly if you are an active investor, you should take trading costs into account when selecting an ETF for your portfolio. The less actively traded sector ETFs are liable to have higher bid-ask spreads than the more broadly diversified index ETFs.

A number of ETFs, especially sector ETFs, have relatively high expense ratios, almost at the level of available actively managed mutual funds. (We saw this with the iShares Dow Jones U.S. Utility

Sector Index Fund, whose expense ratio of 0.6 percent per year is almost as high as the 0.8–1.0 percent per year charged by the less-expensive actively managed utility funds such as Fidelity Select Utilities Growth or FBR Gas Utility Index. When you are evaluating a high-expense ETF (which I define as one with expenses of 0.4 percent per year or higher), you should take the time to search for available mutual funds before you make a final investment decision. In many cases, the ETF will still be more economical or otherwise more appealing than competing mutual funds, but it can only be to your benefit to weigh all your options.

The bottom line is that the rich variety of ETFs that are now available and the degree of competition among different ETF sponsors and index providers offer you the opportunity to be selective when you are shopping for ETF investments. Take advantage, and you will have a leg up on most other investors.

Endnotes

1   *Book value per share* is the value of all of a company's assets less its liabilities *as recorded in its financial statements*, divided by the number of outstanding shares. For example, if a company has 1 million shares of stock outstanding, assets of $10 million, and liabilities of $6 million, the book value per share is $4. Note that the book value of assets can be very different from their fair-market value. For example, real estate is valued in financial statements as the purchase price less accumulated depreciation. Companies that purchased property long ago are generally carrying them on the books at well below market value.

2   Data regarding the Dow Jones Utility Average going back to 1929 is available from the Dow Jones Indexes website, at www.djindexes.com/mdsidx/index.cfm?event=showavgIndexData&perf=Historical%20Values.

3   Source for Figure 12.5 and Table 12.5: Investors FastTrack Database.

13

THE ULTIMATE ETF INVESTMENT PROGRAM FOR 30 MINUTES PER MONTH

Now that you have learned different strategies, it is time to apply them as part of an overall, personal investment program. Here you will see that in terms of beating the market and reducing risk, the final result is greater than the sum of its parts. Following are the pillars of this unified strategy:

- Diversification to reduce risk
- Reduction of market exposure during unfavorable interest rate climates
- Active asset allocation between small- and large-cap ETFs
- Active asset allocation between growth and value ETFs
- Active asset allocation between U.S. and international equity ETFs

The Ultimate ETF Investment Program

You have already seen that some investment decisions have been more important than others in terms of the impact on your bottom-line results. The research underlying Chapter 9, "Boring Bargains or Hot Prospects? Choosing between Growth and Value," and Chapter 7, "The One-Decision Portfolio," shows the following.

- The decision to overweight growth versus value has had the greatest potential to increase the long-term profitability of an investment program.

- Diversification has had the greatest impact on the safety of investments.

The ultimate investment strategy starts with these two principles and then applies the other asset allocation tools presented in Chapters 8, "When to Live Large: An Asset Allocation Model for Small- versus Large-Cap ETFs," 10, "When Is It Safe to Drink the Water? International Investing," and 11, "What Bonds Can Tell You about Stocks: How to Use Interest Rates."

Step 1: Diversification

Recall from Chapter 7 that the building blocks of the one-decision portfolio include U.S. investment-grade bonds, real estate stocks (REITs), small-cap value stocks, and the S&P 500. In later chapters, you have seen how to improve the performance of a strategy that stays continuously invested in the S&P 500 and in small-cap value ETFs. However, the premise that bonds and REITs are effective diversifiers of a stock portfolio remains important.

Therefore, the first step in the ultimate strategy is to allocate 25 percent of your assets to investment-grade U.S. bonds and 25 percent to REITs using ETFs. The best bond ETFs currently available for long-term holding are the iShares Lehman Aggregate Bond Index Fund, ticker symbol AGG and the Vanguard Total Bond Market ETF, ticker symbol BND. (The Vanguard offering has a lower expense ratio but the iShares ETF is more liquid. Both track the same benchmark.) The REIT ETF that I recommend is the iShares Cohen & Steers Realty Majors Index Fund, ticker ICF.

In just two transactions, you can invest half of your capital in a productive and cost-effective way. Table 13.1 shows the historical performance of a hypothetical ½-bond, ½-REIT investment. The best demonstration of the benefit of diversifying between investment-grade bonds and REITs is that the worst drawdown for the combined portfolio is less than the worst drawdowns for either bonds or REITs separately.

Available ETFs should allow you to closely match the performance of these benchmarks in the future. The iShares Lehman Aggregate Bond ETF (ticker symbol AGG) is designed to track the Lehman Aggregate Bond Index, less the impact of its 0.2 percent expense ratio. The iShares Cohen and Steers Realty Majors Index Fund (ICF) was not designed specifically to track the NAREIT Equity REIT Index that is used in the example because of its long history.[1] However, since the inception of ICF in 2001, ICF and the NAREIT Index have behaved similarly.

TABLE 13.1 Performance of REIT and U.S. Investment-Grade Bond Benchmarks Separately and as a 50/50 Portfolio

Based on Monthly Total Return Data 1/1/1979–4/30/2008	Lehman Aggregate Bond Index	NAREIT Equity REIT Index	50/50 Bond/ REIT Portfolio
Compounded annual gain	8.7%	14.4%	11.8%
Maximum drawdown	–13%	–26%	–11%

After the experience of high volatility and low overall stock market returns from 2000 to 2008, an investment that returns nearly 12 percent per year with only 11 percent drawdown seems too good to be true. Unfortunately, it probably is, at least for now. Looking ahead, it is unlikely that the coming years will see the same level of returns from REITs and bonds that were enjoyed from 1979 to 2006. Although the 1979 to 1982 period was one of extremely high interest rate volatility, for most of the time from 1979 to 2006, both interest rates and inflation were in long-term downtrends, developments that have acted as tailwinds for REITs and bonds. This halcyon environment had to end eventually, if for no other reason than that by the end of 2002, inflation and interest rates had virtually no room to move lower. (See Table 13.2.)

TABLE 13.2   Inflation and Interest Rates at Year-End 2002 and May 2008

	Year-End 2002	May 2008
10-year Treasury note yield (%)	4.0%	4.0%
Inflation (12-month change in Consumer Price Index)	1.6%	3.9% (latest report available as of 4/30/2008)

Indeed, as of 2008, inflation has already perked up, spurred by rising energy and commodity prices. Interest rates rose in 2006 but fell again in 2007, leaving them near the low levels seen in late 2002. It is surprising that long-term rates have remained low in an environment of high inflation. However, the outlook for bond total returns remains muted because, over the long term, the expected gains are simply equal to the current interest rate.

REITs did not do well in 2007. From January 2007 to February 2008, the NAREIT Index lost 26 percent: its worst decline in more than 30 years. As of mid-2008, housing and real estate markets around the country remain depressed, and it has become more difficult for potential real estate investors and developers to borrow money. On the plus side, even though real estate was at the epicenter of the financial storm that began in 2007, REITs have actually been outperforming the overall stock market in 2008, suggesting that they have hit bottom. Nevertheless, REITs are not expected to match the 14 percent annual returns they generated through 2006.

Why, you might ask, should you consider incorporating REIT and bond ETFs into your investments given this outlook? The answer is twofold. First, the projection of lower returns in the coming decade is not limited to REITs and bonds. The end of the downtrends in inflation and interest rates is equally likely to produce lower returns in the coming decade in stocks, compared to the level of profits earned in the 1979 to 2006 period.

Second, the expectation is that REIT and bond holdings will continue to be effective at reducing overall risk through the diversification of an all-stock portfolio. If anything, bonds have been more effective at reducing risk as part of a stock/bond portfolio since 1998 than was the case previously because during much of the time since 1998, stocks and bonds have moved in opposite directions. Moreover, in an environment of high inflation, you can increase your returns from bonds by waiting for a more favorable interest rate climate. I have described a simple method of profiting from major interest rate trends in *Beating the Market, 3 Months at a Time* (Gerald Appel and Marvin Appel, FT Press, 2008, Chapter 6).

Step 2: Decide Whether International or U.S. Stocks Are Favored; If U.S. Stocks Are Favored, Evaluate the Interest Rate Climate

So far you have seen that 50 percent of your investment capital should be invested for the long term, equally balanced between REITs and U.S. investment-grade bonds using two ETFs: ICF and AGG. Your next decision, for 25 percent of total investment capital, is whether to go abroad or to invest at home. For this purpose, you should utilize the asset allocation model presented in Chapter 10. Recall that the foreign stock benchmark used in that chapter was the Morgan Stanley Capital International EAFE Index. The U.S. stock benchmark was the S&P 500 Index. ETFs are available that track both of these benchmarks: the iShares EAFE Index Fund (ticker symbol EFA) and the S&P 500 Depository Receipts (ticker symbol SPY).

It turns out, not surprisingly, that interest rate trends in the United States have had significantly less predictive value for investors in foreign stocks than for U.S. investors. As a result, if the model presented in Chapter 10 favors international stocks, you should go ahead and hold 25 percent of your investment capital in EFA, regardless of what interest rates are doing in the United States. However, if the international/U.S. model favors the United States, you should evaluate the interest rate environment as discussed in Chapter 11 to decide how you will manage this part of your portfolio.

If the yield curve is inverted[2] or interest rates are rising,[3] you should move 25 percent of your total portfolio into the money market. These negative factors are *not* required to be in effect at the same time. It takes only one of these interest rate criteria to keep you out of stocks with this part of your investments. The hypothetical past results of applying the asset allocation strategy from Chapter 10 and the composite interest rate indicator from Chapter 11 (the latter only when invested in U.S. stocks) appear in Table 13.3.[4]

TABLE 13.3   Performance of Foreign Stocks (MSCI EAFE Index), U.S. Stocks (S&P 500 Index), and the Hypothetical Results from Switching between them.

Based on Monthly Total Return Data 1/1/1979–4/30/2008	Foreign Stocks (EAFE)	U.S. Stocks (S&P 500)	Switch Between EAFE and S&P 500	EAFE/S&P 500/Money Market
Compounded annual gain	11.6%	12.8%	14.0%	15.2%
Maximum drawdown	–47%	–45%	–53%	–36%

Step 3: Select the Best Investment Style from Large-Cap Value, Small-Cap Value, Large-Cap Growth, or Small-Cap Growth

Up to this point, you have allocated 25 percent of your total portfolio to investment-grade bonds (AGG), 25 percent in REITs (ICF), and 25 percent to large U.S. company stocks (SPY), foreign stocks (EFA), or the money market. 25 percent of the total portfolio remains to be allocated, and the four choices available for this final portion are small-cap value, large-cap value, small-cap growth, and large-cap growth. Historically, the major divergences between the performances of different investment styles have depended most heavily on whether growth or value was favored. Therefore, the next step in allocating the final 25 percent of your portfolio is evaluating whether growth or value is stronger. After you have made this decision, you can select a small- or large-cap ETF.

The way to accomplish this is to utilize the growth/value asset allocation model presented in Chapter 9 to analyze both large-cap and small-cap benchmarks.[5] This will give you two selections: one small-cap style (either growth or value) and a large-cap style (either growth or value). More than 83 percent of the time, both small- and large-caps have favored growth or value concurrently. However, roughly 17 percent of the time, a different style has been favored for large-caps than small-caps. (For example, large-cap value is favored over large-cap growth at the same time that small-cap growth is favored over small-cap value, or vice versa.)

In the event of a split decision, go with value. Only if growth is favored over value among both large- and small-caps will you invest in a growth ETF. If value is favored in small-caps, large-caps, or both, invest in a value ETF. This decision rule does stack the deck in favor of value. Table 13.4 summarizes the possibilities. It is not surprising that better investment performance results from avoidance of growth ETFs during all but the most conducive market environments, because over the long term, value stocks have performed better than growth stocks on a risk-adjusted basis.

TABLE 13.4   Combining the Results of Small-Cap Value versus Growth and Large-Cap Value versus Growth into a Single Overall Selection of Value or Growth

If the Small-Cap Growth/Value Model Favors . . .	And if the Large-Cap Growth/Value Model Favors . . .	The Overall Style Selection Is . . .
Value	Value	Value
Value	Growth	Value
Growth	Value	Value
Growth	Growth	Growth

After you have identified whether value or growth is favored overall using the decision process, the next step is to evaluate the relative performance of small- and large-caps using the asset allocation model presented in Chapter 8. Note that even though you will ultimately select either small-caps or large caps, the determination of whether growth or value is favored always requires you to use all four benchmarks: large-cap value, large-cap growth, small-cap value, and small-cap growth. As of June 2008, growth is favored over value, and large-caps are favored over small-caps.

The profitability achieved from 1979 to 2008 by using this two-step sequence to identify which of the four investment styles (large value, small value, large growth, small growth) to use has been an impressive 17.6 percent per year compounded. However, the maximum drawdown of 31 percent represents a higher level of risk than most individual investors should expose themselves to. Aggressive investors can utilize this as a standalone investment strategy if they are willing to live through at least this much drawdown in the future.

You have already seen how the composite interest rate indicator improved returns and reduced risk when applied to the S&P 500 Index, and even when applied to the S&P 500 Index only during periods when U.S. stocks were favored over foreign stocks. Therefore, it is natural to ask whether attention to interest rates might reduce the risk of the strategy that selects the best investment style.

Doing so did reduce risk historically, but at a significant reduction in profitability by more than 3 percent per year. (See Table 13.5.) This is in contrast to the case with the S&P 500, where long-term profitability was *enhanced* by switching into the money market during unfavorable periods (as seen in Chapter 11). The relatively modest reduction in past risk (from 31 percent to 22 percent drawdown) is not sufficient to warrant the loss of return that using the composite interest rate indicator would have entailed. As a result, I recommend that the 25 percent of your investment portfolio that you allocate to identifying the best of the four investment styles remains invested in the market at all times.

TABLE 13.5   The Effect of Taking Interest Rates into Account in Addition to Selecting the Best of the Four Investment Styles (Large Value, Small Value, Large Growth, or Small Growth)

1/1/1979–4/30/2008 (Monthly Total Return Data)	Best Style (Always in Stocks)	Best Style/Treasury Bills (Switch According to Composite Interest Rate Indicator)
Compounded Annual Gain (GPA)	17.6%	14.2%
Maximum drawdown	–31%	–22%

Results of the Ultimate ETF Strategy

Historically, the three-step ultimate investment approach outlined in this chapter has delivered attractive returns at reasonable risk, as shown in Table 13.6. The portfolio in the Ultimate Strategy with bonds is comprised of 25 percent bonds (AGG); 25 percent REITs

(ICF); 25 percent allocated to EFA, SPY, or money market, and 25 percent allocated to the best investment style (that is, the strongest of small-cap value or large-cap value or small-cap growth or large-cap growth). The Ultimate ETF Strategy using only equity ETFs has one-third allocated to REITs (ICF); one-third allocated to EFA, SPY, or cash; and one-third allocated to the best style.

I recommend maintaining a 25 percent allocation to bonds in your long-term portfolio. However, more aggressive investors may want to forego making a commitment to bonds in favor of staying with stocks only. The historical (hypothetical) results of both options are presented in the table. In terms of both risk and rewards, the Ultimate ETF strategy has outperformed relevant market benchmarks.

TABLE 13.6   Investment Results for the Ultimate ETF Strategy Described in This Chapter

1/1/1979– 4/30/2008 (Monthly Data)	Ultimate ETF Strategy (with Bonds)	Ultimate ETF Strategy (Equity ETFs Only)	S&P 500 Index	Russell 2000 Value Index	Russell 2000 Growth Index	MSCI EAFE Index	Russell 1000 Value Index	Russell 1000 Growth Index	NAREIT Equity REIT Index
			All Index Performances Are Based on Monthly Total Return Data						
Compounded annual gain (GPA)	14.3%	16.3%	12.8%	14.6%	9.8%	11.6%	13.7%	11.5%	14.4%
Maximum drawdown	–12%	–19%	–45%	–33%	–63%	–47%	–28%	–62%	–26%

Conclusion

You will need to expend relatively little effort in order to maintain your ETF portfolio. The specific steps are listed below:

1. Start out by placing 25 percent of your total portfolio in U.S. investment-grade bonds (AGG) and 25 percent in REITs (ICF).

2. At the end of each year, select either small- or large-caps as the favored style for the coming year, as described in Chapter 8.

3. At the end of each month, evaluate whether value or growth is favored, as described in Chapter 9. Perform this for both large- and small-cap benchmarks by comparing the Russell 1000 Value and Growth Index ETFs (IWD and IWF, respectively) to each other, and the Russell 2000 Value and Growth ETFs (IWN and IWO, respectively) to each other. If either the Russell 1000 Value Index ETF or the Russell 2000 Value ETF (or both) is favored, value is the selected style. Only if both small-cap growth and large-cap growth are favored over their value counterparts is growth selected as the style.

4. Invest 25 percent of capital in the ETF that meets both of the criteria selected in the previous two steps.

5. At the end of each month, evaluate whether U.S. stocks (S&P 500 Index ETF) or foreign stocks (EAFE Index ETF, ticker EFA) are favored, as described in Chapter 10. If foreign stocks are stronger, invest 25 percent of your total portfolio in EFA.

6. If U.S. stocks are favored over foreign stocks, evaluate the composite interest rate indicator, as described in Chapter 11. If both of the interest rate features are favorable, invest in the S&P 500 Depository Receipt (SPY) or in the similar iShares S&P 500 Index Fund (IVV). If either one or both of the interest rate indicators is unfavorable, place this part (25 percent) of your capital into the money market.

Rebalance your portfolio as often as transaction costs (see Chapter 1, "Exchange-Traded Mutual Funds: Now Individuals Can Invest Like the Big Players") and tax considerations allow.

Figure 13.1 shows a flowchart of the decisions you have to make to implement the ultimate portfolio strategy.

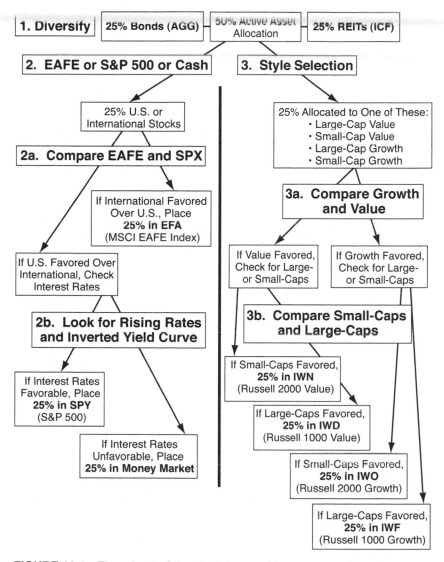

FIGURE 13.1   Flowchart of the decision- making process that allows you to maintain the ultimate ETF investment strategy portfolio.

As a closing comment, remember that you might have many ETF options available with which to implement the investment strategies described. Although I encourage you to consider every possible option when you purchase an ETF for yourself (as discussed in Chapter 12, "It's a Jungle Out There: Selecting from among Different ETFs with Similar Investment Objectives"), I do recommend using the Russell Index ETFs and the other index and interest rate data exactly as I have specified when you implement any of the models from this book that you might want to use. Once you have used the models presented here to select the most promising areas of the market, you are then free to choose from among the available ETFs to gain exposure to the areas you have identified.

For example, if you determine using the iShares Russell Index ETFs that small-cap value happens to be the favored investment style, my current recommendation for investing in that style is the StreetTracks Dow Jones U.S. Small-Cap Value Fund (ticker symbol DSV). On the other hand, if you determine that small-cap growth is the style of choice, I recommend the iShares S&P 600 Growth Index ETF (ticker symbol IJT). These recommendations are a good place to start in your small-cap investments, but you might find it valuable to evaluate all the alternatives on your own in case new ETFs arrive or market conditions change significantly in the interim.

At this time, I recommend the iShares Russell 1000 Growth and Value Index ETFs (ticker symbols IWF and IWD, respectively) based on the performance of the various alternatives from 2000 to 2006. However, in December 2005, the methodologies that were used to construct the benchmarks for the iShares S&P 500 Growth and Value Index ETFs (ticker symbols IVW and IVE, respectively) were changed. Moreover, ETFs tracking Morningstar-style indexes were introduced in early 2006. As a result, you will have some new options available to you for large-cap value and growth investing. Some of these newer options might prove to be superior to the Russell Index ETFs in the future.

At this point, the only remaining task required for you to be on your way is to identify a low-cost broker in which to trade ETFs. The choice you make will depend on a number of factors applicable to you individually. In general, individual investors should not have much difficulty getting good execution on orders for the ETFs discussed here, which tend to be among the most easily traded. As a result, getting a low transaction cost will likely be the most important criterion that determines whether a broker works well for you. You should aim to pay $10 or less per trade for your ETF transactions.

If you follow the specific steps outlined in this chapter, you will be well ahead of the crowd in terms of making reasoned decisions and keeping your investment risk under control. The models and ETFs that I have discussed in detail can serve as the foundation of a well diversified long-term investment program.

The ETF world is an exciting place because new investments and new sources of insight are becoming available all the time. If you want to broaden your investment horizon to take advantage of the most recently launched ETFs, you can still use the tools provided in this book along with the Internet resources cited. (A list of free sources of ETF information on the Web appears at the end of this book.)

1 Because REIT ETFs are fairly new, having been launched in 2000, it was necessary to select a REIT benchmark with a longer history than the benchmarks used for REIT ETFs. The NAREIT Equity REIT Total Return Index represents the performance of all publicly traded REITs that hold or manage real estate. (REITs that issue mortgages are excluded from this index.) Its history goes back to the start of 1972. Its data is available online at www.nareit.com.

2 If the yield on 10-year Treasury notes is higher than the yield on 90-day Treasury bills, as reported under monthly data on the Federal Reserve Web site, the yield curve is inverted. (See Chapter 11.)

3 If the yield on 10-year Treasury notes is higher at the end of the most recent month compared to six months prior, as reported under monthly data on the Federal Reserve Web site, rates are said to be rising.

4 The hypothetical results in Table 13.3 are based on monthly total returns translated into U.S. dollars without allowance for taxes or transaction costs.

5 Recall that the large-cap growth and value benchmarks are the Russell 1000 Growth Index and the Russell 1000 Value Index. The ticker symbols of the ETFs that track these benchmarks are, respectively, IWF and IWD. The small-cap value benchmarks are the Russell 2000 Growth Index and the Russell 2000 Value Index. The ticker symbols of the ETFs that track these small-cap benchmarks are, respectively, IWO and IWN.

14

ETF STRATEGIES FOR INVESTMENT INCOME

We are fortunate that advances in health care and greater awareness of the benefits of healthy lifestyles has increased the likelihood of living past age 80. In fact, if a couple makes it to age 65, at least one of the spouses is expected to live until 91.[1] Greater longevity means that one of the major challenges for today's investors is to devise ways of making consistent withdrawals from their savings without depleting their principal over time. The task is rendered all the more difficult by the need to keep up with inflation.

As of this writing (June 2008), inflation is running at roughly 4 percent per year, which is high by the standards of the past 20 years but is actually consistent with the average inflation rate that has prevailed since 1945. That poses a big problem for bond investors, because the average investment-grade bond in the United States currently pays little more than 5 percent per year. Bonds do have the advantage of being safe, which is why many advisors recommend them for retirees. However, any bond position you might take at age 65 (under current inflation and interest rates) will not by itself provide for your likely needs over the 15 to 30 years you can expect to live in retirement. That is where high-dividend equity ETFs should enter the picture.

The Ideal Income Investment—A Payout That Grows over Time

The ideal investment for retirement would be one that pays interest at the same rate as a bond (say, 5 percent of principal annually) with the safety of an investment-grade bond, but whose payout grows with inflation. Inflation-protected Treasury bonds (TIPS) would be perfect, except that they pay only 0 to 2 percent above inflation.

Dividend-paying stocks offer another alternative. Their dividend payouts (as a group) have increased over time. Although the dividend yield of the S&P 500 Index is just 2.1 percent, many stocks pay 4 percent or more. Even better, under current tax law (which may change in 2011), "qualified" equity dividends are taxed at a lower federal rate than taxable bond interest. Figure 14.1 shows the growth of the dividend payout of the S&P 500 Index since 1971.

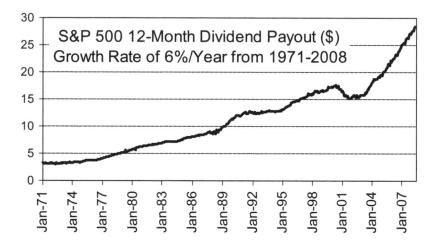

FIGURE 14.1 **Growth of dividends paid by the basket of stocks in the S&P 500 Index, 1971 to 2008.**

You won't be limited to spending only investment income to meet current expenses, however. You could, for example, invest in an S&P 500 Index fund and withdraw 5 percent of your principal each year.

Assuming that the total return of your fund exceeded 5 percent per year, which has certainly been the case historically, your withdrawals would be able to grow over time as the value of your principal increased.

Nonetheless, even if you are not looking for current investment income, there is another advantage to high-dividend stocks: They have historically been safer than the overall stock market. This was especially true from 2000 to 2003, when the damage sustained by value stock strategies in general was far less than the losses seen in growth stocks. Safety is important for everyone, but especially for people who are living off their savings.

Even though high-dividend stocks as a group have been safer than the stock market, they are still far riskier than investment-grade bonds. Unlike a bond, a company isn't guaranteed to maintain or grow its dividend payout or a stock price to hold steady. Formerly high-dividend stocks such as Washington Mutual, Eastman Kodak, or General Motors attest to the dangers of putting too much into any one company.

This is where ETFs come in. Since 2003, numerous ETFs designed to pay above-average dividends have come to market. Each ETF typically has 50 individual stocks, which mitigates the single company risk. The remainder of this chapter highlights a few selected high-dividend ETFs and shows you how to reduce your stock market risk by holding both a U.S. and a foreign high-dividend ETF.

If You Want High Dividends, You Have to Like Financial Stocks

A disproportionate share of high-dividend stocks are banks. Utilities have traditionally also been overrepresented among the ranks of high-dividend stocks although, since the 1990s, some utilities have morphed into growth stocks. Others, like Consolidated Edison (New York City's electric company), continue in the traditional pattern of the regulated utility with a protected monopoly, low growth, and a high dividend yield (5.6 percent).

In the 1990s (before the explosion in energy prices), integrated oil companies such as ChevronTexaco or ExxonMobil were above-average dividend payers. However, the growth in their profits and stock prices has outstripped growth in dividend payouts. One reason is that all the oil in the world that is easy to extract has already been tapped. Future development of offshore rigs or heavier oil require a much greater capital investment than did past exploration and drilling projects, which leaves less free cash flow to pay dividends.

In the future, if either of these oil companies, which are in the Dow Jones Industrial Average, should again become one of the top ten highest-yielding stocks among the 30 that comprise the Dow Industrials, I would recommend buying them. Under current market conditions, that would require a drop of more than 20 percent in ChevronTexaco (to less than $80 per share) and a drop of more than 46 percent in ExxonMobil (to less than $50 per share). Of course, it is also possible that these companies will eventually increase their dividend payouts to catch up with the increases in their profits. The easiest way to keep track of where the dividend yields of these companies stand in relation to the other components of the Dow Jones Industrial Average is to check the Web site www.dogsofthedow.com.

Where to Find High-Dividend ETFs

iShares launched the first high-dividend ETF: the Dow Jones Select Dividend Index ETF (ticker DVY). It remains one of the most actively traded high-dividend ETFs, which is an important virtue for a money manager, because I've been able to buy or sell significant numbers of shares without moving the market against me. The current dividend yield is an attractive 4.6 percent. As with most high-dividend ETFs, the largest sectors represented in DVY are financials (47 percent) and utilities (18 percent). DVY has the advantage of diversification across market capitalization: Large, small, and mid-sized companies are represented almost equally. This ETF pioneered the use of dividend-weighting rather than market capitalization weighting and is a valuable addition to an investor's arsenal. A simplified example illustrates how a dividend-weighted index is calculated.

If Company A pays $1 per share in annual dividends and a billion shares are outstanding, the total dividends that Company A pays are $1 billion per year. Suppose Company B also pays $1 per share in dividends but has only 500 million shares outstanding. That means Company B pays a total of $500 million in dividends each year. The total dividends that Companies A and B pay amounts to $1.5 billion. A dividend-weighted index of Companies A and B would consist of two-thirds of stock in Company A and one-third in Company B, because Company A represents two-thirds of the total dividends of $1.5 billion that both companies pay out. Note that the actual dividend *yield* (that is, the dividend payment as a fraction of the stock price) does not enter the index calculation. However, as a practical matter, a dividend-weighted index will have an above-average dividend yield.

Wisdom Tree, a newer entrant to the ETF landscape, has heavily exploited the concept of dividend-weighting. Wisdom Tree ETFs (see http://WisdomTree.com) total 34, with yields ranging from 1.3 percent (Japanese equities, ticker DXJ) to 6.1 percent (Pacific ex-Japan ETF, ticker DNH). Wisdom Tree's high-dividend offerings include U.S. equities (segregated by market capitalization), international equities, and individual foreign sectors. Table 14.1 highlights four of Wisdom Tree's ETFs that have attractive dividend yields.

TABLE 14.1   Selected Wisdom Tree ETFs with High-Dividend Yields (Net of Expenses and Withholding Taxes)

ETF Name	Ticker Symbol	Dividend Yield[2]	Expense Ratio	Objective	Percent in Financials
High-Yielding Equity	DHS	5.4%	0.38%	U.S. large-cap value	55%
Small-Cap Dividend Fund	DES	5.3%	0.38%	U.S. small-cap value	56%
Pacific Ex-Japan High Yielding Equity Fund	DNH	6.1%	0.58%	Large-cap value (86% Australia)	52%
Emerging Markets High Yielding Equity Fund	DEM	4.2%	0.63%	Emerging markets large-cap value	15%

Keep in mind that just because a high-dividend ETF sounds unusual does not mean that its risk profile will be all that different from more conventional ETFs. For example, the stocks in the iShares Emerging Market ETF (EEM) are yielding 2.3 percent, whereas those in the Wisdom Tree Emerging Markets High Yielding Equity Fund (DEM) are paying 4.8 percent. Clearly, the two ETFs have different portfolios. Yet, the short-term fluctuations between these two ETFs have been highly correlated, as shown in Figure 14.2. Although DEM had a smaller drawdown than EEM from July 2007 to February 2008 (15 percent for DEM versus 22 percent for EEM), the similarity in the price movements shown in Figure 14.2 makes it clear that when you hold DEM, you are generally exposing yourself to the high-risk levels characteristic of emerging market stocks.

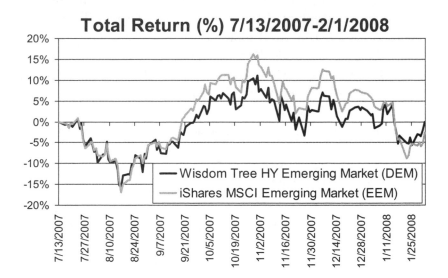

FIGURE 14.2

Total returns for two emerging market ETFs: iShares MSCI Emerging Market Index Fund (EEM) and Wisdom Tree High-Yielding Emerging Markets Fund (DEM) from July 2007 to February 2008.

A Unique High-Dividend Portfolio

The data in Table 14.1 exemplifies that the Wisdom Tree Emerging Markets High Yield ETF (DEM) is unique among high-dividend ETFs in that financials are not the predominant industry sector. Rather, materials and energy stocks are the largest groups. This observation raises the possibility that you could pair DEM with a U.S. equity high-yield ETF for a well-diversified portfolio. That indeed turns out to be the case.

Figure 14.3 shows the hypothetical history of the benchmarks for the Wisdom Tree Emerging Market High Yield and the U.S. High Yield ETFs (DEM and DHS, respectively).[3] Note that from 1997 to 2002, DEM and DHS moved almost like mirror images of one another: From 1997 to 1998, emerging markets fell while U.S. equities rose. From mid-1999 to mid-2000, U.S. high-dividend stocks fell while emerging markets rose. A bull market for both the Emerging Market and U.S. high yield ETF benchmark indexes ran from January 2003 through mid-2007.

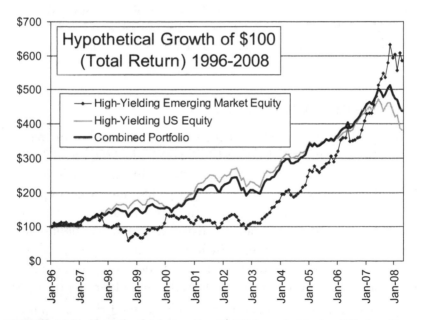

FIGURE 14.3   Hypothetical growth of $100 invested in two Wisdom Tree Dividend ETFs individually (DHS and DEM), and in a portfolio of 80 percent DHS and 20 percent DEM.

Even though the emerging market ETF has returned more than the U.S. equity ETF over the entire 1996 to 2008 period, it also has had far larger drawdowns. As a result, the risk-adjusted performance of the U.S. ETF has actually been superior. But you can do even better.

A hypothetical portfolio of 80 percent DHS (U.S. high dividend) and 20 percent DEM (Emerging Market high dividend) would have a lower drawdown than either ETF would individually. Yet its return would be higher than that of DHS alone. In other words, adding 20 percent high-dividend emerging market stocks to a portfolio of high-dividend American equities would have increased return and slightly decreased risk. The growth of this combined portfolio is plotted in Figure 14.3.

It turns out that from 1996 to 2008, DEM has outperformed the MSCI Emerging Market Index (tracked by two ETFs: iShares' with ticker EEM and Vanguard's with ticker VWO) by 5 percent per year. It's safe to say that you should not expect this level of outperformance to persist in the future. Nonetheless, because the sectors represented in DEM and DHS are so different, it is reasonable to expect that you will continue to improve the balance between risk and reward if you use both DEM and DHS as part of a diversified portfolio.

Preferred Stock ETFs

Preferred stocks represent a small corner of the broad stock market but one that should be of interest to investors looking for high-dividend yields. Until now, all the stock market indexes you have read about have represented common stocks—literally ownership of a piece of a collection of individual companies. In addition to issuing common stock, a company can sell shares that represent debt obligations rather than ownership. Such shares are called *preferred*, because if funds are insufficient to pay dividends to both common and preferred shareholders, the preferred shareholders get paid first.

In fact, a preferred stock is more like a bond than a common stock, except that individual shares are listed on the same stock exchanges that trade the far larger volume of common stocks.

Although preferred shareholders are ahead of common shareholders when it comes to receiving dividends in the event of insufficient free cash flow, they are behind bondholders. That makes preferred stocks riskier than bonds issued by the same company.

Preferred shareholders must also bear an additional risk: refinancing risk. Preferred stocks are like mortgages in that the debtor can refinance if interest rates drop. Although you can refinance your mortgage at any time, preferred stocks can only be called after five years, typically for the issue price of $25 per share. As a result of this provision, preferred shareholders reap little benefits if interest rates fall once a preferred issue has been trading for five years. On the other hand, if interest rates rise, preferred shareholders are liable to see their share price fall, just as bond prices fall when interest rates rise. In contrast, corporate bonds are redeemable only at the maturity date. If interest rates stay below where they were when a bond was issued, bondholders reap the benefits until maturity, not just for the first five years.

Given that preferred stock is more exposed to default risk and to refinancing risk than corporate bonds from the same company, it would be natural to ask what attraction preferred stocks hold. The answer is higher dividends and, frequently, better tax treatment (at least under current regulations that are scheduled to remain in effect until 2010). In May 2008, preferred stocks were typically yielding 7 percent to 8 percent, which is two percentage points higher than corporate bonds of similar credit rating. Preferred stock yields are currently about the same as many junk bond yields even though the default risk has historically been much lower with preferred stocks. (High-yield bonds do not bear refinancing risk, however.) Most preferred shares currently listed represent financial company debt, so in the interest of diversification, you should take into account the need to avoid excessive exposure to this one industry. Figure 14.4 shows how similar the price movement of the preferred stock ETF (ticker PFF) has been to that of the Financial Sector SPDR (XLF) that is composed entirely of common shares in financial companies.

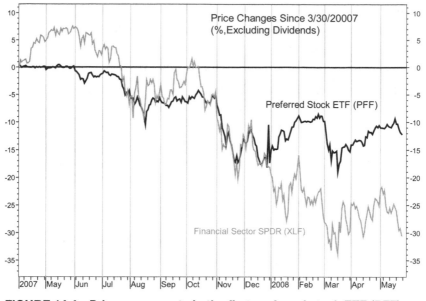

FIGURE 14.4   Price movements in the first preferred stock ETF (PFF) and in the Financial Sector SPDR (XLF), 2007 to 2008.

One potential advantage of preferred stocks over bonds is that many preferred shares pay *qualified dividends*, which are corporate dividends that are taxed at federal long-term capital gains rates (maximum tax rate of 15 percent) rather than as ordinary income as bond interest is (maximum tax rate of 35 percent). Unfortunately, the tax break afforded to qualified dividends is scheduled to terminate in 2011. More precisely, my observation is that American banks tend to issue preferred shares whose interest is taxed like bonds so that they can deduct the amount paid out as interest expense. However, European financial companies and American utilities more frequently pay out qualified dividends on their preferred shares listed in the United States.

iShares launched the first preferred stock ETF (ticker PFF) in 2007, and PowerShares launched its own version in January 2008 (ticker PGX). The ETFs have similar expense ratios (0.48 percent for PFF and 0.50 percent for PGX). The big attraction of preferred stock ETFs over individual preferred stocks is the ease of diversifying a debt portfolio with ETFs. As with individual corporate bonds, each preferred stock has its own specific terms and credit rating. When you own preferred stock in a company, you are assuming that company's credit risk. Each of the preferred stock ETFs holds more than 50 separate issues, so individual company risk is limited to approximately 10 percent of the ETF's portfolio. (That is, the largest allocation to preferred shares of any one company represents roughly 10 percent of these ETFs' portfolios.)

Owning preferred stocks through ETFs offers another big advantage: New preferred issues will find their way into the ETF portfolio without your having to pay the 4.5 percent to 5 percent sales commission that brokers typically charge for selling initial public offerings of preferred shares to individual retail clients. It is harder to keep up with developments in the preferred stock universe than it is to follow common stocks, because preferred stocks do not attract the same level of public interest. In contrast to common stocks, preferred stocks have no uniform system of ticker symbols, which often makes it difficult to find information about them on the most popular Web sites, such as Yahoo Finance. The best resource for preferred stocks is QuantumOnline (www.quantumonline.com).

The best time to buy one of the preferred stock ETFs is when its dividend yield is sufficient to meet your income needs. Also, as a rule of thumb, you should require that the dividend yield be 2 percent (200 basis points) higher than the yields on comparably rated 7- to 10-year investment-grade corporate bonds to compensate you for price volatility and refinancing risk. You could use the 30-day SEC yield of the iShares Lehman Intermediate Credit ETF (CIU) as a reference. This information is available on www.ishares.com/home.htm.

After you invest in preferred stocks or in one of the preferred stock ETFs, the amount of dividend income you receive either remains constant or decreases. If interest rates fall, preferred stocks in the ETF portfolio are called, and the ETF is forced to reinvest the proceeds in the lower-yielding issues that remain. On the other hand, if interest rates rise, the interest income generated by preexisting preferred stocks remains the same as when you purchased them.

Conclusion

Many new ETFs allow you to reap more generous dividend income than is available from mutual funds. Only mutual funds that invest in high-yield bonds (junk bonds) and other debt rated below investment-grade can compete with some of the ETFs presented in this chapter, such as the Wisdom Tree High Yielding Pacific Ex-Japan Index Fund (DNH). Other high-yielding equity ETFs pay dividends in the 4.5 percent to 5.5 percent range, which is commensurate with the yields available from most investment-grade bond mutual funds. High-dividend equity ETFs are expected to be riskier than investment-grade bond mutual funds, but their returns are also likely to include capital gains on top of dividend income over the long term (say 10 years), even though nothing can be guaranteed.

The particular portfolio that I recommend if you are seeking long-term investment income is 80 percent Wisdom Tree High-Yielding U.S. Equity ETF (DHS) and 20 percent Wisdom Tree High-Yielding Emerging Market ETF (DEM), because the diversification between U.S. and emerging market stocks has improved the balance between risk and reward compared to holding only U.S. stocks. If you want to take advantage of the lower tax rate on qualified dividends, you can simply hold the iShares Dow Jones Select Dividend Index ETF (DVY) for as long as the tax break remains in effect.

Finally, you can diversify 5 to 10 percent of your holdings in investment-grade bonds by adding one of the preferred stock ETFs to your portfolio. As of June 2008, the PowerShares Preferred Stock Index ETF (PGX) has a higher yield. Remember, if you do invest in preferred stocks or in any of the developed-country high-dividend ETFs, beware of placing too many holdings from financial companies elsewhere in your portfolio.

---

1 Source: Life expectancy table II in IRS publication 590, "Individual Retirement Arrangements" (2007), www.irs.gov.

2 You can find the latest updates to this data at www.wisdomtree.com/etfs/estimated-dividend-yield.asp. Note that many foreign countries withhold taxes on dividends paid to American investors. As a result, the yield you receive is often less than what the underlying stocks actually pay on a pretax basis. The amount you would get net of taxes if you held the underlying stocks directly is called the net dividend on Wisdom Tree's Web site. The dividend yield reported in Table

14.1 is the net portfolio dividend yield (as reported by Wisdom Tree) less the expense ratio. It is the dividend income you can actually expect to receive assuming that the past 12 months' dividend payouts continue for the next 12 months.

3 These ETFs were launched in 2006 and 2007, but Wisdom Tree provides the hypothetical performance back to 1996 of portfolios constructed according to the rules currently in effect.

15

THE HOTTEST INVESTMENTS AROUND: COMMODITY ETFS

Up until now, we have been discussing stocks and bonds, which are tied to individual corporations. In recent years, a different type of investment has come to the fore: investments in commodities. Commodities are physical raw materials or agricultural products. Following are examples of the numerous commodities in which investors can trade:

- **Energy**—Crude oil, gasoline, natural gas
- **Agricultural products**—Wheat, corn, soybeans
- **Industrial metals**—Copper, aluminum
- **Precious metals**—Gold, silver, platinum

Trading in commodities has been around for decades and was especially popular in the 1970s. Because the 1970s were years of high inflation, commodity prices were strong. Indeed, they performed far better than the stock and bond markets during that decade. However, commodities lost their appeal (and market leadership) in the disinflationary 1980s and 1990s.

Starting in 2003, commodity prices have advanced more strongly than at any time since 1973. Figure 15.1 shows the history of the Bridge-CRB Commodity Spot Price Index since 1973. The gain since 1973 has averaged only 4 percent per year. However, commodity prices have jumped 17 percent per year from October 2001 to May 2008.

FIGURE 15.1   **Bridge-CRB Index of Spot Commodity Prices, 1973 to 2008.**

Many argue that commodity prices, high as they are in 2008, remain in just the initial phase of a long-term bull market. According to the bullish scenario for commodities, demand from China and India will continue to grow as the standard of living of their population increases. Their large trade surpluses give China and India the economic muscle to bid as much as is needed to attract a growing share of the world's resources to meet their own needs. With the majority of their populations still in poverty, potential demand from these two countries (which together account for almost half of the world's population) could be insatiable.

The skeptical case for commodities anticipates that, at some point, prices will become so high that they decrease demand, either through forced conservation borne of economic necessity or through the development of alternatives. Skeptics also assume that the surge in commodity prices in recent years owes more to speculators than to a sustainable imbalance between supply and demand.

Regardless of which view is correct, investing in commodities offers a major advantage: diversification. Historically, commodity prices have been negatively correlated with stock prices over the long term. During multiyear periods of strong commodity prices, stocks have returned less than usual. Conversely, prolonged periods of weak commodity prices have been good for stocks overall. In the shorter term, commodity prices and stock prices have either been uncorrelated or negatively correlated much of the time.

A simple example that shows the power of diversification between stocks and commodities will illustrate the point. A portfolio composed 50 percent of the S&P 500 Index and 50 percent of the Dow Jones-AIG Commodity Index from 1974 to 2008 would have had just half the drawdown (that is, –25 percent) of either index separately (that is, –44 percent to –46 percent).

It would be great to be able to recommend holding commodity-related investments at all times based on this big reduction in maximum drawdown, but unfortunately for such a strategy, commodity prices have gone through long periods of low or negative returns. For example, Figure 15.1 shows that commodity prices were 45 percent lower by October 2001 than they were in November 1980. During the entire 1974 to 2008 period, commodity prices rose just 3.7 percent per year, compared to 6.6 percent for the S&P 500. (Dividends are not included here.)

The implication is that *if* past patterns repeat themselves, any allocation to commodities (up to the amount you have in equities) should result in lower drawdowns than an all-equity portfolio. However, it is uncertain what effect commodities will have on your overall level of profits. If the inflationary environment of 2008 continues, commodities could continue to outperform stocks. However, a worldwide economic slowdown could derail the seven-year old commodity rally.

Primer on Commodity Investing

You might think that trading commodities is like trading stocks: You buy oil at $100, sell at $110, and pocket a $10 profit, for example. However, you face a big hurdle when trading or holding commodities that you would not face as an investor in stocks or bonds.

That hurdle is the *cost of carry*, which is the jargon for the cost of storing physical commodities while you wait for their prices to rise. If you buy a share of stock for $100, leave it in your brokerage account for a year, and then sell it for $110, your profit is $10 less commissions. However, if you buy a barrel of oil for $100, store it for a year, and sell it for $110, your profit is *not* simply $10 less commissions because you also had to pay the costs of storing oil for the year. That cost might be $0.30/month, so the cost of carry in this case would be $3.60 per year. At current oil prices of $130/barrel, the cost of carry reduces your profits by about 3 percent per year. The cost of carry generalizes to any physical commodity. Even in an ideal world, your returns from trading commodities will be less than the reported increase in prices. In contrast, there is no cost of carry for stocks (unless your broker charges you for inactivity). In fact, you might benefit from holding stocks to the extent they pay you dividends while you wait for the time to sell.

You might raise the question as to whether the cost of carry would apply to you as an ETF trader, because a commodity ETF would reside in your brokerage account like a stock rather than in a storage facility for physical commodities. In the next section, you will see that some commodity ETFs represent a share of a physical store of commodities, in which case the ETF's expense ratio accounts for the cost of carry. In other cases, commodity ETFs represent financial instruments (called *futures contracts*) tied to the prices of physical commodities. This arrangement also imposes the cost of carry on investors. Unfortunately, there is no escape.

A second reason why commodity investing can be difficult is the high level of volatility that commodity prices can display. For example, the average daily price change in the PowerShares DB Liquid Commodity Index ETF (DBC) was 1.4 percent in May 2008. This was twice the size of the average daily move in the S&P 500 Index during the same time. (Risk is proportional to volatility.) DBC tracks a diversified basket of commodities. As we will see later (Figure 15.6), the volatility of specific commodities has been even higher than that of the diversified basket. High price volatility is not an insurmountable obstacle in the absence of leverage, but it is something of which to take note when deciding how many commodities to include in your portfolio.

There is one additional risk unique to most commodity ETFs (as compared to the others discussed in earlier chapters): *derivatives*. This means that not only do you have to worry about the risk of the commodities, you also need to be concerned about the integrity of the financial system and, in some cases, of the individual ETF sponsor. The next section explains why some commodity ETFs have this particular risk. Fortunately, this risk is low for ETF investors. Although many large financial firms, including some ETF sponsors, were hurt by the credit and housing crises in 2007-2008, no ETF assets have been compromised.

Absentee Ownership of Precious Metals

The simplest way to trade commodities without physically taking possession is to use a *warehouse receipt*. You deposit a known quantity of gold (for example) in a vault, and the bank gives you a claim check. Whoever presents that claim check (warehouse receipt) to the bank can take possession of the gold. If you want to sell the gold, you do not have to physically move it. You only have to sell the claim check. Even if the bank holding the gold fails, your claim check should remain valid since banks, brokerages, and so on are supposed to keep clients' assets separate from their own. Only in the case of actual embezzlement from clients would the failure of a bank affect the owners of the contents in its safe deposit boxes.

One last point: Banks do not give away space in their vaults for free. Gold does not pay dividends, so if you did not have cash, you would have to sell off a fraction of the gold each year to pay the cost of storage. That would mean that, each year, the claim check would represent slightly less gold than the year before.

This is basically how ETFs that track gold and silver bullion work. Each share of the ETF represents a quantity of the underlying physical metal. The first ETF to adopt this format was the SPDR Gold Shares, ticker symbol GLD, launched in November 2004. Each share of GLD represents approximately one-tenth of an ounce of gold bullion, stored at HSBC. The expense ratio is 0.4 percent per year.

In 2005, iShares launched its two precious metal ETFs: the Comex Gold Trust (IAU) and the iShares Silver Trust (SLV). As with SPDR Gold Shares, these ETFs own physical bullion: one-tenth ounce in the case of IAU (gold) and one ounce in the case of SLV (silver) for each share. The expense ratio of SLV is 0.5 percent per year, and IAU is 0.4 percent per year. Gold and silver are relatively inexpensive to store, making it efficient for investors to track the changes in the price of these metals. Just as if you were to own gold bullion directly, these ETFs are taxed like collectibles: ordinary income if held a year or less, or at 28 percent if held for more than a year.

Figure 15.2 shows that GLD has done an excellent job of tracking the price of gold bullion. From the start of 2005 through mid-2008, GLD has returned 108 percent, while the price of gold has risen 111 percent. This discrepancy can be explained entirely by the 0.4 percent per year expense ratio of GLD.

FIGURE 15.2   GLD has tracked gold bullion closely for more than three years.

Become a Futures Trader

Most commodity ETFs do not represent ownership in a physical commodity. Rather, they represent ownership in a portfolio of contracts to buy the underlying commodity at a specified future date. Such contracts are called *futures*, and an investment consisting of a group of futures contracts and Treasury bills is called a *commodity pool*. When you buy shares of commodity ETFs, such as those offered by PowerShares, you are participating in a commodity pool. Power-Shares launched its DB (Deutsche Bank) Commodity Index series of ETFs in 2006 and 2007. Table 15.1 lists some of the PowerShares Commodity ETFs.

TABLE 15.1   Selected PowerShares DB Commodity Index ETFs

PowerShares Commodity ETFs	Ticker Symbol	Commodities Included	Expense Ratio[1]
DB Commodity Index Tracking Fund	DBC	Aluminum, corn, gold, heating oil, crude oil, wheat	0.83%
DB Agriculture Fund	DBA	Corn, soybeans, sugar, wheat	0.91%
DB Base Metals Fund	DBB	Aluminum, copper, zinc	0.78%
DB Energy Fund	DBE	Brent crude, light crude, heating oil, natural gas, gasoline	0.78%
DB Precious Metals Fund	DBP	Gold, silver	0.79%

Another set of ETFs that invest through the use of futures are the energy ETFs that Victoria Bay Asset Management sponsors. The first of these is the United States Oil Fund (USO), which attempts to track the price of West Texas Intermediate Crude Oil. Its expense ratio is 0.81 percent (including brokerage costs). The other ETFs in this family track natural gas, gasoline, and heating oil.

The problem with investing in futures directly or indirectly is that the futures contract might fail to track closely with the investment you intended. This was a particular problem with the U.S. Oil Fund (USO) in 2007. Figure 15.3 shows how far USO has diverged from the underlying price of oil in 2007. Between the start of 2007 and August of that year, USO underperformed the price of crude oil by more than 12 percent. That discrepancy is far more than can be blamed on just the cost of carry. Strangely, USO has actually *outperformed* crude oil in the ten months through May 2008. In fact, USO does state in its prospectus that it may trade in other energy futures besides crude oil in its attempt to track the price of West Texas Intermediate Crude. Perhaps noncrude oil futures in its portfolio account for these discrepancies.

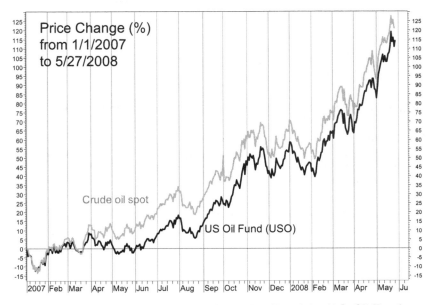

FIGURE 15.3   Percentage changes in crude oil and the U.S. Oil Fund, 1/1/2007 to 5/27/2008.

It is beyond the scope of this book to describe the futures markets in more detail. The important risk that ETF investors need to know is that for every buyer of a futures contract, a seller exists. Like any other contract, its ultimate worth is limited by the solvency of the person on the other side of the agreement.

When you buy an ETF that represents a share in a commodity pool, you are implicitly betting that the people who sold you the futures contracts will be able to meet their obligations. Fortunately, you do not have to worry about who those people are—the commodity exchange and network of commodities brokers keep track. The odds that any particular futures investor will end up across the table (metaphorically) from a deadboat have been low, but unfortunately, that risk is not zero.

The main reason why the risk of default in a futures position is low is that you must place collateral with a broker to help guarantee that you can make good on the obligations implied by the futures contracts in which you have positions. That collateral is in the form of Treasury bills, which pay interest that the commodity pool investor receives in addition to changes in the value of the underlying futures contracts. The ETFs' expenses come out of the interest income from the Treasury bills in the portfolio, so unlike the case with GLD or SLV, the ETFs do not need to sell off bits of their portfolios each day to meet expenses.

Unfortunately, futures investments do not allow you to avoid the cost of carry. In addition to reflecting the day-to-day price fluctuations of the underlying commodity, the price of a commodity futures contract normally declines a bit each day to reflect the cost of carry of the underlying physical commodity. If this were not the case, no user would ever need to store a commodity. Commodity consumers could meet all their needs by buying futures contracts set up to expire when they need the product. There would be an imbalance between a high demand for futures and a low demand for physical commodity. That imbalance would drive up the price of futures contracts relative to the physical commodity until the cost of buying commodities for future use was the same whether achieved through buying and storing the physical commodity or through the use of futures contracts.

One last note on taxes: The government taxes futures contracts differently from shares of stock. The applicable rate for futures contracts lies between the long-term capital gains rate and the ordinary income rate. (The tax rate is a 60 percent weighting of the long-term capital gains rate and 40 percent of the ordinary income rate regardless of how long you hold the futures position.) Mutual funds and brokerages send out 1099s by the end of January reporting how your different sources of investment gains should be taxed. Futures-based ETFs send out a different form called a K-1. It usually arrives much later than a 1099—after the middle of March. This is important to keep in mind (and can be an irritant) if you take significant positions in futures-based ETFs.

A Virtual Commodity Investment

Barclays Bank, the sponsor of iShares ETFs, came up with a way to invest in commodities with a vehicle that technically is not really an ETF. Barclays' product line is called iPath Exchange-traded notes (ETNs). Rather than buying physical commodities or taking positions in publicly traded futures contracts, shares of iPath ETNs represent Barclays Bank's promise to redeem each ETN in 30 years for the value of the underlying commodity index. Therefore, each ETN is actually a piece of unsecured debt issued by Barclays, so it carries the credit risk of the sponsoring bank.

If Barclays fails, shareholders in its iShares ETFs should not be hurt because the shares of underlying baskets of stocks are independent of Barclays' assets. However, iPath ETN shareholders would be out of luck, because the only thing that gives ETNs their value is the faith that Barclays will be able to honor its obligations down the road. In addition to the reliance on Barclays' solvency, there is a second disadvantage to the ETNs. As a practical matter, ETNs have traded with wider bid-ask spreads than similar PowerShares DB Commodity Index ETFs. ETNs have a similar expense ratio (0.75 percent) to the PowerShares Commodity Index ETFs in Table 15.1.

So why bother using ETNs? First, iPath ETNs track the well-established Dow Jones-AIG family of commodity indexes that were established long before the first ETF came into being. This is a big advantage of the ETNs. Second, there is no actual trading in an ETN portfolio, so each ETN should in theory be able to closely track its underlying index (after expenses). That actually has been the case so far. Figure 15.4 shows how well the diversified iPath Dow Jones-AIG Commodity Index ETN (DJP) has tracked its benchmark commodity index.

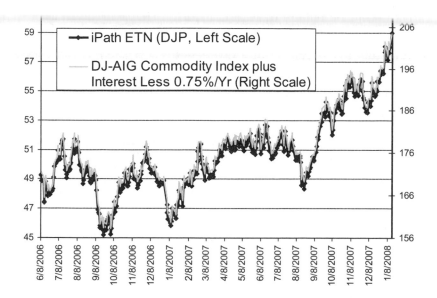

FIGURE 15.4   The Dow Jones-AIG Commodity Index and its iPath ETN, 2006 to 2008.

For the moment (mid-2008), ETNs enjoy better tax treatment than other types of commodity ETFs in that they can be taxed as long-term capital gains if held for more than a year. However, the tax treatment of ETNs is a matter of active debate in Washington and could change at any time.

How to Invest in Commodity ETFs

The price history shown in Figure 15.1 suggests that individual investors should not hold big positions in commodities for extended periods. On the other hand, some exposure to commodities is likely to be favorable because of the potential risk reduction they can provide to an all-equity portfolio. A compromise solution would be to allocate 10 percent of your equity capital to a diversified commodity ETN such as the iPath Dow Jones-AIG Commodity Index ETN (DJP). I prefer DJP because it tracks the better established benchmark and because it happens to be one-third less volatile than the PowerShares

DB Liquid Commodity Index ETF (DBC). However, if you are concerned about the risk of depending on just Barclays, some of your commodity assets can be in a diversified ETF, such as the Power-Shares DB Liquid Commodity Index ETF (DBC). Certainly, if you do invest in iPath ETNs, you need to follow the news for any sign of financial distress in Barclays Bank. Any worries about Barclays should lead you to sell your ETNs.

If you are going to hold commodities in your portfolio as a hedge against inflation, diversify across different sectors. Figure 15.5 shows that DJP is diversified across several types of commodities. As a result, the price risk in DJP has been significantly lower than the risks of its individual components.

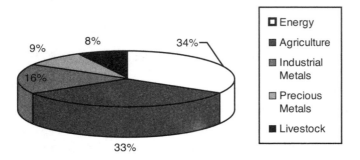

FIGURE 15.5   Sector composition of the iPath Dow Jones-AIG Commodity Index ETN.

For example, Figure 15.6 shows three months' history (percent price change, 10/29/2007 to 1/14/2008) of three of the iPath ETNs that track different commodity sectors and of the broad commodity index ETN (DJP). Note that, during this period, the worst drawdown for DJP was 4 percent, which isn't trivial, but it's not disastrous either. Two sectors—industrial metals and energy—had far worse drawdowns of 15 percent and 10 percent, respectively. Agriculture fared well during this particular period, gaining more than 18 percent and suffering no significant drawdown. However, from March to May 2008, energy rallied and agriculture suffered an 18 percent drawdown (not shown in the figure). Meanwhile, DJP lost just 3 percent.

The bottom line is that DJP, at roughly 1.5 times the volatility of the U.S. stock market, is risky enough. I do not recommend buying and holding individual commodity sectors.

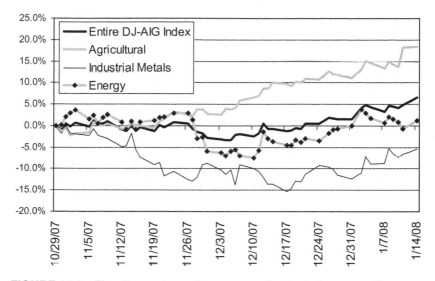

FIGURE 15.6   The disparate performances of selected commodity sectors, October 2007 to January 2008.

The Outlook for Commodities

Even though I do not recommend long-term holdings in single commodity sectors, as of mid-2008, energy has the best outlook. Even as other commodities (industrial metals, precious metals, agriculture) had significant corrections between March and May 2008, energy has held up. Energy also faces the greatest supply risk because so much oil is produced in unstable areas of the globe.

For example, Venezuela is a major oil supplier to the United States. Apparently, its government is failing to maintain the physical infrastructure of the Venezuelan oil industry and instead is diverting oil profits to other domestic projects. As a result, oil production in Venezuela is slipping and is likely to continue to decline for years. Meanwhile, Nigeria (another member of OPEC) has faced recurrent supply disruptions as the result of civil unrest. If you do want to overweight energy over the long term, it would be safer to buy stocks in blue chip integrated oil companies such as ExxonMobil (XOM) or in the Energy Sector SPDR (XLE).

Agricultural commodities were strong until the second quarter of 2008. For example, the Dow Jones-AIG Grains Index nearly doubled between September 2006 and January 2008. However, a good part of the current supply-demand imbalance in agriculture is the result of U.S. government policies favoring the diversion of corn to produce ethanol even though that is inefficient. (The same mass of sugar cane from Brazil would produce 33 percent more fuel than an equal weight of corn, since the process of deriving ethanol from corn consumes a significant fraction of the fuel energy produced.) If the U.S. government changed its ethanol policy to allow imports from Brazil, a significant source of demand for crops would disappear. No such political risk threatens the demand for energy or for precious metals.

Conclusion

In summary, commodities have been excellent investments during prolonged periods of high inflation (such as the 1970s), and they have been good diversifiers of U.S. equities. However, they are volatile and have an inconsistent record of profitability. In the 1970s, it was hard for individual investors to access the commodities markets (they needed an account at a commodity broker), but recent ETF and ETN offerings allow anyone with a discount brokerage account to make bets on commodity prices.

The best way for you as an individual investor to add commodities to your portfolio is to allocate up to 10 percent of equity capital into diversified commodity index funds, such as the iPath Dow-Jones AIG Commodity Index ETN (DJP) or the PowerShares DB Liquid Commodity Index ETF (DBC). The latter is more volatile (greater price risk), but the iPath has more risk exposure to the welfare of the single financial institution (Barclays Bank) that sponsors it.

An argument can be made for overweighting energy in a long-term portfolio. However, rather than holding a long-term position in crude oil (and bearing the cost of carry, which can be a significant drag on returns), you are likely better off holding stocks in integrated oil companies. The Select Sector Energy SPDR (XLE) is a handy vehicle with which to maintain long-term exposure to the energy sector.

Finally, do not forget that although trends in commodity prices have not correlated with U.S. stock market movements, emerging market stocks and commodity prices have trended together. If you already have a significant allocation (more than 20 percent of equity capital) to emerging market stocks, be wary of piling into commodities, too.

---

1 The expense ratio includes 0.75% percent for PowerShares plus estimated brokerage costs. Source: http://www.invescopowershares.com/products.

Appendix

INTERNET RESOURCES FOR ETF INVESTORS

Five categories of Web sites are valuable in managing investments and in performing research:

- ETF Sponsor Web sites
- General ETF Web sites
- Index provider Web sites
- Current and historical market data Web sites
- Fundamental economic data Web sites

ETF Sponsor Web Sites

These are the best sources of information if you know which ETF you are looking for. However, if you are looking for which ETF might be best for you, you should consult the Web sites from multiple sponsors or one of the general ETF Web sites.

Web Site Address	Comments
www.ishares.com/home.htm	This is easy to navigate and has a rich source of information about individual stock holdings and a distribution history for all of its ETFs. In addition, it is an excellent source of valuation measures for equity ETFs.
www.ssgafunds.com/	This site provides a rich source of information about individual stock holdings for the SPDR ETFs, is an excellent source of valuation measures for equity ETFs, and is easy to navigate.
www.sectorspdr.com/	This Web site, for the sector SPDRs, is not as easy to navigate as the others. (You have to open the fact sheet to get valuation information.) A unique advantage is the excellent link to a third-party research provider (Altavista Independent Research).
www.invescopowershares.com	This easy-to-navigate site offers a great source of information about individual stock holdings for all of its ETFs and is an excellent source of valuation measures for equity ETFs.
www.holdrs.com/holdrs/main/index.asp	The Web site for HOLDRs offers extremely easy access to the individual stocks in each ETF but has no valuation information (such as current dividend yield).
www.wisdomtree.com	The unique advantage of this Web site is the link Dividend Yield Analysis, which is helpful if high-dividend yield is your objective. The site reports dividends net of foreign withholding taxes, which is also important.

General ETF Web Sites

These sites are not affiliated with any one ETF sponsor, so they are good for screening the ETF universe. (For example, if you are looking for a utility ETF, iShares, HOLDRs, and State Street Global Advisors offer one. Any of the Web sites listed here could point you to all three, whereas none of the sponsor's Web sites would.) Although the Web sites that follow provide information about all ETF sponsors' products, the sponsors' own Web sites go into greater detail. The disadvantage of ETF screening Web sites is that they focus on past performance to the exclusion of risk. As a result, I use ETF screeners to make sure I do not overlook a potentially useful ETF, but I almost never use them to make a final selection. The short list here is not intended to be exhaustive. You can find more ETF Web sites using Google to search for "ETF screener."

Web Site Address	Comments
www.amex.com	The American Stock Exchange was the first to get into the ETF market in a big way. Its Web site has an ETF screener. If you look up an individual ETF on this site, click the button labeled "tear sheet" for basic information, including the expense ratio, ticker symbol and IOPV (see Chapter 1, "Exchange-Traded Mutual Funds: Now Individuals Can Invest Like the Big Players"), and recent distribution history.
www.marketwatch.com/funds	Select the ETF Tools tab to access a quick screener or advanced screener.
www.etfconnect.com	Although sponsored by Nuveen Investments (a purveyor of closed-end funds), this Web site also has basic information about ETFs (ticker symbol, expense ratio, objective) and links to the SEC Web site, where you can review relevant regulatory filings.

Index Provider Web Sites

These Web sites are often more difficult to navigate than the ETF sponsors' Web sites, but they are good to visit if you want detailed information about the construction of the indexes that are used.

Web Site Address	Comments
www.djindexes.com	This Web site includes information on the venerable Dow Jones Averages (Industrials, Utilities, and Transportation) and on the indexes originally developed by Wilshire Associates. One user-friendly section is also devoted to indexes underlying ETFs. The rest of the Dow Jones Indexes Web site can be frustrating to navigate.
www2.standardandpoors.com	This is the site for Standard and Poor's Indexes. It has no historical data.
www.russell.com/us/SiteNav.asp	This site contains information about the Russell Indexes. Of the three index providers, Russell has by far the best Web site in terms of the quality of the information provided and the ease of navigating. You can find daily historical data dating back to 1995 on this site.
www.nareit.com	The NAREIT Indexes available (for free) on this Web site offer the best long-term monthly historical data available for investment research.

Current and Historical Market Data Web Sites

These sites are excellent for retrieving the data you need to implement the models presented in this book.

Web Site Address	Comments
http://finance.yahoo.com	This is an excellent source of daily historical ETF pricing that you can easily export to Excel. You can also find data on distributions on this site. In addition, the Web site provides back-adjusted prices that include the impact of distributions and splits. It's an excellent tool, but you should verify ETF distributions from an independent source (such as the ETF sponsor Web sites listed earlier).
http://moneycentral.msn.com/investor/home.asp	This site offers excellent charting capability. Historical price data is also available that you can download into Excel. In addition, it has good information on top holdings, sector representations, and expense ratios.

Fundamental Economic Data Web Sites

The Federal Reserve Web site is excellent for current and historical interest rate data, some of which is required to implement the models in Chapter 11, "What Bonds Can Tell You about Stocks: How to Use Interest Rates." The data on other Federal government Web sites makes it into the business news headlines (such as unemployment, inflation, gross domestic product, productivity, balance of trade, and so on). Visiting these Web sites can provide some deeper background for those of you who are interested.

Web Site Address	Comments
http://www.federalreserve.gov/releases/H15/data.htm	This site offers a treasure trove of historical interest rate data. It has spartan formatting but is easy to import into Excel. The information on this site is required to implement the interest rate indicators presented in Chapter 11.
http://www.bls.gov/data/	The Bureau of Labor Statistics Web site, is the place to visit for inflation data (as well as for data on employment, unemployment, wages, and productivity.) Navigating takes a little practice.
http://www.bea.gov/	You need to come here, to the Bureau of Economic Analysis Web site, for gross domestic product data. There are also Web pages that contain the balance sheet and income statement for the entire country, and information about the balance of trade, taxes, and government spending. (The Bureau of Economic Analysis is part of the Commerce Department of the Federal government.)

INDEX

Note: Page numbers followed by *n*
are located in footnotes.

A

ADRs (American Depository
  Receipts), 175
agricultural commodities,
  supply risks in, 264
all-cap ETFs, 37-38
American Depository Receipts
  (ADRs), 175
American Stock Exchange
  website, 20
analysis, fundamental/technical, 41
annual gain-to-drawdown
  ratio, 88-90
ask, 9
asking price, 9
asset allocation
  domestic versus international
    stocks, 179-185
  for selecting small-cap versus large-
    cap stocks, 138-142
  growth versus value stocks. *See*
    growth stocks, value stocks versus
  ultimate ETF investment strategy,
    223-224
    diversification in, 224-227
    growth/value evaluation in,
      228-230
    interest rate evaluation in,
      227-228

performance of, 230-231
rebalancing, 231-233
authorized participants, 16
avoiding fund managers, 3

B

bankers' risk aversion, 149*n*
Barclays Bank, 260-261
bear markets, 79
  40-year history of, 70
  investments that have not been
    around during, 70-72
*Beating the Market, 3 Months at a
  Time* (Appel and Appel), 188, 227
benchmarks, 44, 70
  benchmark index performance,
    47-48
bid, 9
bid-ask spread
  for ETFs, 7-9, 15-16
  for international stocks, 175-176
blend indexes, 39
bond ETFs, 224-227
bond market, 192-193. *See also*
  interest rates
bonds
  credit risk of, 129-130
  defined, 129
  interest rate risk of, 130-131
  intermediate-term bond ETFs, 132
  performance, 26, 29
  preferred stocks versus, 245-246

book value, 39, 214, 222*n*
Bridge-CRB Commodity Spot
  Price Index, 252
Buffett, Warren, 106

C

calculating
  compounded annual rate of
    return, 96-98
  drawdown, 79-82
  Sharpe ratio, 98-101
capital gains, 21-22
capitalization weighting, 54-55
cash component
  eliminating from one-decision
    portfolio, 123-124
  performance, 26, 29
charts, drawdown, 208-210
Comex Gold Trust (IAU), 256
commodities
  commodity ETFs
    for precious metals, 255-256
    futures contracts and, 257-259
    recommendations, 261-263
  commodity pools, 257
  correlation with emerging market
    stocks, 265
  defined, 251
  future outlook for, 263-264
  investment risk with, 254-255
  negative correlation with stocks, 253
  performance of, 251-253
  tracking with ETNs, 260-261
common stocks, preferred stocks
  versus, 244-245
companies, size of, 29-34
comparing mutual fund performance
  to benchmark index performance,
  47-48
composite interest rate indicator,
  203-204
compounded annual rate of return,
  calculating, 96-98, 172*n*
corporate bonds, preferred stocks
  versus, 245-246
correlation in investment mixes, 116

cost of carry
  defined, 254
  in futures contracts, 259
credit risk of bonds, 129-130
currency risk in international
  stocks, 173-174
custodians, 16

D

defaults, 129
deferred sales charge, 5
deflation, 205*n*
derivatives, 255
developed market stocks,
  performance versus emerging
  market stocks, 185-188
distributions
  evaluating ETFs, 142-143
  taxes and, 146-148
diversification, 113
  with commodities, 253, 262
  creating a good mix of stocks and
    bonds, 108
  with emerging market stocks, 187
  in high-dividend ETFs for
    investment income, 243-244
  one-decision portfolio. *See* one-
    decision portfolio
  with preferred stock ETFs, 246
  reducing risk, not profits, 104-105
  Sharpe ratio, 110
  in ultimate ETF investment strategy,
    224-227
  uncertainty of future investment
    returns, 110-112
  versus picking only the best, 106-
    107
dividend-weighted indexes, 240-241
domestic stocks
  future outlook of, 188-189
  performance versus international
    stocks, 176-179
    recognizing trends in, 179-185
  in ultimate ETF investment strategy,
    227-228
Dow Jones-AIG Commodity
  Index, 253

Dow Jones-AIG Grains Index, 264
Dow Jones Select Dividend Index
ETF (DVY), 240
Dow Jones U.S. Utility Index Fund
(IDU), 218
Dow Jones Utility Average, 71-72
drawdown, 58-64, 79, 208
   annual gain-to-drawdown ratio,
      88-90
   bear markets (40-year history of), 70
   calculating with spreadsheets, 79-82
   drawdown charts, 208-210
   of one-decision portfolio, 121
duration (of bond), 205*n*

E

EAFE Index
   EAFE Index ETF (EFA), 232
   performance versus S&P 500
      Index, 176-179
      recognizing trends in, 179-185
economic data Web sites, 272
economic trends
   effect on small-cap stock
      performance, 136-138
   future outlook of, 188-189
EEM (iShares Morgan Stanley
   Capital International Emerging
   Market Index Fund), 73-76
emerging market stocks, 73-77
   correlation with commodities, 265
   one-decision portfolio and, 127-128
   performance versus developed
      market stocks, 185-188
energy stocks
   as high-dividend, 239-240
   supply risks in, 263
equal weighting, 53
ETFs (exchange-traded funds), 1-2
   avoiding the expense of fund
      managers, 3
   bid-ask spread, 7-9, 15-16
   distributions
      evaluating, 142-143
      taxes and, 146-148
   emerging market stocks, 73-77, 188

   evaluating, 142-143
   growth and value, 39
   growth ETFs, 214-217
   intermediate-term bond ETFs, 132
   of investment-grade bonds, 132
   investment styles, 34
   midcap, 35-36
   in one-decision portfolio, 124-125
   performance, 21
   recommendations for, 233-234
   resources
      *ETF general information
         Web sites, 269*
      ETF sponsor Web sites, 268
   risks, 22
   share prices, 16-20
   taxes and, 21-22
   total market ETFs, 37-38
   tracking growth and value stocks,
      169-171
   tracking large-cap and small-cap
      stocks, 142-144
   trading on exchanges, 4-7
   utility sector ETFs, 218-220
   value ETFs, 214-217
ETNs (exchange-traded notes),
   260-261
evaluating ETFs, 142-143
ex-date, 148
examples
   growth versus value ETFs, 214-217
   small-cap ETFs, 211-213
   utility sector ETFs, 218-220
exchange-traded funds. *See* ETFs
exchange-traded notes (ETNs), 260-
   261
exchanges, trading ETFs, 4-7
expense ratios for precious metal
   commodity ETFs, 256
ExxonMobil (XOM), 215-216

F

fair value, 19
fast markets, 22
Fidelity Contrafund (FCNTX), 50
Fidelity Magellan, 50

Fidelity money market funds, 40
financial stocks as high-dividend,
    239-240
finding quantitative investment risk
    information, 79
foreign stocks. *See*
    international stocks
free-float weighting, 55
fund managers, 3
fundamental analysis, 41
future
    future outlook of international
        versus domestic stocks, 188-189
    planning for, 77-78
futures contracts, 254
    commodity ETFs and, 257-259
FVINX (Vanguard's S&P 500
    Index Fund), 4

G

gain per annum (GPA), 88
Gateway Fund (GATEX), 50
gold, commodity ETFs for, 255-256
GPA (gain per annum), 88
growth ETFs, 39
    defined, 152
    versus value ETFs, 152-154,
        214-217
growth indexes, 39
growth stocks
    tracking with ETFs, 169-171
    value stocks versus
        *evaluating in ultimate ETF
        investment strategy, 228-230
        history of relative strength,
        156-160
        recognizing new relative
        strength trends, 161-168*

H

high-dividend ETFs
    diversification in, 243-244
    finding, 240-242
high-dividend stocks for investment
    income, 238-240
high-yield bonds, 130
Hussman Strategic Growth
    (HSGFX), 50

I

IDU (Dow Jones U.S. Utility Index
    Fund), 218
income. *See* investment income
index construction
    capitalization weighting, 54-55
    equal weighting, 53
    free-float weighting, 55
    price weighting, 53-54
index provider Web sites, 270
indexes, 3, 44
    benchmarks, 44
    blend indexes, 39
    comparing mutual fund
        performance to benchmark index
        performance, 47-48
    Down Jones U.S. Utility Index Fund
        (IDU), 218
    growth indexes, 39
    Lehman Aggregate Bond Index, 108
    market indexes, 44-47
    mutual fund managers, 50-52
    in one-decision portfolio, 119
    Russell 2000 Index, 51, 211-213
    S&P 500 Growth Index, 216
    S&P 500/Citigroup Value Index, 216
    S&P 600 Small-Cap Index Fund,
        211-213
    S&P Value Index, 214
    small-cap, 49
    value indexes, 39
Indexfunds.com, 20
Indicative Optimized Portfolio
    Value (IOPV), 19
inflation
    effect on bonds and REITs, 225-226
    investment income and, 237
    risk of, 198-199
inflation-protected Treasury bonds
    (TIPS), 238
interest rate indicators
    composite indicator, 203-204
    inverted yield curve, 197-203
    10-year Treasury note yield
        change, 196-197
interest rates, 191
    bond market explanation, 192-193
    bonds and, 130-131

effect on bonds and REITs, 225-226
effect on stock market, 193-195
evaluating in ultimate ETF
investment strategy, 227-228
interest rate indicators
composite indicator, 203-204
inverted yield curve, 197-203
10-year Treasury note yield
change, 196-197
intermediate-term bond ETFs, 132
international stocks
currency risk in, 173-174
emerging market stocks, 185-188
future outlook of, 188-189
one decision portfolio and, 127-128
performance versus domestic
stocks, 176-179
recognizing trends in, 179-185
transaction costs in, 174-176
in ultimate ETF investment
strategy, 227-228
inverted yield curve indicator,
197-203
investment-grade bonds
defined, 129
ETFs of, 132
investment income
high-dividend ETFs
diversification in, 243-244
finding, 240-242
high-dividend stocks for, 238-240
inflation and, 237
preferred stock ETFs, 244-247
recommendations for, 248
investment mix in one-decision
portfolio, 116-118, 123-124
investment risk. See risk
investment styles in ultimate ETF
investment strategy, 34, 228-230
investment transparency, 3
investments, tracking with market
indexes, 46-47
IOPV (Indicative Optimized Portfolio
Value), 19-20
iPath Dow Jones-AIG Commodity
Index ETN (DJP), 260-261, 264
iPath ETNs, 260-261

iShares Cohen & Steers Realty
Majors Index Fund (ICF), 224
iShares Dow Jones Select Dividend
Index ETF (DVY), 248
iShares Dow Jones Total Market
Index Fund (IYY), 37
iShares EAFE Index Fund
(EFA), 227
iShares Emerging Market ETF
(EEM), 242
iShares Goldman Sachs $ InvesTop
Corporate Bond Fund (LQD), 132
iShares Lehman 1-3 Year Treasury
Index fund, 26
iShares Lehman Aggregate Bond
Index Fund (AGG), 224
as bond fund, 132
in one-decision portfolio, 126
iShares Lehman Intermediate Credit
ETF (CIU), 132, 247
iShares Morgan Stanley Capital
International Emerging Market
Index Fund (EEM), 73-76
iShares MSCI Emerging Market
Index ETF (EEM), 188
iShares Russell 1000 Growth
Index Fund (IWF), 170, 234
iShares Russell 1000 Index Fund
(IWB), 142-144
iShares Russell 1000 Value Index
Fund (IWD), 170, 234
iShares Russell 2000 Growth
Index Fund (IWO), 169
iShares Russell 2000 Index Fund
(IWM), 142-144
iShares Russell 2000 Value Index
Fund (IWN), 169
iShares Russell 3000 Index Fund
(IWV), 37
iShares Russell Index ETFs, 234
iShares Russell Microcap Index
Fund (IWC), 30
iShares S&P 500 Growth Index
ETF (IVW), 234
iShares S&P 500 Index Fund
(IVV), 232
iShares S&P 500 Value Index ETF
(IVE), 234

iShares S&P 600 Growth Index ETF
  (IJT), 234
iShares Silver Trust (SLV), 256
IWC (iShares Russell Microcap
  Index Fund), 30
IWV (iShares Russell 3000 Index
  Fund), 37
IYY (iShares Dow Jones Total Market
  Index Fund), 37

J-K-L

JDSU (JDS Uniphase), 215
junk bonds, 130

large-cap stocks, 29
  asset allocation model for, 138-142
  defined, 148*n*
  growth versus value
    history of relative strength,
    158-160
    recognizing new trends in, 168
  large-cap growth mutual funds, 52
large-cap value ETFs, 217
  performance versus small-cap
    stocks, 135
  small-cap stocks versus, 228-230
  tracking with ETFs, 142-144
Legg Mason Value Trust
  (LMVTX), 45-46
Lehman 7–10 Year Treasury Index
  Fund (IEF), 132
Lehman Aggregate Bond Index, 108
  components of, 132
  in one-decision portfolio, 119
liquidity, 32
LMVTX (Legg Mason Value
  Trust), 45-46
loans. *See* bond market
long-term interest rates. *See*
  interest rates
LVB (Steinway Musical Instruments
  Company), 31

M

market data Web sites, 271
market indexes, 44-47
market size, 190*n*

maturity (of loan), 205*n*
microcap, 30-32
mid-sized companies (midcap), 29
midcap (midsized companies),
  29, 35-36
money market funds, 26, 40
MSCIEmerging Market Index,
  187, 244
MSCIWorld Index, 187
municipal bonds, 126
mutual fund managers, 50-52
mutual funds, 2
  comparing performance to
    benchmark index performance,
    47-48
  tracking investments with market
    indexes, 46-47
  trading on exchanges, 4

N

NAREITEquity REITTotal Return
  Index, 235*n*
NASDAQ Composite, 71
90-day Treasury bills, 119, 199-201
noise, 164

O-P

one-decision portfolio, 27, 115
  without cash component, 123-124
  ETFs in, 124-125
  indexes used in, 119
  international investments and,
    127-128
  investment mix in, 116-118, 123-124
  performance history of, 119-123
  rebalancing, 126-127

passive management, 3
performance
  bonds, 26, 29
  cash, 26, 29
  commodities, 251-253
  emerging market versus developed
    market stocks, 185-188
  ETFs, 21
  large-cap versus small-cap
    stocks, 135

long-term performance histories for
  U.S. stocks, bonds, and cash, 26
mutual fund performance versus
  benchmark index performance, 48
one-decision portfolio, 119-123
small-cap stocks, 136-138
risk-adjusted performance. *See* risk-
  adjusted performance
S&P 500 Index versus EAFE Index,
  176-179
    recognizing trends in, 179-185
stocks, 26, 29
ultimate ETF investment strategy,
  230-231
picked off, 20
planning for your future, market risks
  and, 77-78
portfolios
  creating a good mix of stocks and
    bonds, 108
  creating the optimal portfolio, 107
  one-decision portfolio. *See*
    one-decision portfolio
PowerShares DB Commodity Index
  ETFs, 257
PowerShares DB Liquid Commodity
  Index ETF (DBC), 254, 261, 264
PowerShares Preferred Stock Index
  ETF (PGX), 248
PowerShares Zacks Microcap
  Portfolio (PZI), 30
Pradhuman, Satya, 136
precious metals, commodity ETFs
  for, 255-256
preferred stocks
  common stocks versus, 244-245
  corporate bonds versus, 245-246
  preferred stock ETFs, 244-247
price weighting, 53-54
price-to-book ratio, 214-215
prime rate, 149n
profit summary for two large-cap
  value ETFs, 217
PZI (PowerShares Zacks Microcap
  Portfolio), 30

Q-R

qualified dividends, 246
QuantumOnline Web site, 247

ratios
  annual gain-to-drawdown ratio,
    88-90
  price-to-book ratio, 214-215
  Sharpe ratio, 91-93, 108-110
    calculating, 98-101
real estate investment trust (REIT),
  104-105
rebalancing
  growth versus value stock, 161
  one-decision portfolio, 126-127
  ultimate ETF investment strategy,
    231-233
recession, 206n
recommendations for ETFs, 233-234
reducing risk, 192
refinancing risk of preferred
  stocks, 245
REIT (real estate investment
  trust), 104-105
  REIT ETFs, 224-227
relative strength
  explained, 154-156
  history of changes between growth
    and value, 156-160
  recognizing new trends in, 161-165
    *large-cap value versus growth
      stocks, 168*
    *small-cap value versus growth
      stocks, 165-167*
relative strength indicator, 172n
resources for information. *See*
  Web sites
retirement income. *See*
  investment income
returns, uncertainty of future
  investment returns, 110-112
risk
  bear markets (40-year history of), 70
  in commodities investing, 254-255
  credit risk of bonds, 129-130

drawdown, 58-64
   calculating with spreadsheets,
     79-82
ETFs, 22
emerging market stocks, 73-77
finding quantitative investment risk
   information, 79
of inflation, 198-199
interest rate risk of bonds, 130-131
investments that have not been
   around during a bear market,
   70-72
large-cap value ETFs, 217
planning for future, 77-78
in preferred stocks, 245
reducing, 104-105, 116-118, 192
supply risk
   in agricultural
     commodities, 264
   in energy, 263
utility sector ETFs, 220
volatility of past returns, 83-85
risk-adjusted performance, 96
annual gain-to-drawdown ratio,
   88-90
review of, 94
Sharpe ratio, 91-93, 98-101
Rothschild, Baron, 165
RSP, 35-36
Russell Indexes
Russell 1000 Growth Index ETF
   (IWF), 232, 235*n*
Russell 1000 Index
   results for 1979–2007, 139-142
   selecting as benchmark, 139
Russell 1000 Value Index ETF
   (IWD), 232, 235*n*
Russell 2000 Growth ETF (IWO),
   232, 235
Russell 2000 Index, 51, 211-213
   results for 1979–2007, 139-142
   selecting as benchmark, 139
Russell 2000 Value Index (IWN),
   119, 125, 232, 235
Standard & Poor's
   Index versus, 149*n*
Rydex Funds, 35

S

S&P 500 Depository Receipts
  (SPY), 227
S&P 500 Growth Index, 216
S&P 500 Index, 194, 232, 253
   performance versus EAFE Index,
   176-185
S&P 500 Value Index, 214
S&P 500/Citigroup Value Index, 216
S&P 600 Small-Cap Index Fund,
  211-213
S&P 500 Depository Receipt
  (SPY), 232
sales charge, 5
sales loads, 5
Select Sector Energy SPDR
  (XLE), 265
Select Utility Sector SPDR
  (XLU), 218
selecting
   ETFs, 233-234
   growth versus value stocks. *See*
     growth stocks
   large-cap stocks versus small-cap
     stocks, 138-142
share prices of ETFs, 16-20
Sharpe ratio, 91-93, 108-110
   calculating, 98-101
   of one-decision portfolio, 122
short-term interest rates. *See*
  interest rates
SHY (iShares Lehman), 26
silver, commodity ETFs for, 255-256
size of companies, 29-34
Small Cap Dynamics
  (Pradhuman), 136
small-cap stocks, 29-30, 33, 43
   asset allocation model for, 138-142
   defined, 148*n*
   economic factors, effect on
     performance, 136-138
   ETFs, 211-213
   growth versus value
     history of relative strength,
     156-158
     recognizing new trends in,
     165-167

indexing, 49
large-cap stocks versus, 220-200
performance versus large-cap
stocks, 135
tracking with ETFs, 142-144
SPDRGold Shares (GLD), 256
spreadsheets, calculating drawdown,
79-82
Standard & Poor's Index, Russell
Indexes versus, 149n
Steinway Musical Instruments
Company (LVB), 31
stock market
effect of interest rates on, 193-195
interest rate indicators
10-year Treasury note yield
change, 196-197
composite indicator, 203-204
inverted yield curve, 197-203
stocks
emerging market stocks, 265
high-dividend stocks, 238-240
negative correlation with
commodities, 253
performance, 26, 29
preferred stocks versus common
stocks, 244-245
recognizing new relative strength
trends, 161-165
in large-cap value versus
growth stocks, 168
in small cap value versus
growth stocks, 165-167
relative strength history of changes
between growth and value,
156-160
size of company, 29-34
StreetTracks Dow Jones U.S. Small-
Cap Value Fund (DSV), 125, 234
StreetTracks Total Market ETF
(TMW), 37
supply risk
in agricultural commodities, 264
in energy, 263

T

taxes
ETF distributions and, 146-148
ETFs and, 21-22
ETNs and, 261
on futures contracts, 259
rebalancing portfolios and, 126
technical analysis, 41
Technical Analysis: Power Tools for the
Active Investor (Appel), 165
10-year Treasury note yield, 199-201
10-year Treasury note yield change
indicator, 196-197
10-year Treasury Note Yield
Index, 194
term (of loan), 205n
TIPS (inflation-protected Treasury
bonds), 238
TMW (StreetTracks Total Market
ETF), 37
total market ETFs, 37-38
Total Market Vipers (VTI), 37
tracking investments with market
indexes, 46-47
tracking error in ETFs, 127
trading on exchanges, 4-7
trading costs, 34
transaction costs
ETF performance, 21
in international stocks, 174-176
Treasury bills. See U.S. Treasury bills

U

U.S. Equity REIT mutual fund
average, 119
U.S. High Yield ETF (DHS), 243
U.S. stocks. See domestic stocks
U.S. Treasury bills
alternatives to, 126
bond market explanation, 192
interest rate risk of, 130
ultimate ETF investment strategy,
223-224
diversification in, 224-227
growth/value evaluation in, 228-230

interest rate evaluation in, 227-228
performance of, 230-231
rebalancing, 231-233
United States Oil Fund (USO), 257
UTH (Utilities HOLDR), 71, 218-219
utility sector ETFs, 218-220

V

value ETFs, 39
defined, 152
growth ETFs versus, 152-154
versus growth ETFs, 214-217
value indexes, 39
value stocks
defined, 151
growth stocks versus
  *evaluating in ultimate ETF
  investment strategy, 228-230
  history of relative strength,
  156-160
  recognizing new relative
  strength trends, 161-168*
tracking with ETFs, 169-171
Vanguard money market funds, 40
Vanguard Emerging Market ETF
  (VWO), 188
Vanguard S&P 500 Index Fund
  (VFINX), 4, 119
Vanguard Tax-Exempt Money
  Market Fund, 126
Vanguard Total Bond Market
  ETF (BND), 224
Vinik, Jeffrey, 50
volatility
in commodity prices, 254
as risk measure, 83-85
VTI (Total Market Vipers), 37

W

Wal-Mart, free-float weighting, 55
warehouse receipts, 255
Web sites
economic data, 272
ETF sponsors, 268
general ETF information, 269

index providers, 270
market data, 271
Wisdom Tree Emerging Markets
  High Yield ETF (DEM), 243
Wisdom Tree Emerging Markets
  High Yielding Equity Fund
  (DEM), 242
Wisdom Tree High Yielding Pacific
  Ex-Japan Index Fund (DNH), 248
Wisdom Tree high-dividend
  ETFs, 241
Wisdom Tree High-Yielding
  Emerging Market ETF (DEM), 248
Wisdom Tree High-Yielding U.S.
  Equity ETF (DHS), 248

X-Y-Z

XLU (Select Utility Sector
  SPDR), 218
XOM (ExxonMobil), 215-216

yield curve indicator. *See* inverted
  yield curve indicator